Theaters
of Occupation

Theaters
of Occupation

Hollywood and
the Reeducation of
Postwar Germany

Jennifer Fay

University of Minnesota Press   Minneapolis / London

A previous version of chapter 1 was published as "Germany Is a Boy in Trouble," *Cultural Critique* 64 (Fall 2006): 196–234. A previous version of chapter 3 appeared as "Becoming Democratic: Satire, Satiety, and the Founding of West Germany," *Film History* 18, no. 1 (2006): 6–20; copyright 2006 by Indiana University Press. A previous version of chapter 4 was first published as "'That's Jazz Made in Germany!' *Hallo, Fräulein!* and the Limits of Democratic Pedagogy," *Cinema Journal* 44, no. 1 (2004): 3–24; copyright 2004 by the University of Texas Press; all rights reserved.

Published by the University of Minnesota Press
111 Third Avenue South, Suite 290
Minneapolis, MN 55401-2520
http://www.upress.umn.edu

Library of Congress Cataloging-in-Publication Data

Fay, Jennifer.
    Theaters of occupation : Hollywood and the reeducation of postwar Germany / Jennifer Fay.
        p.   cm.
    Includes bibliographical references and index.
    ISBN-13: 978-0-8166-4744-6 (hc : alk. paper)
    ISBN-10: 0-8166-4744-5 (hc : alk. paper)
    ISBN-13: 978-0-8166-4745-3 (pb : alk. paper)
    ISBN-10: 0-8166-4745-3 (pb : alk. paper)
    1. Motion pictures—Germany—History.   2. Motion pictures, American—Germany—History.   3. Germany—History—1945–1955.   I. Title.
    PN1993.5.G3F33 2008
    791.430943'09045—dc22
                                                            2007031971

Printed in the United States of America on acid-free paper

The University of Minnesota is an equal-opportunity educator and employer.

15 14 13 12 11 10 09 08   10 9 8 7 6 5 4 3 2 1

For Scott Juengel and Abby Wells

and in memory of G.

Contents

Introduction
Theaters of Occupation

The German language is uniquely poised to reflect the militarization of entertainment and the theatricality of occupation that became evident in the days following Germany's unconditional surrender to World War II Allies in 1945. For example, the noun for military occupation, *Besetzung,* has another definition: the casting of actors for a film or show.[1] The verb *besetzen,* to occupy militarily, also means to take on a role in a play or to adorn or decorate. A *Besitzer* is an occupier; a *Theaterbesitzer* is a theater owner or exhibitor. To occupy a country means not only to assume sovereignty over the people, it may also mean to take possession of its theaters and thus its culture and to cast a population in a role commensurate with its defeat. In Germany, the Americans exhibited their film culture to the defeated population to make a show of U.S. military and moral superiority and to offer American culture as a model for imitation. The Germans in turn, and in order to regain independence, were expected to enact and make visible their rehabilitation by behaving like their wardens.

Occupation Mimicry

In 1949, after four years of Allied occupation and just months before Germany was to become a semisovereign state, the *New York Times* Berlin correspondent offered this unsettling portrait of occupation life. Driving on the autobahn to Munich, our reporter pulls into a gas station at a military base where the attendant "in denims" saunters up and asks in proper Americanese, "Fill her up, boss?" Next to the pumps is a diner where the waitress, wearing a "blue and white uniform," announces the daily specials: "We got hamburgers, cheeseburgers, bacon and eggs, ham and eggs. No chicken. And no milk. It ain't come in yet." Nothing is remarkable about these two encounters except, as the reporter stresses, neither the attendant nor the waitress is American. They are Germans who, as a result of living in the American zone of occupation, have adopted "the accents, the manner and even the clothes" of "the conqueror." So typical is this diner that it "could be situated outside any American city."[2] Of course, the American influence on West Germany is neither new nor surprising; rather it is the similitude between occupier and occupied that disturbs the reporter on another level:

> Perhaps it is because these Germans are so much like Americans outwardly that many earnest and thoughtful Military Government officials have become convinced that there is an inner likeness as well; that inside the German likes freedom and liberty and believes in democracy. Something must account for the great illusion, shared by so many, that the mass of Germans are good little democrats after four centuries of authoritarianism and four years of occupation.

The putative Americanization of the two roadside workers is not a sign of a coming democracy—unthinkable for the reporter, given Germany's history—but a symptom of U.S. military gullibility and earnestness coupled with German cunning. As his driving tour through the Western zones progresses, he finds that the locals are far from embracing the liberal ideology that we might associate with the manners of colloquial America. Many of the Germans he meets harbor simmering resentment toward Jews and refugees and, in Munich in particular, against the very American occupation forces some of them imitate so well. Americans, he fears, are under a mimetic spell, convinced that Germans have changed, have disavowed authoritarianism, because where before U.S. officials saw only Nazis, they now see and hear only versions of themselves. And this copying phenomenon is not limited to the American territory. In the British zone "the Americanisms disappear and the bartender reports that a new restaurant is 'jolly good.'" The disconnect between *acting* and *being* has, in the words of the reporter, rendered Germans "rudderless" and occupation soldiers susceptible to all manner of deception. The accents, the clothes, and the menus may be different, but the Germans, one officer remarks, "haven't changed. If we left tomorrow [Nazi authoritarianism] would all come back."

The larger conundrum for the reporter is perhaps troubling to any occupier. How can the conqueror be sure that these denim-wearing Germans who look American on the outside are indeed "good little democrats" on the inside? How can one distinguish between the German who has sincerely embraced American ways from the one who is merely pretending? And what exactly is the connection between an ideology and an idiom? Why would acting like an American serve as an index of democratic vitality in the first place?

Leaving Germany and these questions for a moment, I want to turn to another example of occupation mimicry. The conqueror's fear that his wards are not as they appear finds a rejoinder from the perspective of the occupied in the aptly titled 1942 satire *To Be or Not to Be,* Ernst Lubitsch's incendiary send-up of life in Nazi-occupied Poland. The film opens in Warsaw, where a repertory acting troupe, rehearsing their anti-Nazi play *Gestapo,* learns that their government has canceled the play out of fear that it "might offend Hitler." Thus the troupe must go back to performing *Hamlet* until even this performance is upstaged by what the actors refer to as Hitler's own "show," the bombing and invasion of Poland—an offensive act, they observe, no censor can stop. The theater is shut down and the actors, who become entangled in the Polish resistance movement, take their Nazi act to the streets using the fake guns, the Nazi costumes, and even some of the Nazi dialogue from the canceled *Gestapo* play. One of the film's many running jokes is that the actors are successful in duping Nazis not only because the Poles have learned to mimic them, but because Nazis themselves behave just like Poles acting like Nazis. In the end, the troupe manages to escape Warsaw when one of them imitates the führer himself, a performance so convincing that even Hitler's own guards (who have commandeered the theater to put on a show for their leader) escort the actors to Adolf's private plane.

As Stephen Tifft explains in discussing Lubitsch's film, Hitler fashioned his political career around his "unparalleled sense of theater."[3] Biographer R. G. L. Waite remarks that Hitler "saw himself as a clever dissimulator who could 'fool people' into believing anything and who was, he said, 'the greatest actor in Europe.'"[4] In the

Actors from the Polski Theater rehearsing the anti-Nazi play *Gestapo* pause to listen to Hitler's radio address just before the Nazi invasion of Poland in *To Be or Not to Be* (Ernst Lubitsch, United Artists, 1942). Production still courtesy of Photofest.

Lubitsch film, the Poles' enactment makes abundantly clear that the führer, like the actor who plays him, is "just a man with a little mustache" with a flair for performance. If Nazism is essentially a matter of pageantry and showmanship, if Hitler is nothing more than a performance of himself, then he and his minions may fall prey to the very terms of their own illusion making. Ratcheting up the mimetic bombast, Lubitsch's film exposes the simulacral nature of Nazi posturing and, just as important, the power of the copy whose "original" is in any case a fiction. Mimesis becomes not only a means of surviving an occupation by pretending to be other, it is a political, even martial act of defeating that other. As the troupe flees to the airport, the resistance movement, undetected thanks to the actors' shenanigans, blows up the Nazi headquarters in Warsaw.

These two examples—one an eyewitness report from American-occupied Germany, the other a Hollywood film about Nazi-occupied Poland—illustrate that occupation mimicry is more than mere imitation. Mimicry may camouflage the occupied and in this way serve as a mechanism of subterfuge and resistance. Power (Nazi or American) becomes disarmed and even entranced when it sees itself reflected in the enemy. On the other hand, as Tifft notes, mimicry may function as a technology of "unwitting collaboration" and perhaps even authentic ideological conversion. Sometimes you are what you pretend to be or cannot escape becoming what others believe you resemble. For Adorno and Horkheimer, fascist indoctrination is predicated on precisely this instrumentality. The purpose of the fascist cult of formulas, "the ritualized discipline, the uniforms, and the whole allegedly irrational apparatus, is to make possible mimetic behavior. . . . The *Führer,* with his ham-actor's facial expression and the hysterical charisma turned on with a switch, leads the dance."[5] In mounting his attack on Nazism, Lubitsch, writes Tifft, mobilizes the "powers of rhetorical coercion akin to those of Nazi propaganda and power of histrionic and mechanical replication that are associated with the image of Hitler." But he does so "in the Allied cause."[6] That is, using Nazism against itself, Lubitsch stages the mimetic volleys between Germans and Poles in such a way that Nazism is undone when Germans become copies of their Polish imitations.

In a manner prefigured by the theatricality of Lubitsch's satire, U.S. occupation policy in Germany was also constructed as a mimetic pedagogy. U.S. authorities shipped close to two hundred Hollywood films and documentaries across the Atlantic to tutor Germans in the gestures, speech, and affect of democratic sociality. *Theaters of Occupation* is an extended meditation on the film culture produced in U.S.-occupied Germany, a culture that reverberated with the theatrical touchstones of occupation mimicry and the performative force of America's democratic fantasies. The U.S. military government believed that Germans would develop a politically enlightened culture, in part, if they could learn to act like Americans or like Hollywood actors portraying Americans, and to this end required that Hollywood films be screened in German theaters so that audiences could study the behaviors of everyday democratic life. As an industry and signifying system, Hollywood was held up as a model democratic institution that was replicated piecemeal in the American zone. But why use Hollywood films for democratic instruction?

Reflexive Democracy

The purpose of the occupation was to transform Germany from a totalitarian dictatorship into a peaceful, prosperous, and democratic republic that would no longer pose a military threat to its neighbors or to the rest of the "free" world. From 1945 to 1949, Germany was under the control of a foreign military government and for much of that time partitioned into four zones, one for each of the Allies (France, Britain, United States, and the Soviet Union) to govern and rebuild. Though the victors initially agreed on the basic tenets of demilitarization, deindustrialization, de-Nazification, and democratization in Germany (referred to as the "four D's"), they interpreted these directives differently and, with democratization especially, shaped policy according to their own national heritage and political myths. As Fritz Erler remarks, each power "tried to make out of its portion of Germany a kind of copy of the homeland. We had a little France, a little United States, a little England, and of course a little Russia."[7] Because the Allies promoted themselves as democracies and encouraged Germans to imitate their example, "democracy" became an elusive and always shifting abstraction that each of the Allies had to tether to other, more tangible concrete practices and systems of value. In each zone, motion pictures from the home country were part of a larger politico-cultural effort to remake Nazis into liberal democrats. Feature films, documentaries, and newsreels screened in the occupied country provided the experiential tropes, genres, structures of feeling, and images of democratic life that both tutored the Germans and differentiated the Allies from each other. Political propaganda became especially baroque when the Allied alliance gave way to the cold war.

For the Americans, democracy was never understood merely as a matter of voting, political self-determination, or the creation of parliamentary and juridical systems. Democracy was also a type of behavior, a public attitude, and an affective relationship to the state, independent of these other political institutions. In his memoir of the occupation, General Lucius D. Clay, who served in Germany as the U.S. military governor, devotes only one chapter of his book specifically to the question of democracy. Curiously, he does not discuss elections or political process but rather the importance of using "every available means" to "penetrate the German consciousness" with "hard, convincing facts" about "the ways of democracy." To this end, he writes, "the magazines, the press, the radio, books, moving pictures, the theater, music, lectures, and town meetings" were used to spread the gospel of democracy "in the meeting halls of trade unions, in the schools, and in the churches," and, of course, in movie theaters.[8] But what is democracy, and how do these media convey its hard, convincing facts? Clay discusses the details of military information infrastructure and the pressing need to politically "reeducate" Germany away from Nazi authoritarianism. But he offers no factual particulars because democracy is supposed to be a self-evident political and cultural truth. One of my projects in this book, then, is to read the American films screened in Germany for the "hard facts" and slippery truths that American democracy communicates.

Indeed, in the minds of U.S. occupation officials, American democracy was inseparable from its culture, a proposition supported by academics associated with the emerging field of psychoculturalism, an interdisciplinary movement devoted to the study of national character. Anthropologist Margaret Mead and neurologist Richard Brickner were among those psychoculturalist policy advisers who fervently believed that the United States produced a democratic character structure that could be the model for a new German citizen.[9] Specifically, they argued that German reeducation could be modeled on immigrant assimilation in the United States. Because immigrants became democratic citizens by embracing U.S. culture and everyday American habits, the immigrant narrative confirmed that character structure was not a genetic given but formed in relation to the political and economic culture of a nation. The project in Germany was not education—for everyone acknowledged that Germans were educated—but *reeducation* meant to undo the deep structures of the German collective identity in the way that U.S. immigrants learned to become democratic Americans, regardless of their birthplace or ethnic heritage. Mead and Brickner were particularly focused on reforming, even curing, Germany's national mental health and its citizens' "primitive" belief in the superiority of their race. Social groups who abided by racial determinism and tribal hermeticism, they argued, were blind to the work of culture and duped by the magic of blood. In the psychoculturalist view, Germany and Japan shared with primitive people a false sense of their racial formation and were given to a mass form of delusion, even psychosis. But mentally stable Americans, immigrant Americans especially, fully understood that culture and not blood is the basis for national belonging. How else could people from so many places all call themselves Americans?

Russ Castronovo and Dana D. Nelson discuss how the concept of democracy-as-culture has its own history, one that finds its most pronounced articulation in immigrant literature such as Andrew Carnegie's 1886 *Triumphant Democracy*. Of his book, they write:

> Here democracy is neither a moral category nor a neighborly virtue: it is a physiological response like swallowing or like what one's leg does when the doctor taps the knee. Democracy is America's default reflex, its parameters and properties rarely subjected to a critical view that could suggest that political forms and rhetoric are other than the result of a natural course of events.[10]

As a default reflex, democracy is hardly something learned through conventional education (or even reeducation) so much as acquired through mechanistic repetition of the body's hardwired responses to the state (one that modern authoritarian regimes perversely recondition, very often through cinema).[11] In the 1940s, this uniquely American idea of reflexive democracy was imported to and implemented in Germany with the effect that culture was highly politicized, gestures instrumentalized, and politics a matter of performance. The myth of immigrant assimilation became the master trope for German rehabilitation, and Hollywood films were screened to foster an imitative, virtually biomechanical relationship to politics.

The connection between democracy and immigration, however, suggests something more. Ali Behdad explains that "to be accepted as immigrants and to be eligible for citizenship, newcomers [to the United States] have had to forsake their ethnic identities and relinquish their political and cultural differences."[12] Considering that Germany's political reeducation is imagined as a process similar to assimilation, democracy is not an enlightened pluralistic philosophy so much as a homogenizing force. The logic of reeducation, if we want to call it that, is that "democracy" depends on a mimesis that erases difference. Is it little wonder that the gas station attendant and the hostess described earlier do not act just like Americans but, as if out of a B-movie, like stereotypes of Americans? We could make the case that Germans were primed for this kind of democratic pedagogy by Hitler's own mimetic indoctrination. Both Lubitsch and the *New York Times* correspondent caution, however, that we should not confuse Americanisms (or Nazisms) with Americanization or presume that Americanization is itself a sign of democratization. Mimicry is a close cousin to mockery, and outer and inner likenesses do not always correspond.

A Liberal Project

In their response to the U.S. film program as manifest in opinion surveys, film criticism, and German feature films produced under American military censorship, German spectators and filmmakers did not merely imitate Hollywood examples; they reinterpreted, adapted, and domesticated these fictions. German directors even managed to subtly mock, boldly contest, and at times empty these constructs of American citizenship by inverting the conventions of Hollywood genres.[13] These transmutations merit our attention because they animate some of the darker features of America's long historical project (particularly as celebrated in Hollywood westerns, World War II films, and musicals) and its short-term goal of rehabilitating Germans by molding them in and through the American image. Because of the rapid acceleration of American exceptionalism and Hollywood's global domination after the war, this study theorizes the limits and varieties of America's so-called democratic culture through the texture of its filmic representations at a moment and place where democracy was multiple, malleable, and culturally diffuse. Above all, film culture in Germany illuminates without resolving the inherent illogic of using a military occupation as a mechanism of regime change and democratization. Again Fritz Erler argues that "to introduce democracy by military government is a contradiction in itself," and, we might add, such an introduction puts pressure on democracy's relationship to collective will and desire, to say nothing of freedom.[14]

Democracy in post–Nazi-occupied Germany was riddled with the problems that complicate democracy's relationship to economic and political liberalism more generally. As a political process, democracy presumes an equal and fully enfranchised citizenry whose government carries out the popular or general will, even when that will moves to eliminate democratic institutions and processes. Liberalism, on the other hand, holds that individuals possess inalienable rights (to life, liberty, happiness, security, etc.) that the state *must* protect. But what if the *demos* chooses to impose limits on and/or circumscribe access to these rights? Either liberalism must give way to democracy or democracy to liberalism, or both give way to something else entirely. Numerous political theorists have noted that though we tend to think of democracy in tandem with liberalism, there is no guarantee that the process of the former will ensure the longevity of the latter. The paradox, as Chantal Mouffe argues, is that "both perfect liberty and perfect equality" are impossible.[15] According to the Public Opinion Survey Branch of the U.S. military government, even in 1948 the majority of Germans living in the American zone were in favor of a national policy determined by popular vote. Yet 46 percent of those questioned felt that human rights should be suspended when the state deemed it necessary, and 48 percent of respondents felt that some races were more fit for public office than others.[16] Further, with the onset of the cold war, the Western Allies feared that a minority of Germans could be swayed by the Soviet economic model. In the best scenario, the Americans did not want Germans to vote until Germans were sufficiently democratic, by which the Americans really meant liberal. But even liberalism became secondary to anticommunism. Reeducation then aimed at disposing Germany's general will toward democratic capitalism compatible with U.S. economic and political interests. American film propaganda tethered democracy to capitalism and liberalism and, beginning in 1948, to anticommunism. Capitalism, particularly as it was given representational form in Hollywood films and newsreels, was associated with a sensual mode of being (of smiling, laughing, eating, drinking, buying goods, and generally partaking of bodily delight) in contrast to the belt-tightening, anticonsumerist Soviet culture. Given the choice, American propaganda makes the decision easy, and it suggests that consumer freedom is the basis of the liberal state. This campaign evinced the logic of what Victoria de Grazia calls the "sociability" of market empire, which "defined liberty as the freedom of choice, privileged the marketplace and individual acquisitiveness as the means to access it, and tranquilly asserted that a vote in politics was not significantly different from making a choice in the market."[17] Where today we have become so saturated in this consumerist logic that we have to be reminded of what "democracy" really is, during the occupation the competing models of civic virtue and liberty so disentangled democracy from capitalism and liberalism that U.S. film propaganda strained to bring these terms into interchangeable relation.

Hollywood features were the perfect "democratic" medium for the occupation because, as the captains of industry argued, these films were produced in a market economy free from government censorship. To profit, they argued, Hollywood had to respond to (as opposed to dictate) American consumer desires. As a commodity and signifying medium, Hollywood films were presumed to be naturally imbued with the democratic sensibility of American spectators and thus could be shipped abroad as democratic products. In his statements before the House of Representatives' Special Committee on Postwar Economic Policy and Planning, Eric Johnston, president of the Motion Picture Association of America, asserted that, during the war, Hollywood films had effectively communicated the "story of America as the arsenal of democracy." In the postwar period, film had taken its place "beside the press and radio as one of the great media for the dissemination of information and enlightenment."[18] But, he argued, Hollywood films could not carry out their mission if beholden to trade restrictions in the United States or abroad or to government censorship (the former, in fact, was a means of carrying out the latter). Indeed, what for Johnston marked the Nazi film industry as fascist was "the complete ban on the importation of foreign [especially American] films." "This form of restriction," Johnston explained,

> dishonest in concept and purpose, too often arises from the fact that American pictures inescapably reflect our way of life. Some foreign critics fear our American system. Consequently, under one guise or another, they would keep out American pictures. They prefer to see the screen used as a weapon of ideological warfare.[19]

Out of political or economic self-interest, foreign governments erect trade barriers to Hollywood because, without such measures, their citizens would certainly pay to see films about the American way of life. Another Hollywood representative argued that in the United States, by contrast, "we have an absolutely free market for any country in the world to bring their pictures . . . but [to be successful] they must be pictures of the type that the American audience desires and wants to see."[20] What differentiated Hollywood as a democratic industry from its fascist counterparts was that the free market allowed consumers and not governments to choose

the films national audiences saw. Thus free trade was the economic cornerstone of free speech and trade barriers were indicators of totalitarian mind control.[21] This was Hollywood's brand
of market empire that was pointedly obscure in its description of
a democratic film defined as anything the American people will
pay to see. Based on the Hollywood model, the American occupation forces insisted that the German film market be open to free
trade, that the film industry abide by self-regulation as opposed
to government or civic censorship, and that any form of subsidies
or quota systems be banned. Yet as Johnston and others extolled
the virtues of Hollywood's free-trade ethos in Washington, in another part of D.C., Hollywood moguls were literally on trial for
violating Sherman antitrust legislation. In 1948, the U.S. Supreme
Court ruled that the major studios had colluded to maintain dominance in the American market through unfair exhibition practices
of block booking and blind buying and through control of the first-
run theater chains. As a result of these practices, independent and
foreign producers did not have access to American theaters and
thus to the American public.[22] Even by its own problematic definition, Hollywood did not abide by free-market democracy and the
German film industry would be held to "democratic" standards
Hollywood itself failed to meet. I dwell on this example not only
because it tidily illustrates Hollywood's bad-faith sociability abetted by a willful collapsing of democracy with market freedom, but
also because it shows how notions of reflexive democracy could
intersect with the democracy of market empire in the medium and
business of motion pictures. Hollywood films were brought to
Germany not because they conveyed some particular idea about
democracy, but because Germans could study them as artifacts of
a free-market, putatively democratic worldview. As both products
and instruments of democratic culture—as mass-produced fictions
for the heterogeneous, immigrant American masses—Hollywood
films also could be easily enfolded into the psychoculturalist pro-
scriptions for German reeducation.

Occupation Spectatorship

In Germany, film was at the periphery of the daunting tasks of reconstruction and even reeducation, and yet films brought to and
made in the occupied territory were shot through the complex negotiations that arise when nations create democratic fictions for
themselves and each other. In fact, *because* it was at the margins

of official life, film became a medium through which Germans rearticulated the relationship between culture and politics, democracy and consumerism, and contested the American model of each. Several chapters of this book are concerned with theorizing occupation subjectivity through German filmmaking and spectatorship. How, I ask, do German productions address themselves to the mandates of reeducation? How does the experience of filmgoing under the conditions of defeat and the loss of sovereignty change the way people read films? How do Hollywood genres become politically reenergized models within the occupation's image world? What is striking about the U.S. film program in Germany is that none of the Hollywood films shown there were made for German audiences or for the purpose of political pedagogy. Yet because of the circumstances of exhibition, these films were understood and interpreted through America's reeducation mission, though often in ways that turned these films against the Allied cause.

Again Lubitsch's film provides one exaggerated example of how a besieged population appropriates texts that initially have nothing do to with occupation. The actors, recall, are forced by Polish censors to cancel *Gestapo* because it explicitly critiques Nazi secret police tactics. But they are permitted to perform *Hamlet* because the world and poetics of Shakespeare are putatively so remote from the war that the play may pass as mere entertainment. Hamlet's soliloquy, after which Lubitsch's film is titled, however, serves mostly to highlight the hamming antics of the lead actor, Joseph Tura (Jack Benny), who is incensed when a young man in the audience leaves the auditorium (for a secret rendezvous with Mrs. Tura backstage) just as Mr. Tura begins his showstopping speech. It is rather the Rialto scene from *The Merchant of Venice* that becomes, with each of its iterations, an increasingly biting commentary on life in Nazi-occupied Poland. I briefly describe the three moments in Lubitsch's film in which the Rialto scene figures.

We first hear lines from *The Merchant of Venice* before the occupation begins. While *Hamlet* unfolds on stage, backstage two of the troupe's bit actors bemoan their lowly roles in this play in which they do little more than carry spears. Consoled in the belief that "they can't keep real talent down forever," Bronski (Tom Dugan) clings to the day he'll finally get his big break playing Hitler in *Gestapo*, and Greenberg (Felix Bressart), convinced that Shakespeare wrote Shylock with him in mind, rehearses a redacted version of Shylock's famous speech for his winsome, spear-carrying colleague:[23]

In *To Be or Not to Be,* Greenberg (Felix Bressart) recites the Rialto scene to Bronski (Tom Dugan) backstage in their costumes for *Hamlet.* Production still courtesy of Wisconsin Center for Film and Theater Research, University of Wisconsin, Madison.

Have I not eyes? Have I not hands, organs, senses, dimensions, affections, passions? Fed with the same food, hurt with the same weapons, subject to the same diseases? If you prick us, do we not bleed? If you tickle us, do we not laugh? If you poison us, do we not die?

This bit of rhetorical showmanship is initially quotation for the sake of highbrow quotation, though it hyperbolically intimates that these ambitious actors are "victims" of a coldhearted director whose casting decisions recognize neither their talent nor their humanity.

Greenberg later repeats Shylock's lines just after Hitler bombs and invades Warsaw and institutes the violent regime of occupation. As the voice-over phrases it, "The curtain has fallen on the Polish drama, a tragedy with no relief in sight." Accordingly, the theater is closed and the actors reduced to manual laborers. Bronski and Greenberg take a pause from shoveling snow as Greenberg once again delivers Shylock's speech. Dejected and genuinely moved to tears by the Nazi invasion, Greenberg need not summon his actorly skills to convey Shylock's abjection. What earlier was merely a backstage appeal to his absent *director* is transformed into a poignant plea to the absent *dictator* on all of Poland's behalf. As this scene ends, the actors wonder aloud if they (and perhaps all of

Bronski and Greenberg shoveling snow just before Greenberg recites the Rialto scene the second time. Production still courtesy of Wisconsin Center for Film and Theater Research, University of Wisconsin, Madison.

Poland) will ever carry spears again, a question that has as much to do with Poland's sovereignty as it does with their stalled careers.

It is during the final citation of the speech, however, that Bronski and Greenberg perform their coveted roles before an audience. The Polish troupe dresses in their Nazi costumes and plans a distraction in the lobby on the occasion of Hitler's visit to the Polski theater. The real Hitler takes his seat in the auditorium, and while his troops sing "Deutschland, Deutschland über alles," the fake Hitler (played by Bronski) is confronted by what the Nazi guards assume is a Polish resistance fighter who, in fact, is played by Greenberg. Before an audience of Nazi troops the actors perform the following lines:

JOSEPH TURA (dressed as a Nazi general, to Greenberg): How did you get here?

GREENBERG (dressed as Polish resister): I was born here!

TURA: And what made you decide to die here?

GREENBERG (gesturing to Bronski disguised as Hitler): Him!

TURA: What do you want from the Führer?

GREENBERG: What does he want from us? What does he want from Poland? Why all this? Why? Aren't we human? Have we not eyes? Have we not hands, organs, senses, dimensions, affections, passions? Fed with the same food, hurt with the same weapon, subject to the same diseases, healed by the same means, cooled and warmed by the same winter and summer? If you prick us, do we not bleed? If you tickle us, do we not laugh? If you poison us, do we not die? If you wrong us, shall we not revenge?

Shylock's humanist entreaty is now a forthrightly political and threatening remonstrance that beseeches Hitler/Bronski to consider the injustice of occupation and Nazi brutality in Poland. Gerd Gemünden points out that in this final version the line "If you wrong us, shall we not revenge?" withheld from the two previous rehearsals, resounds with Poles' "refusal of victimhood."[24] To be or not to be under Nazi occupation: that is the film's guiding question.

This accumulated, layered meaning stages the manner in which texts—even seemingly escapist Hollywood films—may become politicized when read through the material and experiential conditions of occupation. It is significant, moreover, not only how the inflection of this speech changes each time, but how the performance venue alters the meaning of Shylock's appeal. Greenberg's final act, delivered not on stage but in the theater's lobby, is perceived not as a performance in the theatrical sense, but, to the German soldiers who think they have apprehended a Polish terrorist, performative in the very real and transformative sense. As I discuss throughout this book, the German movie theater became a site of protest and film criticism, a venue for political critique. And while few of the Hollywood films shipped to Germany lent themselves to such virtuosic manipulation as Shylock's speech, German audiences read them in rather unexpected ways that exposed the hypocrisy of the re-education campaign and the perils of genuinely imitating America's contemporary culture or its developmental experience. Chapter 2, for example, concludes with a discussion of how Hollywood westerns, screened to "inspire" Germans with stories of America's pioneers, could be read as confessions of the United States' own genocidal origins. Later in the book I return to Lubitsch in my analysis of *Ninotchka* (Lubitsch, 1939), the centerpiece of the U.S. military government's anti-Soviet campaign in Germany. Though made on the eve of World War II, this film uncannily anticipates both the mimetic and sensual tropes of America's cold war propaganda and the American caricature of capitalist democracy in contrast to communist totalitarianism. In Berlin, especially, where the cold war was experienced through the Soviet blockade and Allied airlift, *Ninotchka* was not received as just *anti-Soviet* propaganda. As political satire, it poked fun at America's binary political logic, its hunger diplomacy, and its attempts at ideological manipulation. In another context, I consider how "female gothic" films, especially George Cukor's *Gaslight* (1944), offered Germany's predominantly female spectators an emotional and political narrative that was especially resonant with and critical of occupation life. Studies in film reception have long shown us how meaning is destabilized when films are shown to different audiences in different time periods.[25] In Germany, where Hollywood cinema was part of an official platform of nation building and civic rehabilitation, the stakes of these interpretations were of considerable consequence, not only to the narratives that would shape West Germany's national founding but to America's postwar democratic image.

Occupation Cinema

This book is also concerned with German films made under the authority of the U.S. military government. The Americans granted production licenses only to directors whose political history

cleared them of Nazi involvement and whose screenplays broadly
supported the reeducation dicta that held Germans responsible for
the war, the Holocaust, and even for the privations of the occupation itself. The standard scholarly approach to films of this era is
to assess how they negotiate Germany's complicated relationship
to anti-Semitism and to the country's National Socialist past.[26] I
venture a reading that builds on this scholarship but argues that we
can best appreciate these postwar films as responding to the more
proximate experience of occupation, reeducation, and Hollywood's
own mode of historical reckoning as it played out in the American
zone. For example, Rudolf Jugert's 1949 *Hallo, Fräulein!* is a hybrid, folk-jazz German–American musical about fraternization in
which a character's political sympathies are transparently reflected
in his or her cultural aptitude. In this film, being democratized
amounts to little more than throwing off a convincing jazz performance. Produced at the end of foreign military rule, the film slyly
critiques the cultural logic of reeducation as a mode of political
performance. More distressing, this film holds a mirror to the racial
politics of Hollywood musicals and myths of multiethnic America
by reproducing this logic in the postwar German context. These
gestures problematize the proposition of reeducation through imitation and expose the process by which democratic myths come
into being.

   In a similar vein, Helmut Käutner's 1948 *Der Apfel ist ab* is
a musical satire that allegorizes life under military occupation
through the story of Adam and Eve's fall from grace and expulsion
from paradise. Upon its release, *Der Apfel* was denounced by the
Catholic Church and turned into a cause célèbre for more stringent
film censorship. Such that it has been taken up in scholarly literature, this debate is what makes the film important.[27] But I read
Der Apfel not as a satire of original sin but as a parable of democratic beginnings and the particular problems of national founding
in West Germany. Adam's inability to choose between two women
(Eve and Lilith) and between heaven and hell reflects his inadequacy
for political choice making even as it pokes fun at the limited range
of choices he can make. In Adam's world, decisions are a matter
between two premade options, a choice in 1948 that mirrored the
binary logic of the cold war. Both *Der Apfel* and *Hallo, Fräulein!*
do not simply look back to and then evade Germany's past; they
ironically and obtusely critique their contemporary moment and

anxiously look forward to Germany's political future and cultural life in the occupation's wake. Coupling these Germans films with their Hollywood examples, I am interested in the generic resonances of the two national cinemas and, in particular, how these genres emplot the politics and experience of occupation and national founding. Thus, there is one chapter on satire, another on the musical, and a final chapter on the female gothic.

Occupation and the Contact Zone

My approach to occupation film culture is informed by political theory (especially theories of democracy), literary criticism, psychoanalysis, and ethnography, and I borrow from the disciplinary models of film studies, German history, the history of U.S. foreign relations, and cultural studies. My readings, however, are grounded in the archive of the U.S. military government and inspired by the films brought to and shot in the U.S.-occupied zone. Though the chapters proceed in roughly chronological order, this is not to be taken as a history of the occupation. I have organized material thematically to underscore the call and response of occupation pedagogy. The first chapter lays the historical and conceptual groundwork for reeducation, with particular attention to cinema's relationship to national character and the psycho-culturalist research on Nazi Germany. I focus on Leslie Fenton's 1944 *Tomorrow—the World!* a film that dramatized for American audiences the urgency of reeducation and, in many ways, staged the reorientation-as-assimilation paradigm that would be imported to Germany. Chapter 2 is itself contrapuntally organized. The first part mines the U.S. military government's archive and tracks how and to what pedagogical ends Hollywood films were selected for political modeling. The second part of the chapter decodes the "hard facts" about democratic life these Hollywood films encrypt. The cold war, beginning in 1947, necessitated a revision of reeducation policy, and chapter 3 considers how American films, including the newsreel *Welt im Film (World in Film),* constructs a sensual basis for West German democratic citizenship, which also suggested, in its many rhymes between Americans and West Germans, that the mimetic pedagogy of the occupation's first years had succeeded in making former Nazis into America's democratic allies. *Der Apfel ist ab* not only questions German readiness for self-rule, it parodies this cold war campaign. Jugert's 1949 *Hallo, Fräulein!* made at the end of the occupation, is at the center of chapter 4. Here I analyze how German filmmakers, now with a few years of American propaganda under their belts, create their own discourse of German multiculturalism and democracy under the pressure of cold war politics, a discourse that is informed by Hollywood and Allied film censorship as well as by the structure of the nascent West German film industry's self-regulation. The book's final chapter is a meditation on occupation subjectivity as read through the genre of the female gothic, specifically through Cukor's *Gaslight*, which premiered in Germany in 1948. Inspired by Bonnie Honig's reading of the female gothic as the genre of democracy, I argue that this film not only captures the gothic edges of occupation experience, it actually teaches important lessons about democratic citizenship.

This transatlantic, comparative approach to film culture will, I hope, allow us to understand the occupation as a political and signifying phenomenon that transcends its designation as merely a phase in German history or a discreet project of U.S. foreign policy. Though Germany is my example, *the politics and culture of occupation* is my subject. Where today Germany stands as a shadow paradigm for U.S. nation building in Afghanistan and Iraq, we should look to this historical example for what it tells us about an occupation more generally. The contestations over culture and identity, guilt and accountability, mimicry and invention in Germany suggest first that an occupation is a military affair far more intimate and transculturally generative than war. Where occupier and occupied must negotiate their relative positions of power and powerlessness daily, in close proximity, and rather closed off from the rest of the world, the occupied territory produces a unique interpretative space and politicized culture, one akin to what Mary Louise Pratt famously calls "the contact zone." In this geographic and social space "disparate cultures meet, clash, and grapple with each other, often in highly asymmetrical relations of domination and subordination—like colonialism, slavery, or their aftermaths as they are lived out across the globe today." The contact zone refers not just to the space, but to the nature of "relations among colonizers and colonized, or travelers and 'travelees' . . . in terms of copresence, interaction, interlocking understandings and practices."[28] Obviously the American occupation of Germany is *not* an example of colonial encounter insofar as it is a contact between two imperial and familiar peoples at the frontier of "first world" postwar reconstruction. Yet there are several features of this occupation that merit this comparison.[29] The Allies argued that Germany's unconditional surrender and the collapse of its civil institutions granted the occupation administration complete power over the country *and* its people. Functionally stripping Germans of their sovereign rights, the Allies declared that Germany as a state no longer existed. Eyal Benvenisti explains that the occupation was a hotly debated interpretation of the Hague Regulation, prescribing that "sovereignty may not be alienated through the use of force."[30] The Hague Regulation is but one mechanism that legally sanctions occupation as a martial enterprise distinct from colonization. It is little wonder that "occupation" was semantically contested by some German legal scholars for whom the years 1945 to 1949 were a period of "alien domination."[31] Germany's exceptional status intimates how the politicization of culture as an instrument of both occupation rule and occupied resistance may be informed by the colonial context. This should not be taken to suggest that we should in any way sympathize with unreconstructed Nazis as we might with colonized subjects or that the power imbalances between occupier and occupied in Germany were as asymmetrical or as brutal as other examples of military occupation and colonial rule. But on legal grounds alone, Germany is a limit case. Further, the pedagogical discourse of cultural/political mimicry and German primitivism, combined with America's explicit desire to remake Germans into immigrant Americans, indicates that the occupation of Germany heralded a new imperial paradigm for America's post-imperial, soon-to-be preemptive foreign policy. Because this was an occupation involving two Western, Europeanized, predominantly white cultures, and because Nazism was so reviled the world over, we tend not to question the efficacy of America's German project in the way we might the occupation of Japan. Because postwar Germany is rather unthinkable in a colonial context, it has served as an exemplary template for subsequent occupations to deflect accusations of U.S. imperial designs on the Middle East and to justify or bury the cultural evisceration that accompanies foreign military rule.[32]

With this in mind, I conclude the book on the fiftieth anniversary of the Berlin airlift and President Bill Clinton's commemorative visit to Tempelhof International Airport. A refurbished plane from the original Berlin Allied airlift mission, named *The Spirit of Freedom*, was exhibited on the tarmac while Clinton and Chancellor Helmut

Kohl christened a new C-17 Globemaster cargo plane *The Spirit of Berlin*. Among its first missions was to fly U.S. CARE packages to beleaguered Afghanistan. The airlift, I argue, has not only eclipsed all other aspects of occupation, it has become shorthand for American military operations that "rescue" foreign populations from dictators and that, in the wake of war and Allied bombing and in Helmut Kohl's own words, turn "victors" into "protectors and partners."[33] It is beyond the scope of this book to map a cultural history of American occupations. I focus on Germany and can gesture only to a few of the rhymes between the 1940 campaign in Europe and the turn-of-the-century campaign in the Middle East. It is my hope, however, that this study of cinema and occupation in Germany may help generate a comparative study of occupation policy that questions the relationship between culture and politics and that seeks to understand occupation as a military operation with a historical and interpretative force of its own.

1. Germany Is a Boy in Trouble

One of the leading nations within the framework of our civilization, Germany, has to be handled as a gifted but dangerous boy who must be watched and controlled by strict though well-meaning masters.

—How to Treat the Germans (1943)

In 1944, in anticipation of the American occupation of Germany, Leslie Fenton's star-studded *Tomorrow—the World!* dramatized for U.S. audiences the urgent proposition of reeducating Nazi youth in the wake of Allied victory. Based on the successful Broadway show that earned the New York Theater Club's medal for the best American play of the year, *Tomorrow—the World!* was named *Redbook*'s "Film of the Month" and granted the *Senior Scholastic* Blue Ribbon. It also won the first Hollywood Writers Mobilization Award for distinctive film entertainment for its politically trenchant, reasoned, and timely depiction of the psychological effects of Nazi education on German youth.[1] While wartime Hollywood typically represented Nazi cunning and militarism as dangerous but still recognizably human impulses, *Tomorrow* was the first film to provide the narrative contours of German postwar rehabilitation and to depict the inherent mutability of the enemy's disposition such that one of *them* could become one of *us*.

The plot centers on Emil Bruckner (Skippy Homeier), a fully indoctrinated but orphaned Hitler fanatic who comes to live with his American uncle, Professor Mike Frame (Fredric March), in small-town USA. Rather than accept his refugee status, Emil is deliriously convinced that he has been sent to the United States as a Nazi spy and thus mounts a one-child attack against the Frame family and the town. As Emil lashes out with ever-escalating violence toward Jews, women, and immigrant-American schoolchildren, he becomes an experiment in German reeducation and a limit case of immigrant assimilation. Emil rejects as degenerate the examples of liberal citizenship he encounters, such as the assimilated German-immigrant housekeeper Frieda (Edit Angold), the interethnic romance between Mike and his Jewish fiancée Leona (Betty Field), and Emil's multiethnic classroom where students abide by the "all are created equal" creed. Rather than becoming "less different" (to use Mike's tendentious expression) through his contact with American schoolchildren, Emil begins to influence the small town by teaching Boy Scouts to be soldiers, by atomizing the melting-pot classroom into its discrete ethnic and religious types, and by adapting Nazi "divide and conquer" strategies to the territory of the Frame household. As a threat to the unity of his family, classroom, and town, Emil must either learn the codes of American sociality or spend his remaining adolescence in a reformatory.

To encourage American audiences to discuss publicly the connections between the film's plot and America's commitment to Germany, the film's distributor, United Artists, recommended that the following editorial be sent to local newspapers:

> Can we, having defeated in battle an army and a people imbued with the Nazi ideology, turn our backs on our victory and face the possibilities that our children will in twenty years once more face these boys as full-grown enemies? We believe that our attitude towards the Germans, our willingness to accept our responsibilities to the world along with our allies, is the first test of how we understand the issues of this war and the nature of the present German state.

United Artists' publicity department suggested that exhibitors invite mayors and town officials, school principals, and ministers to the film's opening, entreating, "[G]et them to talk about the picture from their pulpits!" The conversations the film was to inspire would have been enriched by the spate of social scientific research and political analysis increasingly pitched to American citizens to mobilize consent for a prolonged foreign occupation by outlining how the Allies would democratize and thus fundamentally alter the national character and collective psychology of an enemy population. In a 1942 national radio address, Vice President Henry Wallace put the vocabulary of this process into the public record:

> The German people must learn to un-learn all that they have been taught, not only by Hitler, but by his predecessors in the last hundred years, by so many of their philosophers and teachers, the disciples of blood and iron. . . . We must de-educate and re-educate people for Democracy. . . . The only hope for Europe remains in a change of mentality on the part of the German. He must be taught to give up the century-old conception that his is a master race.[2]

Here postwar plans to "un-learn," "de-educate," and "re-educate" explicitly connect foreign policy to a political pedagogy designed to radically alter the deep structures of German history. Elsewhere the lexicon of German reeducation mingled with biological, neurological, and even mystical tropes of "re-birth," "mental reconstruction," and "de-hypnosis."[3] James Tent notes that however diffuse the jargon, German reeducation was popularized as a fundamentally "rehabilitative process based on the assumptions of the Enlightenment that human nature is essentially rational and 'good.'"[4] In academic circles, this terminology grew out of an emerging interdisciplinary field of psychoculturalism. Advocated by such luminaries as Harvard sociologist Talcott Parsons, cultural anthropologist Margaret Mead, Columbia neurologist Richard Brickner, and child psychoanalyst Erik H. Erikson, psychoculturalism analyzed German economic, political, and social institutions as well as individual patterns of behavior as expressions of a unified "national character structure." A product of traditions passed on from one generation to the next, character structure was an evolving cultural construct that, while manifested and reinforced in all aspects of a national, social, and psychic life, could nonetheless be changed: "The psycho-cultural approach . . . proposes not only a new approach to Germany, but presents a novel problem of deliberately seeking the transformation of a people by altering their traditional culture and methods of carrying on social life."[5] Once wrested from the everyday regimentation of Nazism and subjected to the crippling circumstances of defeat, Germans would be able to form new traditions, orient themselves toward the political and economic promises of liberalism, and develop a democratic character structure of their own.

And who better to provide a model of the democratic character than Hollywood? At home, motion pictures could promote the re-education process to the American citizen whose tax dollars would finance the occupation, while in Germany Hollywood films would model for German citizens and filmmakers alike the codes and affects of democratic comportment. In this connection *Tomorrow* is particularly interesting for the way it maps out and participates in a democratic pedagogy intended to construct Nazism as a form of primitive regress and to naturalize American citizenship as the rational embodiment of enlightenment thought. In this chapter, I trace the formulation and popularization of America's reeducation campaign in Germany by mapping the discursive image world it produced. For American audiences, Hollywood depicted reeducation as assimilation in terms strikingly similar to those advanced by the American social scientific community. Mining the archives of the U.S. military government in Germany, I also begin to explain how and by what logic Hollywood features were shipped to the occupied territory to teach Germans about democracy. By reading *Tomorrow—the World!* through popular and contemporary studies on national character, group psychology, and America's own ethnographic imaginary, we can unpack the particularities of this enlightened and uniquely American humanism and specify the process by which the U.S. government would transform Nazis into democratic citizens.

Tomorrow—the World! and the Case of Emil Bruckner

Tomorrow—the World! is a study of Nazi culture as expressed through a thirteen-year-old boy whose fanatical allegiance to the führer is an expression of both political will and pubescent rage. What makes Emil threatening, however, is the sway he has over the other boys in his class, who, for a short while, make him their leader. In keeping with Erik H. Erikson's landmark study "The Legend of Hitler's Childhood," *Tomorrow* suggests that Nazism is a mode of juvenile delinquency and rebellion on a national scale.[6] Hitler, "the gang leader" and self-fashioned "adolescent who never gave in," had, in Erikson's reading, promoted a national culture that "replaced the complicated conflict of adolescence as it pursued every German, with simple patterns of hypnotic action and freedom from thought" so that all youthful energy was spent on the National Socialist cause (337, 342). Rather than pass through puberty, Hitler's Germans were, like their leader, in a state of pro-tracted adolescence. Unquestioningly, they rejected God, parents, ethics, brotherhood, friends, and learning. And they were suscep-tible to a binary racial logic that associated Aryans with all that is light, clean, and pure and Jews with all that is dark, soft, and infectious. Ventriloquizing Nazi propaganda, Erikson explains that in the black-and-white world of the German mentality, all that mattered was "to be on the move without looking backward. 'Let everything go to pieces, we shall march on. For today Germany is ours; tomorrow, the whole world'" (343). Where Erikson proposes to rehabilitate Germany by reviving local and regional culture and by politically empowering women (mothers in particular) to divest the state of its centralized and hypermasculinized military culture, *Tomorrow* (and, as we shall see below, Erikson's fellow psycho-culturalists) proposes to rehabilitate the Nazi by assimilating him into American culture, a solution Erikson's later work revealed as problematic.[7]

As an adolescent boy in trouble, Emil Bruckner seems to ex-emplify all that is wrong with Nazi Germany. So beholden is he to the simple patterns of hypnotic action that he recites with pro-grammatic exactness Goebbels's propaganda, and he mechanically reproduces the *Sieg Heil* and heel clicking of German soldiers. His account of the inequitable Treaty of Versailles and the liberal be-trayal of Germany following World War I—which, in a trance, he precisely repeats twice—is compared by Mike to a phonographic record; Emil's disquisition to the class on Brazil's strategic im-portance is likened by one of his classmates to a national radio broadcast. Dismissing all corrections to National Socialist history as liberal misinformation, Emil is an empty, affectless epigone of Nazi mass culture. Yet most troubling to his Uncle Mike is that Emil often recounts how his father, Karl Bruckner, the celebrated liberal German educator and Mike's own mentor and brother-in-law, committed suicide in cowardly deference to his Nazi challeng-ers, a story Emil believes because he read about it in all the Nazi newspapers.

When Mike's daughter Pat (Joan Carroll) discovers Emil trying to steal Mike's secret government documents related to his academic work for the war effort, Emil's vitriol turns violent. He strikes Pat

In "The Blitz That Failed," Emil (Skippy Homeier) is defeated in a fistfight by
his Polish-American classmate Stan (Rudy Whistler). Promotional material
for *Tomorrow—the World!* (Leslie Fenton, United Artists, 1944). Courtesy of
Wisconsin Center for Film and Theater Research, University of Wisconsin,
Madison.

on the back of the head with a fireplace poker and, under the pur-
suit of Pat's classmates, runs into the woods. In a showdown that
United Artists marketed as "The Blitz That Failed!" Emil is defeated in a fistfight by the Polish-American boy Stan Dumbrowski
and dragged back to the Frame residence for his official punishment. Awakened to Emil's pathological rage, Mike decides to turn
his nephew over to juvenile court. While Emil waits for the police
to arrive, Leona makes one final attempt to reach the boy by having
him open his birthday present from Pat, an expensive wristwatch
with an illuminated face and seventeen jewels, which he has repeatedly requested. When he opens the box, his stoicism gives way
to remorseful sobs, signaling to Leona that he might be a normal
boy beneath his fascist shell. In the film's dramatic apex, Leona
makes the argument that to incarcerate Emil is not only to evade
the larger German question he represents but to admit the failure
of reeducation: "Oh, Mike, don't you see? If you and I can't turn
one little child into a human being, heaven help the world when the
war is won and we have to deal with twelve million of them."

Mike is unmoved until the little Nazi appears to undergo a
more substantive conversion. At Mike's request, Emil once again
rehearses the narrative of his father's betrayal. But when Mike it-
erates this story back to the boy, Emil is caught off guard by his

Leona (Betty Field) presents Emil with an expensive watch for his birthday in *Tomorrow—the World!* Production still courtesy of Wisconsin Center for Film and Theater Research, University of Wisconsin, Madison.

mimetic display. "Uncle Mike, why are *you* saying these things?" Out of this confusion Emil finally speaks, as it were, off the record; he questions the official story, begins to narrate the "correct" version of German history, and, through this arc, the history of his own family and troubled adolescence. His father did not commit suicide, as the Nazis claimed, but died, with his American wife, in a concentration camp because the Nazis were threatened by his revolutionary ideas; because he was Karl Bruckner's son, Emil now claims that he was beaten, isolated, and brainwashed. The boy's reeducation is presented to us not as an education per se, but as a rational confrontation with and correction to Nazi propaganda (though, significantly, Emil is now merely reciting a version of history we have heard Mike explain at least twice before). More important is Emil's psychological rehabilitation and entry into adult subjectivity. Having unlearned Nazi codes, he becomes for the first time a sympathetic and mature subject of feeling. We thus infer that his Nazi performance is not simply the product of indoctrination but a defense mechanism produced by an immature, paranoid, and deeply troubled mind. Even Emil tearfully admits, "I'm all mixed up."

In the film's final sermon, Mike provisionally accepts Emil back into the family and soberly explains the nature of democratic inquiry:

> Anytime anybody tells you anything, you've got to ask why. That's the difference between us and the Nazis. We want people to ask questions. But get this straight, Emil: what happens is really up to you. . . . Whether you like it or not, you'll play according to the rules. And don't kid yourself that just because we want to help you that we're soft or that you can put anything over on us again. In fact, it's about time that you and your people in Germany woke up to the fact that we can be just as tough as you can, and a lot tougher.

Mike addresses the entire German population on behalf of the United States and thus situates this living room drama on the stage of world affairs. Ready now to embrace American conventions of civility and reason, Emil sheds once and for all his Nazi persona and joins the others for breakfast as a member of the Frame family and the American citizenry.

Although Emil's apostasy is dramatized in the film as a renunciation of Nazi propaganda, his conversion was advertised in one of United Artists' promotional photo spreads as the "Making of an American." The chronological triptych begins with Skippy Homeier posing stoically as Emil in his Reich-issued uniform. The accompanying ad copy explains that Skippy "portrays the typical Nazi youth, perverted by the false Nazi claims of a 'super-race.'" The second photo features Skippy now wearing Emil's civilian clothes after losing a scuffle with his Polish American classmate. Here Emil, defeated, with his eye blackened and his fist clenched, "realizes the truth." The iconic transformation concludes in the third shot in which Skippy, healed and kempt, beams before the camera. The caption explains, "The final panel shows how American life and ideals can change at least one member of the 'super-race.'" This series of images attracts patrons to the film with the promise of a "dramatic story of the regeneration of a youth trained in the Nazi tradition who learns the meaning of Americanism in this country." But in this last photograph, Skippy smiles with an exuberance Emil never displays in the film, which speaks to the star power of this

Making of An American!

"Tomorrow, The World!" is the dramatic story of the regeneration of a youth trained in the Nazi tradition who learns the meaning of Americanism in this country. Here Skippy Homeier, phenomenal child star, who plays the Nazi-trained youth, Emil Bruckner, gives a graphic impression of the change of the boy from the first instance of his arrival in America until he casts aside the Nazi uniform forever. ·

In the first panel he portrays the typical Nazi youth, perverted by the false Nazi claims of a super-race. In the second he has met his match in American boyhood and after being beaten in a fist fight with a boy his own age realizes the truth. The final panel shows how American life and ideals can change at least one member of the "super-race."

Fredric March and Betty Field are starred in this challenging film as the lovers who must cope with the problem of Emil. Others in the cast are Agnes Moorehead, Joan Carroll and Edit Angold.

The part of Emil marks Skippy Homeier's first screen appearance. Already he has been hailed throughout the nation for his superb performance. You too will ask, can we save Emil?

"Tomorrow, The World!" which was directed by Leslie Fenton from the screenplay by Ring Lardner, Jr., is now playing at the . . . . Theatre through United Artists release.

Skippy Homeier dramatizes Emil's transformation from a "typical Nazi youth" to a beaming American boy. Courtesy of Wisconsin Center for Film and Theater Research, University of Wisconsin, Madison.

child actor even as it suggests that his German character does not survive the American remaking. The tableaux of regeneration thus erase the Nazi *and* the German and dramatize reeducation as a performance or imitation of national affect.

A Mass-Mediated Pedagogy

Emil's American reeducation does not include going to the movies, listening to American radio, or reading newspapers or pulp fiction. If anything, the film implicitly critiques mass media as a fascist mechanism of mind control in contrast to humanistic pedagogy. Yet *Tomorrow—the World!* preached its tale of rehabilitation within the horizon of American mass culture and mass consumption.

Tomorrow was the subject of a sixteen-page graphic adaptation in *Comic Cavalcade,* which boasted a circulation of nearly three million in 1945. Billed nationally in newspapers, *Tomorrow* was featured in full-page advertisements in *Life* and *Parents* magazines, while *Calling All Girls,* America's most widely circulated magazine for "sub-debs," ran a cover story on Joan Carroll in connection to her role as Pat Frame. On the radio, Betty Field promoted the film on CBS's "Stage Door Canteen," reaching an estimated thirteen million listeners; Fredric March plugged the film on CBS's "Frank Sinatra Show"; and phonographic trailers for the film were distributed to the most prominent national talk shows. In keeping with Hollywood's penchant for product tie-ins, the film was used to sell ladies' and girls' fashions, women's magazines, and comic books. Advertisements for the film featuring a photo inset of Emil opening his birthday present appeared in the windows of neighborhood Harmon brand watch dealers. Though the watch in the film is described but not branded, it is the single commodity that has the power to bring even the staunchest Nazi to tears. Emil's Nazi venom was used to promote local war bond drives, which entreated citizens to support their country by purchasing bonds and seeing the film (in which Emil is framed conspicuously against war bond posters). As both a film and an event, *Tomorrow* brought American adults and schoolchildren together in Hollywood's industrial-commercial public sphere aimed at selling movie tickets through a range of emotional and sensational vectors, all tied to norms of American citizenship, patriotism, and consumerism.

But unique to this campaign, United Artists orchestrated the pedagogical possibilities of cinema in ways suggestive of the democratizing powers of American mass culture. *Tomorrow—the World!* was brought into American schools via *Senior Scholastic* and *Junior Scholastic* magazines, which, in connection to cover stories on the film, asked their five million subscribers to submit to their teachers their essays addressing how they would "re-educate a boy or girl of [their] own age who came from Germany to live in America, so that he or she might become an accepted citizen of the world."[8] *Comic Cavalcade* sponsored a national essay contest based on its own rendition of the plot, which significantly omitted the film's reconciliatory ending, instead leaving Mike suspicious of Emil's conversion. *Cavalcade* thus queried its seventh- and eighth-grade audience:

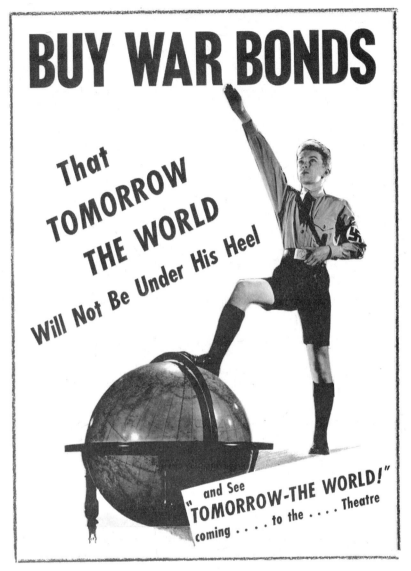

In this poster, Emil is the child threat that may motivate patrons to buy
war bonds. Courtesy of Wisconsin Center for Film and Theater Research,
University of Wisconsin, Madison.

What would *you* do with Emil Bruckner? Those of you who have seen the stirring play or motion picture "Tomorrow—the World!" may or may not agree with its authors and producers as to its ending: Even Professor Frame is not sure in his own mind . . . and so we offer . . . $ONE THOUSAND DOLLARS IN PRIZES$ . . . FOR THE BEST LETTERS TELLING US "WHAT YOU WOULD DO WITH EMIL BRUCKNER!"[9]

Just as the film contrasts the mimetic project of Nazism—wherein children merely repeat what they learn from propagandistic media—against the pedagogy of American individualism and critical questioning, the contests did not ask students simply to replicate the film's discourse but to interrogate its lesson and improvise around its themes. The winning *Senior Scholastic* essay by Kansas high schooler Shirley Deck, titled "Democracy versus Nazism," argued that we could democratize the German student by showing him examples of American cultural life, including a baseball game and American classical concerts that include German music, and, of course, by inviting him to watch an American election "because it is one of the most typically American things we do." She includes no direct references to the film or even to its central character (she calls her Nazi Wilhelm Krueger), but Shirley seems to have learned the film's lesson about democratic nurturing when, echoing Mike Frame, she writes of her ward, "The Nazis robbed him of his inborn capacity to reason and question, and substituted blind obedience. Our first step then would be to reverse the Nazi training and encourage Wilhelm to think and to question."[10] According to this campaign, Hollywood movies could not only model democratic reeducation in their narratives, they could invigorate civic debate outside of the theater and enhance participatory engagement with world politics, or at least provide a forum for students to reproduce a discourse about reason and free thinking.

Hollywood's Liberal Gaze

That *Tomorrow* was not among the hundreds of Hollywood films selected for the German reorientation program suggests that its story about reeducation was not particularly suited to this purpose. Indeed, Emil's Nazism—so stereotyped, unreasoned, and mechanically recited—would no more dissuade a National Socialist than it would convert an anti-Nazi American. Rather Emil is the foil of

American liberalism, there to remind us of everything we are not and to assure us of how completely and reflexively ensconced in liberalism we are. Thus Emil's revulsion at women officials occasions Pat's minisermon on women's suffrage in the United States; Emil's racism gives rise to numerous pronouncements about equality; and his propagandistic speeches prompt lectures on the nature of democratic thinking. These overt lessons directed at Emil and taken up in the essay contests are only reinforcing the film's performative and rather vexed humanism centered on characters who embody progressive ideals so embedded in the American sociality of this film that they come into relief only when Emil questions their legitimacy. Put another way, Emil's bigotry and violence are necessary to produce a discourse about tolerance and reason in a society where such enlightened attitudes are so presumed that they need not be articulated or so volatile that their elucidation requires other forms of compensation.

We can see how the film connects questions of ethnic otherness to citizenship in its depiction of Leona Richard, whose representation telescopes the ethnographic studies discussed later in this chapter. Leona is established early in the film as Mike's beautiful, blonde, light-eyed fiancée and as both an esteemed teacher and child psychologist. It is only in response to Emil's anti-Semitic remark shortly after his arrival (that on the plane he had to sit next to a "big fat Jew") that Mike announces Leona's Jewishness. We not only notice Leona's thin but shapely body (she may be Jewish, but she's neither big nor fat), we also may remark on how little her ethnicity affects her professional, romantic, or interpersonal life in the United States. In fact, throughout the film her Jewishness is so inconsequential, so incidental, that were it not for Emil's vituperations it would remain invisible. There is nothing in the decor of her apartment, her dress, or jewelry that betrays a Jewish identity: even her last name, Richards, is ethno-ambiguous. Significantly, it is Leona who explains to Emil the first rule of American citizenship that she demonstrates so well: "In this country it doesn't matter where you come from. We're all equal, all alike. We're all American." Following a scene in which Emil questions Pat about Leona's ethnicity, we cut to Mike, who remarks to Leona as they make their wedding plans: "You see, intuitively we agree on everything! We think alike, feel alike, act alike!" The very fact of her

"We think alike, feel alike, act alike!" Leona and Mike (Fredric March) make their wedding plans. Production still courtesy of Wisconsin Center for Film and Theater Research, University of Wisconsin, Madison.

Jewishness necessitates emphatic declarations of her similitude to gentile characters.

The film's press books, including all of the suggested reviews, feature stories, and posters, also suppress Leona's Jewishness and instead set up the film's drama around Emil's "unaccountable hate" for her. In a poster that features Leona and Mike embracing under a quote attributed to Emil—"Do you know what that woman is?" (a line he never speaks in the film)—Leona's ethnicity is anticipated as the narrative's dark secret that, once revealed, will turn Mike against her and dash their forbidden love. Of course, the film makes no secret of her Jewishness, it associates no taboo with their interethnic romance, and it is clear that Emil's animosity is directed entirely at her ethnicity. These structured gaps around Leona's Semitism make it more prominent because it is the answer to the questions the publicity begs and it provides the thin psychological motivation for Emil's evildoing. We may then read the press books as preparing American audiences to discover these Semitic indicators so that they may reflect on the extent to which they do not perceive any differences between the Jewish and other characters, a compromised mode of perception that I call "Hollywood's liberal economy of vision."[11] This economy negotiates difference so that all ethnicities are equally marketable and well suited to Hollywood's commercial ambitions.

The press books feature photographs of Betty Field in the outfits she wears in the film for display in lady's sections of department stores. The Jewish part of Field's character, however, is evacuated in the promotion so that all women could identify themselves as Leona and buy clothing that would turn them into visions of her.[12] *Tomorrow* thus attempts to manage a tension between the racially

Poster for *Tomorrow—the World!* Courtesy of Wisconsin Center for Film and Theater Research, University of Wisconsin, Madison.

and ethnically overembodied character and the commodifying trademark of the star. These advertising strategies reveal complicity between an emerging cold war liberalism and Hollywood's system of representation. In 1946 Jean-Paul Sartre witheringly compared the anti-Semite to the democrat: "The former wishes to destroy [the Jew] as a man and leave nothing in him but the Jew, the pariah, the untouchable; the latter wishes to destroy him as a Jew and leave nothing in him but the man, the abstract and universal subject of the rights of man and the rights of the citizen."[13] Liberalism abstracts citizenship through deethnicized political rights. Hollywood, bound to the mandates of photographic representation and the conventions of star personas, whitens. And the white body, in turn, becomes *the* body of American citizenship.[14] The "property of whiteness," Richard Dyer observes, "to be everything and nothing, is the source of its representational power."[15] But even this body is decorporealized. Dyer finds that in Western photography, portraiture, and classical Hollywood cinematography, whiteness is represented cosmologically as "in but not of the body." "Black people" (and we might add ethnically marked people) "can be reduced (in white culture) to their bodies and thus to race. But white people are something else that is realized in and yet is not reducible to the corporeal, or racial."[16] Like the American immigrants and ethnic types he encounters, Emil's civic ascendancy is possible because, once he learns to act like an American, his white body does not betray his foreign origin. In *Tomorrow*'s story, then, American assimilation and citizenship not only obliterate the Jew, they cure and incorporate the Nazi by erasing the differences in others that allow him to exist.

A German National Character

The sublation of difference also functions to dematerialize the basis of Emil's intolerance. With no evidence of Leona's Jewishness, Emil's fervid anti-Semitism is downright phantasmic and pathological. The difficulty in detaching pathology from national identity is what makes Emil's reeducation such a challenge. Leona remarks in exasperation that she has been able to reach hundreds of troubled kids, but "Emil isn't a case of maladjustment. He's perfectly adjusted—to a Nazi society." Separated from the political culture that produced and regulated his behavior, Emil's abnegating patriotism, for which he is ready to die and kill, is in the

American context symptomatic of both an individual and national perversion. Even Frieda remarks to Emil upon discovering him in his Nazi regalia, "You are insane." As he attempts to recruit her for his Nazi spy work, he presumes her incredulity to be a response to his status as a "simple child." She retorts, "A simple child? I think you're simply crazy." And indeed, the film leads us to believe that as a result of his Nazi upbringing Emil is psychically damaged and hopelessly deranged.

In fact, Emil is indicative of what Columbia neuropsychiatrist Richard Brickner diagnosed as the German paranoid trend. Following Freud's work on group psychology and Edward Strecker's study of the modern crowd, Brickner was among the first to adapt the principles of psychoanalysis to the specific national context of Nazi Germany. Published in numerous scientific journals, Brickner's research was made accessible to nonacademic readers in his 1943 book *Is Germany Incurable?* As organizer of

"A simple child? I think you're simply crazy." Emil tries to conspire with fellow German Frieda (Edit Angold). Production still courtesy of Wisconsin Center for Film and Theater Research, University of Wisconsin, Madison.

the 1944 conference "Germany after the War," sponsored by the U.S. State Department and War Department, Brickner not only popularized the idea of German group psychology in the United States, his research shaped U.S. reeducation in Germany.[17] At the core of Brickner's work was the claim that, as a national group, Germans interpreted life in a manner consistent with paranoia as manifested in the individual patient. Attending to an immaterial culture of behavior and feeling (a reading of culture based on his analysis of institutions and widely held suppositions hospitable to paranoid fantasies), Brickner identified four key symptoms animating the German emotional core—megalomania, the need to dominate, a persecution complex and projection, and retrospective falsification—all of which, combined and unchecked, would lead an individual to murder and a group inevitably to war. Whereas in a nonparanoid culture the abnormal individual becomes an outcast, in Germany paranoia had become institutionalized and atavistic such that, "for at least several generations, values congenial to paranoid individuals have been emphasized in German culture, acting selectively on those individuals with the most pronounced paranoid tendencies, giving them leadership and power further to define the paranoid values in the culture." German leaders in this account are not the generators of paranoid culture but symptoms of its excess, or as Brickner vividly phrased it, "the smallpox vesicles on the body of the patient."[18]

Though acutely conditioned to this mental disease through patterns of child rearing and education, Germans were not congenitally mad, nor were they the only examples of paranoid group behavior. As the chapter title in Brickner's book declares, "anthropology testifies" both to the power of culture to produce hypertrophic emotional cores and to the astounding varieties and extremes of group behavior around the globe that, once established, have momentum, "like a rocket with inexhaustible explosive charges in its tail."[19] Margaret Mead's and Ruth Benedict's work in "primitive" cultures provided Brickner with a social–scientific model for the existence of psychic climates. Like New Guinea's pathologically suspicious Dobu tribe, who plotted murder and cultivated the most treacherous community, and the self-aggrandizing Mundugumor, who routinely headhunted their neighbors, the Germans had managed to hold together a rather stable culture based on a normalization of perversions. While primitive tribes were likely to overdevelop certain patterns of behavior given their relative isolation, Brickner observed that at the time of Hitler's rise to power, Germans had approached a hypertrophic pathology equal to these other tribal examples due to the German proclivity toward insular nationalism and racial exclusivity. The very fact that Germans shared with the Dobuians a mystical sense of themselves as a racial totality signaled a confluence of paranoid and primitive modes of thought. But unlike the Dobuians, whose paranoia was of concern only to neighboring tribes, the Germans had the technological means to spread their disease by submarine and airplane and through the printing press, radio, and other forms of mass media, "infecting" its neighboring tribes and those beyond "who constitute the bulk of humanity, all civilized nations, and their appendages." "We have no need to worry if nobody ever does anything to check Mundugumor aggressiveness," Brickner declared. "We have every need to worry—and every need to act—in the case of German paranoid values" (139). In this tropic configuration, the German contagion, including its racism and anti-Semitism, constituted a threat of primitive regress. It is striking that in *Tomorrow,* Emil remarks on his progress in precisely these terms when he observes to Mike, "When I arrived here in America, I was a savage. . . . Now I am a problem, but not a savage."

Though the raced body functions as a placeholder for savagery and biology, Brickner was working against racial determinism and was thus keen to remind us that Germans, like their tribal counterparts in New Guinea, were not all deranged. Those who had been unwilling to participate in this mass mental illness had become either marginalized within German society or had immigrated to healthier shores, a migration that weakened the "anti-paranoid" trend in German social life. Those who remained had adopted the most vacuous crowd mentality, going "through the paranoid motions, often with less and less friction as habit takes over volition." But German immigrants in the United States proved the exception to the rule of derangement and confirmed the positive effects of assimilation:

Consider . . . the type of German who frequently came, as an individual, not a member of a group, of his own volition to the United States, bringing only his family, his skills and his homely instincts, in many cases because he could not stomach the paranoid German

illiberalities that were already developing strongly in the nineteenth
century. He got his V's in the wrong place and his wife still liked to
make apple-strudel, but he plunged wholeheartedly into American
life and found it good, or, if of higher education, he became a
leader in scholarship or civic activities. . . . From their descendants,
profoundly American types in their various ways, including such
figures as Lou Gehrig and Wendell Wilkie, you seldom hear com-
plaints of feeling hemmed-in, encircled. (144–45)

Here, the only healthy, self-possessed Germans are Americans,
an assertion bolstered in Brickner's nondefinition of nonparanoid
behavior. "It seems unnecessary," he writes, "to illustrate the
non-paranoid, although it could be done profusely, it is perfectly
well-known and would be no different from the kind of thought
with which we, as Americans, are thoroughly familiar."[20] So non-
paranoid are we Americans that we can scarcely comprehend the
possibility of a national perversion on Germany's scale. Unable to
fathom paranoia, Americans, in Brickner's view, are the most vulnerable to its manipulations:

> An intrinsic part of the philosophy of democracy is absence of the
> expectation of paranoid behavior. In fact, any antisocial "trend"
> behavior, seen in the light of democratic philosophy, is something
> of an oddity. It is thought of as something more or less distinct and
> separate from any impulse belonging in the democratic way of life.
> Where everyone is born "free and equal" peculiar trends are seen
> more as the fault of abnormal individuals and less as intrinsic prod-
> ucts of the development of society.[21]

Thus in mobilizing for a postwar settlement, Americans must be
prepared, as they were not following World War I, to address the
psychic needs of the defeated people on their own paranoid terms.

Merely ousting the Nazi Party after the war would do little to
eradicate the contagion or foster the mental hygiene necessary to
sustain a democratic government. Germany, Brickner argued, required psychiatric therapy organized around the "clear" mental
areas in the culture "whose emotional values are prevailingly non-
paranoid." For peace to endure, the United Nations would need to
create infrastructures that would make nonparanoia "emotionally
attractive" and foster leaders with new cultural values and "emotional habits."[22] But the most effective therapy would have to be

generated from within; healthy émigrés (from the United States) should return to Germany and commit to living out their remaining years as members of a "cultural army of occupation."[23]

Margaret Mead's America

While Brickner presumed American mental and emotional hygiene as a model for German rehabilitation, Margaret Mead's 1942 ethnographic study of the United States, *And Keep Your Powder Dry: An Anthropologist Looks at America,* explained how the American "democratic character structure" could be a model for German reeducation and global citizenship.[24] Mead strongly advocated applying the social sciences to the practicalities of fighting World War II, a war whose ideological battle could be distilled to the camps of cultural versus evolutionary determinism. In this capacity, Mead advised the U.S. government on techniques of morale building, on psychological warfare, and on strategies for postwar occupation.[25] National reconstruction was perhaps the best application of anthropology, whose purpose, Mead explained, is to "construct a systematic picture of how human culture works, [and] to provide the scientific basis for building an even better world."[26] In Germany, Mead wrote, the social sciences could help the Allies "systematically attempt to alter national character."[27]

Mead's aim in writing this book was to help the American recognize and sharpen "what special or accidental skills he has" that could help him win the war and thereafter reorganize the world. Quite apart from the matériel of war, America's greatest asset, Mead declared, was its national character, one constructed by and predicated on democratic culture. And, what is "democracy," Mead queried, but "merely a word for a type of behavior and an attitude of mind which runs through our whole culture, through our selection of candidates for office, our behavior in street cars, our schools and our newspapers[?] . . . We *are* our culture" (12). In this tautology, American national character is both the foundation of democracy and its effective yield. Mead clarifies that what differentiates the American character from other examples, and what makes it democratic, is the individual belief in and social proof that culture, and not blood, is the basis of national belonging.

Fascinated by the social technologies that turn "a beet-red baby in a hospital delivery room into an American to whom baseball scores and fair play and business and the importance of success all make consummate good sense," Mead argued that national character emerges not from race but from the contingency of birthright and citizenship. For it is in the United States that the anthropologist documents the power of culture to form a nation out of foreigners and rediscovers how "the newborn child, at birth potentially a Chinaman or an American, a Pole or an Irishman, becomes an American" (23) and embodies what she later in the book calls the "democratic character structure" (165). That all children, regardless of ethnicity or race, grow up in the United States to be Americans proves the folly of racial theory. Mead's analysis of American culture is thus an important academic rebuttal to Nazi eugenics and Japanese racism:

> If the Racists were right, if the absolute believers in heredity were right, humanity would be caught in a trap which would—as the Fascists logically enough believe—make Democracy a pipe dream. Because a newborn baby can be brought up to be a Hottentot or a German, an Eskimo or an American, because each group of people seems to be born with the same kinds of individual differences, democracy is not a pipe dream, but a practical working plan. (13)

Democracy is the plan and the United States is the site where Mead discovers a multiethnic place without race, where the free-market economy means that each man who works hard and well is rewarded with material prosperity and an uncontested social position.[28]

Mead does not pinpoint democracy in any one political or economic system, but defines it in reference to the drama of immigration and to the process by which the children of immigrants become unmarked Americans. As sons and daughters surpass their parents in education, affluence, and cultural savvy, the ties that bind them to old world ethnicity cease to matter: "[M]ore surely than ever before in history," the American experience breaks "the tie between blood and ideals, between land of birth and land of political dreaming" (45). The immigrant, both the founding figure of American democracy and one of its most reviled, unacculturated outsiders, brings a supplement of foreignness that marks the United States as a chosen land and a favored citizenship.[29] Third-generation Americans, having long forgotten or turned away from the history that tied them to a different nation, are bound to one another, not through history, ethnicity, or religion but through shared contemporary culture and an ethical relationship to hard and intelligent work. To Americans who are always looking forward, Europe represents "the past which is best left behind."[30] American culture, in Mead's account, is what remains after old world ethnicity, rigid class structure, and history are stripped away.

Mead's project is also important for the ways that it remaps notions of the primitive onto a 1940s globe, inklings of which we find in her statement above, where Europe is a place of the past, of nativity, and where blood is considered the hallmark of belonging.[31] Arjun Appadurai writes that anthropology conceives of the "primitive" as being both geographically and intellectually bound, unable to apprehend his being as an accident of culture rather than the product of nature. As traditional anthropology has it, natives are "confined by what they know, feel, and believe. They are prisoners of their 'mode of thought.'"[32] The mobile anthropologist, the trained outsider, is poised to see and document this incarcerating logic. In Mead's analysis, what distinguishes U.S. citizens from the primitives (Japanese and Germans included) is that Americans implicitly perceive the constructedness of their citizenship. It is little wonder to her that cultural anthropology develops in the United States, where, she asserts, attention has been focused on "the process by which adults reared in one society emigrated and become participants in a very different society, and even more strikingly, the way in which their children entered into the new social heritage." By comparison, in Europe men and women are considered merely "the medium through which the changing traditions of European culture have passed."[33] Americans are conditioned to separate nativity from citizenship, blood from culture, and to accept the ethical mandate to fight a war against racist regimes.[34] In this respect, even the term "native," with all of its primitive resonances, describes less well Mead's American. *Tomorrow—the World!* embraces a similar ethnographic logic. When Emil declares that the only pure-blooded American is the Sioux Indian (a declaration met with faux war cries from the other students), this is really a moment of one native recognizing the blood distinction of another. When earlier Emil confronts Stan with their competing and historically hostile national/ethnic identities, Stan smiles and says in ungrammatical but enlightened American, "I won't hold it against you. It ain't your fault where you're born."

In *Keep Your Powder Dry,* Mead is training Americans to see themselves, and others, through the lens of culture, with the hope that an American victory will spread the gospel of ethnography to the rest of the world. If democratic character (like all national characters) is learned and not genetically programmed, then the whole world, under American guidance, might one day enjoy democracy's peaceful promise. Mead declares:

> The democratic assumption is to say: all cultures are equal in that each is a complete whole, a social invention within which man has lived with man and has found life in some way good. . . . But though all cultures have the dignity of wholes, some of them may be utterly incompatible with living on a world scale. . . . [W]e must accept the responsibility of trying to eliminate in other cultures and our own those particular habits and institutions which lead to war, to separatism, and to a desire to dominate or exploit.[35]

Already accepting that culture is a social invention, Americans—"freedom's own children"—are poised as anthropologists to make themselves and, through their example, the people of the world more enlightened and accepting citizens (16).

In a rather rhapsodic passage, Mead articulates forthrightly the contours of a postwar order in which those values that she has connected throughout her book with the unique circumstance of American citizenship become universal:

> We must see the emerging world as a world of plenty, of great expansion, of room for everybody to make a contribution and succeed. We must see a world in which every human being has a right to develop what he has in him—a right to succeed, a right to the rewards of success. We must see a world built with a moral purpose, built because we think that we are right in building. Above all, we must see ourselves tackling a job which we believe can be done practically, like any other big job. . . . We must believe that we can make war and tariff walls and passports, uneven distribution of the world's goods, and restriction of individuals to the special human inventions of his own society—to one language, one art style, one form of personal relations—as out of date as the cannibal feast, the barter market, the trial by fire, and the sign language of the Plains Indians.[36]

Connecting individual freedom to the development of global free trade, Mead imagines a world without borders in which all forms of cultural and economic nationalism and all institutions that artificially determine individual success are as outmoded as Indian sign language or savage cannibalism.

Powder is a lesser known and certainly less respected anthropological work of Mead; she wrote it in a mere three weeks and conducted no field research as such, relying instead on her own experience and scientific acumen. Under the guise of progressive politics, Mead sweeps under the carpet gross social inequities in wartime America. Absent from this account, except in footnotes and parenthetical asides, are non-European immigrants (those visibly marked by race) and African Americans (brought to the United States as indentured slaves) and the social networks of the entire American South; accordingly, she also overlooks class structures and economic inequality in the United States.[37] Mead's Americans are all white, middle-class, third-generation immigrants whose "European ancestry" is "tucked away and half forgotten."[38] This book does not, as Hervé Varenne notes, describe the United States. Rather, Mead is "educating and prophesizing" the potentiality of an American democracy where assimilation has erased biology.[39]

Brickner and Mead share with the makers of *Tomorrow—the World!* an assumption of American normalcy and enlightened liberalism. They also describe the immigrant experience as the foundation for democracy in America and as a template not only for German reconstruction, but, in Mead's case, for democratic cosmopolitanism the world over. The proceedings from Brickner's "Germany after the War" conference, published as a roundtable summary of the papers presented, urged U.S. policy makers to understand the institutions and practices that compose German society "not as 'forces' or as causes of this or that event or as separate independent activities, but rather as the different patterns of endeavor and of life career which the cultural traditions and the social order offer to individuals as designs for living, for the expression or realization of their character-structure, and for meeting the affective needs of their personalities."[40] Thus Nazism was not an "officially planned, intellectual theory of political procedure," as ideology might be traditionally defined, but an outcome of long cultural conditioning that had reinforced the German predisposition to define all human relations "in terms of dominance, submission and romantic revolt" (397). The only way to change

Germany's national character and political culture would be to replace "self-pictures" and traditional myths of German identity (including German invincibility, racial superiority, Prussian militarism, and authoritarianism as the basis for civil society) with a new, liberal mythology based in part on the idea "that no group is superior or inferior to any other, [that the world] is made up of human beings with the same basic hopes, needs, strengths, and frailties, [who] before God . . . are the same" (413).

While neither Brickner nor Mead discusses motion pictures in their studies (nor is film even mentioned in the seventy-page conference summary), they too were attentive to the power of mass culture, and films in particular, to create "self pictures" and myths of national belonging. For example, Mead stresses early in her book that, in place of shared history and geographical ties that typically produce European national communities, American intimacy is founded on "feverish grabs at a common theme," such as "enthusiastic preferences for the same movie actor, the same brand of peaches, the same way of mixing a drink." Through shared superficial preferences ("that may call forth the same kind of enthusiasm that one might expect if two people discovered that they had both found poetry through Keats"), Americans bridge their "idiosyncratic experience" and overcome the fact that "every American's life is different from every other American's."[41] American mass media enable community in the land of heterogeneous immigrants, and this multiethnic audience is the foundation of what some describe as Hollywood's democratizing power.[42]

Cinema and Germany's National Pathology

The strongest arguments in support of cinema as both a reflective and instrumental technology of national character came from Gregory Bateson (Mead's husband and fellow anthropologist) and cultural theorist Siegfried Kracauer. Their studies of Nazi film culture brought the vocabulary and methods of psychoculturalism to bear on film analysis, and they explained how the gangsterly propaganda of the Third Reich had perverted German sensibilities. While Mead and Bateson had used films and photography to document Balinese culture, Bateson's study of the Nazi-sanctioned *Hitlerjunge Quex* (Steinhoff, 1933) was among the first to analyze a fiction film from a foreign culture as an ethnographic artifact.[43] As he explains of his method, "We have applied to [the film] the sort of analysis that the anthropologist applies to the mythology of a primitive or modern people."[44]

Almost a prequel to *Tomorrow—the World!*, *Hitlerjunge Quex* centers on Heini, a working-class adolescent who, in the course of the film, matures from a disaffected adolescent into a Nazi youth and martyr when he is murdered by the leader of the communist gang. When the film opens, Heini lives in a lower-class urban neighborhood with his violent, communist-sympathizing father and browbeaten mother. Though his father urges him to join the communist club, Heini is attracted to the Nazi youth group, whom he first spies camping in the forest outside the city. Before he may become a uniformed member, however, Heini must extract himself from the plotting communist kids, his suicidal mother (who nearly succeeds in killing Heini along with herself), and his controlling father, who has to be persuaded that the Nazi Party is finally the best family for his son. As the narrative unfolds, Heini is transformed first from an apolitical and lost son into a Nazi and, through his death at the end of the film, into a supreme symbol of the Nazi state. The last three shots of the film are dissolves from Heini's dying body to the Nazi flag, to an image of faceless Nazi youth marching with geometric precision. As Bateson noted, the film offered its viewers a transcendent story of military redemption or, as the Nazi slogan went, "through death to a millennium."[45] The film's implicit critique of the family as harmful to Heini's development (both the mother and father are associated with the degeneracies of communism) means that he must seek out parental surrogates in the Nazi Party. Whereas the communists attempt to lure Heini to their destructive cause, he is of his own volition attracted to Nazi discipline and order. And so *Hitlerjunge Quex* constructs a mythology of citizens who, uncoerced, choose Nazism over other competing ideologies or, in this case, gangs. Like Erik Erikson's analysis of Hitler's childhood, this film too reads National Socialist culture through a narrative of arrested adolescence.

Based on the true story of Hitler Youth Herbert Norkus, a Nazi martyr whose 1932 murder was widely covered in the German press, the film was one of several mass renderings of the story, including songs, poems, plays, and a novel that was mandatory reading for Hitler's youthful following.[46] The melodramatic arc of Norkus's story and its imminent transferability into the codes of cinema functioned, in the context of an emergent fascist public sphere, to synchronize Nazi affect and consolidate the visual and thematic tropes of Hitler's Germany. Bateson selected this film for analysis because, as an overtly political, propagandistic, and pedagogical text about Nazis and their communist enemies, it established "the basic symbolic equations" and narrative themes of Hitler's Germany. "In America," Bateson explained, "we tend to think of propaganda as consisting of a large number of separate utterances, pious sentiments or jokes, inserted into the more or less propagandistically neutral matrix of communication." In contrast, the Nazi method "consists not of isolated utterances but of themes built into the structure of the plot in such a way that the audience, while enjoying the plot, will necessarily accept the underlying themes as basic premises which need never be articulately stated."[47] Bateson implicitly subscribes to the transparency and legibility of American mass culture that does not manipulate its audience with encrypted symbology and that clearly marks propaganda as distinct from entertainment and news.

Bateson was particularly attentive to the filmic and narrative techniques Steinhoff employs that both distinguish communism as Nazism's opposite and obscure the political agenda of Nazi rule. Communist characters are associated with sexual promiscuity, slovenliness, unlawful greed, and political opportunism and are shot against the chaotic mise-en-scène of the local carnival and the smoke-filled rooms of the communist clubhouse. The Nazis are "almost colorless in comparison." "We see their parade-ground smartness, we see them dashing into the sea to bathe; but these behaviors are rather the negative of the excesses that are attributed to communism, and throughout one is left with the feeling that Nazi life is empty."[48] Heini is attracted to the Nazis not for anything in particular that they represent, but out of disgust for the alternative communist youth group. The persistence of oral and anal images the film associates with communism—from the apple of the opening shot that communist boys steal and savagely devour to the bottom-slapping camp games Heini watches in revulsion—construct communism as a politics of regress and moral degeneracy. Such images, Bateson reasoned, create a portrait not of communism but of what the Nazis think that they themselves are like "under the veneer of discipline" (the same, of course, could be said of the portrait of Nazism painted by Tomorrow—the World!). Bateson concluded that the communists in the film represented the other half of a

Nazi split personality that oscillated "between the over-pure and the over-dirty." This pendular mentality exceeded Nazi rule as was evident in the themes of Weimar cinema: "In fact the problem of Germany is in part a problem of preventing a pendulum from swinging too far into aggressive purity in good times and into degenerate self-contempt in bad."[49]

Where Bateson limited his analysis to a single film to unearth a phobic Nazi sensibility, Kracauer, in his well-known *From Caligari to Hitler: A Psychological History of the German Film*, examined the arc of modern German subjectivity through German film culture.[50] Though written as a history of German film, Kracauer hoped that his research, written expressly for an American audience, would provide a model for understanding mass behavior in the United States and elsewhere. In the context of the occupation and postwar reconstruction, his study, he explained, could "help in the planning of films—not to mention other media of communication—which will effectively implement the cultural aims of the United Nations." Significant to my study, Kracauer signaled to his American readers the centrality of cinema to Hitler's ascendancy in Germany but also the potentially vital role films might play in fostering a peaceful and democratic postwar global order.

In preparation for his sweeping, book-length study, Kracauer wrote the 1942 essay "Propaganda and the Nazi War Film" to aid the U.S. government in psychological warfare. Here he explicated the filmic techniques by which the Nazis revived German "antirational" and mythical thinking. Using film to erect what Kracauer described as an "impregnable intellectual 'West Wall' against the dangerous invasion of democratic ideas," Nazi war films rallied Germans to Hitler's cause through elliptical editing, polyphonic montage, and patterns of geometric abstraction that distilled the blitzkrieg and Nazi ascendancy into a series of formal and visceral sensations. In contrast to democratic propaganda, which "appeals to the understanding of its audience," to conscious and rational thought, the Nazi penchant for visual spectacle was aimed at psychological retrogression "addressed directly to the subconscious and nervous system of spectators."[51] In his analysis of the dramaturgy of the Nazi "documentary" *Baptism of Fire (Der Feuerteufel,* Trenker, 1940) and *Victory in the West (Sieg im Westen,* Noldan, 1941), Kracauer notes how the films anthropomorphize Germany in epic heroic terms and present national history through a series of maps in which the white of Germany is contrasted with the black of surrounding hostile states. Refusing to recognize any reality beyond the battle plan, both films depict Germany hemmed in darkness by the Treaty of Versailles; Germany's victimization, Kracauer notes, is purely cartographic. Kracauer also brings his critical acumen to Leni Riefenstahl's 1935 *Triumph of the Will*—the urtext of fascist aesthetics that perfectly illustrates the Nazi transfiguration of reality through perversion of the documentary form. Akin to the visual mastery that maps provide, *Triumph* creates a geometric sublime through the arrangement of human subjects captured with aerial photography. Recalling his Weimar essay on the Tiller girls, Kracauer now sees the mass ornament not as an aesthetic exposé of capitalist rationality, but as a *tableau vivant* in which the masses are convincingly presented as "instrumental superunits" of the party. These formations, staged expressly for Riefenstahl's camera, are fictions of a new reality that captivate the spectator with their formal splendor and lead him to believe in "the solidity of the swastika world." The apogee of totalitarian pageantry, *Triumph* represented "an inextricable mixture of a show simulating German reality and of German reality maneuvered into a show."[52]

Kracauer's book-length study *Caligari to Hitler* tracked the terrifying trajectory whereby the Mabuses and Caligaris of the Weimar screen came to life in the arena of political culture. Widely reviewed in the American press, Kracauer's book provided the most thoroughgoing argument for national cinema as a reflection of the "deep layers of collective mentality."[53] In photographing the visible world—in either the documentary or fictional mode—cinema fulfilled its "innate mission" to ferret out unobtrusive, normally neglected minutiae of everyday life and human relations. Psychic life found external expression in the "imperceptible surface data" of the cinematic screen; film, he famously argued—with its capacity to isolate nuances of gesture, expression, and the bits of incidental busywork—"provide[s] clues to hidden mental processes" and group desires and may thus open a window to the inner life of the nation. To account for the otherwise unaccountable "chronic inertia" of the middle class in the face of Hitler's ascendancy, which neither political, economic, nor social history alone could explain, Kracauer found in German cinema the hieroglyphs of mass fatalism. The thematic oscillation in Weimar films between chaos and autocracy, and the prevalence of character types who were either power-hungry supermen or weaklings over whom these supermen presided, led Kracauer to conclude that the "Germans obviously held that they had no choice other than the cataclysm of anarchy or a tyrannical regime" (88). This paralysis, which found resolution only with Hitler's rise to power, was also evident in film style itself. To take just one example: Walter Ruttmann's montage poem *Berlin, Symphony of a City (Berlin: Die Sinfonie der Großstadt,* 1927) is a film of surface effects that reflect an impression of modern scatter. Cameras mounted on roller-coasters, trains, and automobiles reproduce the dizzying speed of urban life, while shots of rotating spirals, revolving doors, and bustling streets populated by prostitutes and passersby "indicate a society that has lost its balance." Berlin's machine world as captured by Ruttmann's camera is one in which humans are "forced into the sphere of the inanimate," merely "molecules in a stream of matter" (186). As Nazi politics moved toward mass theatricality, German cinema not only captured the pitch of middle-class anxiety but contributed to its psychological stagnation.

Kracauer's indictment of interwar German cinema is also interesting for its celebration of American democratic film culture. As he notes in the introduction, the profit motives of any commercial film industry necessitate that studios attune their narratives to the ever-changing mental climate of their audiences or suffer poor returns on box office receipts: "To be sure, American audiences receive what Hollywood wants them to want; but in the long run public desires determine the nature of Hollywood films." While Weimar cinema abetted Hitler's tyranny, French and American detective films in particular were infused with the spirit of their respective ticket-buying audiences, whose embrace of the genre in turn marked its democratic status as such. The detective, Kracauer mused, is "the single-handed sleuth who makes reason destroy the spider webs of irrational powers and decency triumph over dark instincts." He is "the predestined hero of a civilized world which believes in the blessings of enlightenment and individual freedom" (19). In his Weimar writings Kracauer critiques the detective novel for its plotting rationalism and empty ratiocination indicative of the late capitalist predicament,[54] but in *Caligari* he praises American and French detective films as being "closely related to democratic institutions." German attempts at the genre are indicators of enfeebled republican vitality.[55] It is no surprise to Kracauer that his compatriots, who "had never developed a democratic regime," failed to produce a native equivalent to Sherlock Holmes.

But the very flexibility of a consumer-oriented cinema, beholden to the whims of little shopgirls and white collar workers the world over, was never immune to totalitarian prevarication, even—and perhaps particularly—in the United States. Theodor Adorno comments that the tendencies Kracauer attributes to German cinema could just have easily culminated in *King Kong* (Cooper, 1933), a film Adorno aptly characterizes as "an allegory of the unrestrained and regressive monster into which the public sphere developed." The truth of Kracauer's thesis, Adorno declared, is that "the dynamic that exploded in the horror of the Third Reich extended down into the winding-shafts of society as a whole and for that reason was reflected even in the ideology of nations that were spared the political catastrophe."[56] Indeed, the similarities between *Hitlerjunge Quex* and *Tomorrow—the World!* leave little doubt that American cinema is not Weimar or even Nazi cinema's opposite but its shadow.[57]

How Democracy Looks

For U.S. officials, American cinema was firmly rooted in and integral to the promises of democratic capitalism. It is thus little wonder that in 1944, the Office of War Information declared that motion pictures would be instrumental in "reorienting and reeducating the German mind out of its enslavement to Nazi and militarist doctrine." The very selection of films, the OWI explained, was itself "an act of political warfare—warfare against an idea, against a legacy of ten or more years of Nazi thinking and practice, which a German defeat will not automatically wipe out."[58] Few of the Hollywood films selected touched on the German question as explicitly as *Tomorrow—the World!* yet this film's depiction of German rehabilitation encapsulates America's reeducation policy.

The twelve-page document titled "The Re-education of Germany," produced by the Committee to Reeducate the Axis Powers, provided the U.S. military government with an initial blueprint for the defeated territory. Here the committee argues that before Germans could adopt the codes of a liberal democracy they would first need to undergo a subtractive "unlearning" of Nazi doctrine.

Or, as the committee put it, "the Germans can be educated away from Nazism into what we like to call their better selves and their truer nature."[59] The better German—"industrious, well-disciplined, peace-loving"—can be found where he or she has "had a chance to grow from childhood outside the direct or indirect influence of a Prussian, Pan-Germanist, militaristic pattern." The committee declared that the "millions of American citizens of German descent whose parents left Germany to escape the growing pressure of tyranny and militarism" prove that these people are not without "native virtues"; it is only that these values of "loyalty" and "respect for discipline" have been misdirected by "self-educated gangsters who are skillful at propaganda." Authentic Germans, we may thus surmise, are none other than the emigrated Germans whose innate, native goodness is fully expressed only with the first generation to be born and bred on U.S. soil and who have undergone the process of American acculturation. Echoing the rehabilitative logic of *Tomorrow—the World!* this document proposes to strip Germans of their "attitudes towards life, codes of behavior, and moral and spiritual values" that have hidden their positive qualities. Like immigrants who thrive in the United States, Germans will rediscover who they were before German nationalism and militarism perverted their otherwise virtuous ways of being.

To this end, the committee outlined, in two separate lists, "What Germany Has to Unlearn" and "What Germany Has to Learn." Germans would have to unlearn that they had evolved into a superrace "called by destiny to be the leaders of the world and to rule all other countries in a new order"; that the individual is subordinate to the state over which its leader has supreme authority; that war is the highest, most "holy" manifestation of the state and may thus be carried out with unbridled brutality; that "envy and *Schadenfreude* [. . .] are legitimate and morally justifiable emotions"; and that Germans, envied the world over, should not be "duped into friendship with others." Disabused of Nazi gospel, Germans would be initiated into the second phase of their rehabilitation.

The eleven-point list of "hard lessons to learn" emphasizes above all that Germans "must develop new respect for the truth" by embracing empirical science, valuing individual liberty, and upholding "the fundamental moral and spiritual values of human society." This "truth" was both sociopolitical and historical in nature. Germans had to learn that women are equal and that the civilized are those capable of self-administration and cooperation with other people and nations who may have differing life philosophies. The committee was also invested in shaping German interpretations of their recent history. Thus Germans would have to learn to assume collective responsibility for war crimes; acknowledge that the destruction of German cities was a consequence of German, not Allied, aggression; and concede that at the hands of the superior Allied forces, Germany had been "'really' defeated in this war and the last, and that the notion of the invincibility of the German army is a myth and a lie." Though the document is principally concerned with the implementation of a new, humanist pedagogy, the committee stresses that all available mass media should be mobilized "to help the German people learn the truth about their false doctrines."

Just as *Tomorrow—the World!* invests Emil's wristwatch with a talismanic power to alter his most deeply held commitments, the American authorities believed that Hollywood films, America's most popular consumables, could likewise unsettle the entrenched mysticism of German identity. If *Tomorrow* proposes to cure Emil by transplanting him from Nazi Germany to multiethnic, small-town USA, where he learns the truth about culture, and if the film rehabilitates the Nazi by bringing him into an American living room, then Hollywood films under the aegis of America's reeducation policy could foster German democracy by bringing the American living room (and the American immigrant) to Germany.

In March 1944, OWI German specialist W. D. Patterson explained the contours of the American film policy to reeducate Germany, a country he described as the "problem child of history." "With respect to film," Patterson declared, "Germany will present the same conditions of control as a scientific laboratory. . . . Through this powerful medium, which many people regard as the most powerful of any medium available to modern man, we shall be able to say anything we want to the German people." As the document continues, he imagines a series of documentaries that would systematically deflate German racial science and Nazi self-fashioning. In a contortion of race-effacing liberalism, Patterson proposes the following film, a proposal so strange that I must quote it at length:

The theme [of the film] might be "Germans are blond, English are blond, Frenchmen are blond, Russians are blond, Norwegians are blond, Dutchmen are blond, Danes are blond, Belgians are blond, Austrians are blond, Hungarians are blond." All these people like music, all these people like to drink beer, all these people get married and raise families, all these people work hard, etc., etc. Yet, you Germans act differently. Three times you have set out on a Master Race theory to conquer the world, letting loose the most dreadful blood baths of modern times. Each time you failed. . . . Throughout the film, the differences between the Japanese and the Germans, racially and culturally, should be used as a counterpoint to emphasize that the little men of the Pacific certainly don't appear to be the chosen race, yet they share with the German the responsibility of a vain adventure of world conquest which brought only defeat.[60]

In this statement, the occupied territory is constructed as a site of social scientific experimentation in which motion pictures real and imagined explode the racial uniqueness of German nativity. Film is thus not only a tool of diplomacy; diplomacy itself is written in cinematic terms. Resonant with the racial similitude of both *Tomorrow*'s world and Margaret Mead's America, Patterson's compulsive naming of blond-haired nationals, articulated as a montage of head shots, inscribes the liberal vision of sameness onto white faces the world over. These comparisons deflate Teutonic superiority by showing that Americans and other Europeans are equal to German racial standards. Ironically, however, Patterson's anti-Nazi film hinges on racial difference and the inassimilable Japanese body. According to his view, the German cult of racial superiority may be misguided, but the Japanese as a chosen race is absurd. Axis defeat aside, anyone can see that the "little men of the Pacific" fall short of other national bodies.

As the memo continues, Patterson estimates that nonfiction films, such as the hypothetical one above made specifically for German audiences, could best debunk the particularities of Nazism. But such documentaries would take time to produce, and finally Germans would have to make their own films for rehabilitation. Ready for immediate distribution, the OWI documentaries (made during the war for American and Allied audiences) would illustrate facets of U.S. life, while Hollywood films would provide new heroic models, stress individualism over the "orgiastic" *Sieg Heil* of

German conformity, and feature German immigrant characters who, assimilated into American life, have refused to become "devotees of blood and thunder." Such films, Patterson concludes, could reveal "how the other half, the democratic half of the world, really lives."[61] Responding to this memo, William Harlan Hale endorsed Patterson's assimilationist rhetorical strategy:

> And the theme you propose . . . "a film showing the racial similarities that the Germans share with other nationalities"—could best be carried out, I think, by a picture based on German life in, say, the melting-pot of Milwaukee. In other words, a German edition of "The Sullivans."[62]

The 1944 20th Century Fox epic that follows five Irish American brothers who die while serving in the U.S. Navy during World War II becomes a template for German reorientation precisely because of its focus on the immigrant and second-generation experience. Replace the Irish American with a German American and Nazi audiences would see the triumph of culture over blood. So powerful was the immigrant trope in these planning statements that Bernard Barnes's 1945 "Draft Operational Plan for Germany," sent to all U.S. Information Services division chiefs and section heads, was concerned that using American media to show Germans about the "democratic way of life" might encourage them to literally undertake the immigrant journey: "Our aims should be not to induce the Germans to wish to migrate to the United States, but rather to help create in their own country the conditions of freedom which we enjoy."[63] But exactly what about democracy would such films convey and how were Germans to understand this pedagogical agenda?

Although one confidential memo states that Hollywood films would "demonstrate the great values and strengths of democratic living,"[64] in effect such movies offered spectators an emotionally engaging experience in which the political ramifications of democracy could be diffused into a set of discrete, imitable practices and narrative effects. Another OWI consultant curiously observed that, "in the political realm," Hollywood films emphasizing individual responsibility in public affairs could show Germans that "democracy is possible and desirable, but without any talk about democracy but rather in concrete dramatic terms [sic]."[65] William Hale claimed that Hollywood features could be mechanisms of a counterfactual imaginary; in them, Germans would see what their life could be "in contrast to what they have made it." Carefully vetted, American movies would "graphically but not blatantly," "preferably by illustration, suggestion, implication, story," exemplify to Germans "how Americans live and think."[66] Thus, films were shipped to Germany not expressly to teach democracy per se but as democratic, even ethnographic artifacts that could be studied as cultural fragments of an entire worldview.[67] At such time that Germans were once again given a camera, American films would serve as models for German democratic culture. For as one film officer quipped:

> You can't expect Germans who have been under twelve years of Nazi rule to come up with democratic ideas overnight. Film makers who have made Siegfried their motion picture hero for twelve years cannot understand that Joe Smith (Johann Schmidt for local consumption) is a guy who looks like John Garfield and thinks like Spencer Tracy and acts like James Cagney and thinks he is just as good as anybody else—and not a whit better. [68]

This officer conceives of democracy in terms of how Hollywood actors (including second-generation Irish American James Cagney and Jewish American John Garfield) look, act, and think. Mining American films for democratic ideas, German viewers are supposed to adopt what we might reasonably call an ethnographic mode of spectatorship, i.e., they are expected to learn from these actors the gestures of democracy, gestures that Germans could later perform and film to enact a similar politics. In this imagined interface between Germans and American movies one significant facet of the enlightenment project of reeducation reveals itself: to transform Germans from Nazi *objects* of ethnography into democratic *subjects* of ethnographic knowledge. That is, the Americans assumed that if Germans would consume and imitate these democratic fictions, they would see their own ethnography, disavow their primitive cult of blood, and accept themselves and the rest of the world as products of culture.

Yet if the democratic character could be learned and imitated, it could also be faked and even parodied. It is the suspicion of Emil's rehabilitation that unsettles the end of *Tomorrow—the World!* and prompts *Comic Cavalcade* to draw (literally) an alternate conclusion. If Emil dissimulates his democratic mentors and evades punishment by cunningly parroting their stories and reproducing their affect, how can we discern the difference between authentic conversion and mimetic aptitude? When is democracy real and when is it merely performed? And when Hollywood films are the instruments of pedagogy—when the democratic character is indeed a fiction—can we even speak of a real politics outside of performance? The rest of this book takes place in Germany, and it is attentive to the iterations, filmic and otherwise, of American liberalism in the context of occupation and what its German imitations reveal about America's so-called assimilating (often dissimulating) democratic culture.

2. Hollywood's Democratic Unconscious

The well-known statistical record can only numerically capture the bleakness of Germany in 1945. In the wake of Allied bombing, Cologne, Dusseldorf, Frankfurt, and Berlin were more than 70 percent destroyed.[1] Three and a half million German soldiers were killed in battle and approximately 780,000 German civilians were lost in fire bombings and air raids, while countless more were wounded, rendered homeless, and psychologically scarred.[2] Once the centers of European culture, German cities were now populated by charred corpses and millions of refugees. In the words of W. G. Sebald, these ruins were the new "necropolis," where the stench of decay, the swarms of flies, and small armies of rats overwhelmed those "foreign, mysterious," surviving people who, "torn from . . . civil existence and . . . history," were "thrown back to the evolutionary stage of nomadic gatherers."[3] German film studios that once produced epics rivaling Hollywood's production values were converted to displaced-persons camps and in the process produced of one of the war's more bizarre spectacles. An American officer reported in 1945 that emaciated victims recently released from POW and forced labor camps were scavenging for food around the rubble of the Bavarian Filmkunst studio. In place of their tattered garments, they were adorned like the characters of Nazi cinema in the most lavish costumes from the wardrobe department.[4] These bedraggled refugees became in this moment a palimpsest of the triumph of Nazi hero culture, the brutality carried out in its name, and the mind-boggling devastation and disorder created in the wake of its ruin.

39

With most of the population in desperate need of food and clothing, motion pictures seemed as inappropriate and incongruous as the costumes clinging to these desperate bodies. American officials realized, however, that Germans could not subsist on bread alone. As the Allies tried to address survival necessities, the U.S. military troops immediately took charge of film culture. They impounded extant films in the U.S. zone, banned all German personnel from the film industry pending lengthy de-Nazification procedures, and commenced with the rapid rebuilding of theaters so that Germans would have access to American films and the reorientation messages they contained. Just months after VE Day, film exchanges opened in Munich, Frankfurt, and Berlin to service the 16 movie theaters then in operation. By February 1946 there were 351 cinemas in good working order in the U.S. zone; this number increased to 700 by July.[5] In 1948, there were more than 1,000 cinemas in the U.S. zone alone.[6]

Under military law, movie theaters were initially among the few places where Germans were permitted to gather publicly. Eager to escape the rubble of their once-flourishing neighborhoods and re-establish community, Germans were, in the words of one military historian, "film hungry," even for programs comprised exclusively of Hollywood features, newsreels, and worn-out and outdated documentaries, and even while suffering under near-starvation caloric intake.[7] The *New York Times* reported in 1946 that with little to buy and few entertainments to choose from, Germans willingly waited hours in long queues to see the same Hollywood films "several times over."[8] So dominant was Hollywood that most living in the U.S. zone were convinced that Germany had become an American film monopoly.[9] Though these circumstances would change with the slow revitalization of German film production and the 1948 currency reform that brought more and newer films into Germany, the first postwar years established cinema as the occupation's primary medium of diversion. Cinema was also, however, one of the most potent cultural signifiers of defeat and, significantly, one of the chief means by which Germans came to understand the military government's reorientation policy and democratic vision for Germany.

This chapter considers how the film program, initially imagined in and through the American movie theater, addressed itself to spectators in the German theater of occupation. Given that

Hollywood films were used to teach Germans to behave and think like democratic citizens, how did the circumstances of occupation and the culture of reorientation affect the way these films signified to the defeated audience? What exactly did Americans hope Germans would learn from these films, and how might Germans have construed the political message differently?

The first part of the chapter approaches these questions through the U.S. military government archive. It unpacks the pedagogical rationale for bringing Hollywood films to Germany and mines the numerous documents that outline what American officials hoped to teach the Germans through cinema. The German response to this offensive, however, is far more elusive. Film reviews and questionnaires can give us the most general sense of the film audience and the range of reading practices. But for the early years of the occupation, especially, this documentation is rather scarce and limited in detail. Thus I construct a horizon of reception that is attentive to the material conditions and ideational predispositions of German audiences. By no means passive, occupation spectatorship was a generative (very often oppositional) mode of engagement. To capture the tensions between policy and reception, this part of the chapter shuttles between American policy and expectation on one hand and German experience on the other. That Germans and Americans had different readings of the same text is not only indicative of the radically different position of occupied and occupier, it also speaks to the political polysemy of Hollywood movies that would prove ungovernable in Germany.

The second part of the chapter considers how a cross section of films shipped to Germany under the aegis of reeducation coalesced into a counterfactual politics of American democracy. Based on the filmgoing culture outlined in the first part of the chapter, the second part attends to the interpretative possibilities available to German spectators. But I am also interested in what these films tell us about America as a democratic state, independent of any specifically *German* interpretation. In effect, I turn the psychocultural tables on Hollywood films, reading them as artifacts of America's political and cultural sensibility. The Hollywood features shipped to Germany—films that were selected by U.S. officials for the purpose of political reeducation—encrypt a history and specularity that implicitly question American citizenship as an ideal or enlightened model, especially for post-fascist Germany.

Where later chapters consider German critical and filmic responses to Hollywood narratives, this chapter concludes on a more theatrical note. The postwar German phenomenon of Indian masquerade, as Katrin Sieg discusses it, is a public enactment that may be understood as a rewriting of Hollywood westerns and a literal recasting of Germany's occupation role. Rejecting identification with their occupiers, hobbyists perform their sympathy with Native Americans in response to the German experience of occupation. Based on the popularity of this institution, we may extrapolate that there were numerous instances of generic rewriting and political rereading of Hollywood genres. How then did the occupation condition Germans to reread Hollywood films?

The Psychopathology of Occupied Life

From the rationing of food and the slow restoration of basic utilities, Germans interpreted the everyday living conditions of occupation as calculated effects of Allied policy, a policy many initially saw as unjustly punitive under the early doctrine of collective guilt.[10] This position was conveyed in the documentary *Die Todesmühlen* (*Death Mills,* Signal Corps, 1945), a film exhibited in nearly every theater in the U.S. zone.[11] As one of the first films to reach postwar German audiences and one of the initial few made expressly for reeducation, *Death Mills* established cinema as the occupation's most compelling, even shocking, evidentiary medium, but just as important it performed the pedagogical prompt that would condition German viewers to read even Hollywood films as political, didactic, and historically anchored texts.

Composed of footage shot during the liberation of concentration camps, *Death Mills* is a twenty-two-minute exposé of Nazi war crimes and a testament to German civilian complicity with Hitler's genocide. For as the film repeatedly asserts, German civilians, many of whom lived within walking distance of the camps, had to have known of their existence. Not only might they have heard the victims' cries or caught whiffs of the stench of human death, Germans ate produce fertilized by human bone, wore wigs fashioned from human hair, and purchased goods that once belonged to their disappeared neighbors. Indeed, the film argues that the Nazi political economy rested in part on the camps' efficient, assembly-line operation that produced, processed, and sold the remains of the state's political and racial enemies. Redirecting its gaze, the camera frames the anonymous and naked survivors who have been transformed by "many years of humiliating imprisonment" into "degraded" and "animal-like creatures." Above all, however, the film asserts that Germans are guilty of putting themselves "into the hands of criminals and lunatics without resistance [. . . and permitting] law and justice to be stomped on in the name of the people."[12]

In the film's final sequence, citizens of Weimar are commanded to visit Buchenwald to "take a walk among the corpses." The punishment for these men, women, and even children is also the film's own rhetorical gambit: "They have to see with their own eyes the crime whose existence many of them tried to deny." The townsfolk somberly walk past the death display as the voice-over reiterates that few of these victims suffered a natural death: "They were murdered because they held onto their religion; to their belief; others because they didn't want to be Nazis, because they were Russians, Poles, Belgians, French, Czechs or Jews, because their own neighbors informed against them." Over shots of mass graves the film superimposes images from Leni Riefenstahl's *Triumph des Willens* (*Triumph of the Will*, 1935), a film here used as both a record of the Nuremberg rally and as an example of a Nazi film that mobilized Hitler's star image. This reference makes explicit the pedagogical role of film in the occupation, whereby the United States counters one "successful" use of propaganda by appropriating and reorienting it against itself. Americans share with Nazis the means of swaying public opinion but hope that Germans recognize the different political ends. To reinforce this new reading of *Triumph,* the voice-over momentarily ventriloquizes a would-be German spectator and in so doing offers this admission of guilt:

> Yes, I remember. At the Nuremberg party assembly, I yelled "Heil."
> And then, on another day, when the Gestapo took my neighbor away,
> I turned away and asked, "What do I care?" Do you still remember
> 1933, 1936, 1939? I was part of it. What did I do against it?

The very Germans who are forced to see the spectacle of death at Buchenwald are the same Germans, we are led to believe, who participated in the pageantry of Nuremberg. The image track, however, condemns not just those who were physically present at the rally, but the postwar Germans in the film theater watching this very documentary who, once dazzled by fascist film culture, consented to the genocide it promoted. Indeed, this quotation of Nazi cinema conspicuously enacts a doubleness of historical optics: these images of the Third Reich's populism are to be retrospectively read as enthusiastic endorsements for the death camps that were only *apparently* hidden from view. By causally connecting Riefenstahl's film to Hitler's genocide, *Death Mills* initiates an associative logic between cinema and historical violence. Though there are no explicit traces of the Holocaust in *Triumph,* audiences may in hindsight notice the absence of Russians, Poles, Belgians, French, Czechs, and Jews among the German masses. This citation is meant to teach Germans to look at their own film culture for the signs of historical guilt and denial that were part of the public culture at the time of *Triumph*'s release (this is a mode of reading that Germans could also bring to Hollywood films, as I discuss below). In this respect, film itself becomes a technology of death, and the movie theater is another crime scene, one that some Germans were forced to revisit.

In parts of Bavaria, attendance at *Death Mills* was compulsory if Germans wanted to obtain their food ration cards (a perverse literalization of their film hunger). *Death Mills* was, perhaps for this reason alone, well attended, if unpopular.[13] Yet if its aim was to convince Germans of the existence of the camps, there is some evidence that the film was successful. In one instance, the U.S. military government cast a plainclothes American officer in the role of a Holocaust naysayer. At a screening, he shouted into the crowd that the entire film was American propaganda. The Motion Picture Branch was pleased to report that Germans in the audience threatened the pretender until he was silent.[14] Such was the theater of reeducation.

Ethnography by Hollywood

In contrast to this bleak tour of ethnic erasure, German moviegoers would likely have seen *The Human Comedy* (Brown, 1942), a film about the trials of a typical Irish American family in a small California town during the war. Described by *Variety* as "a brilliant sketch of the basic fundamentals of the American way of life," this was one of the first films to reach postwar German theaters and, in fact, played in Germany throughout the occupation.[15] At least one exhibitor outside of Frankfurt wrote in 1945 that *Human Comedy* played with "great success," attracting more than five thousand patrons in the first two-week run.[16] One scene in particular enacts an uncritical rendition of American multiculturalism that would surely have resonated with German audiences. Newlyweds Tom and Diana Spangler drive through the ethnic expo that is Ithaca, California's Valley Summer Festival, and rather abruptly the film's diegetic world gives way to a kind of educational voice-over documentary. Surveying the fairgrounds from his car, Tom jubilantly enumerates the festival's exhibits: "Greeks, Serbs, Russians, Poles, Spaniards, Mexicans, and all the others. Americans, all of them!" The sound track transitions from one ethnically inflected version of "Let Freedom Ring" to another as the couple drives past a series of ethnic *tableaux vivants*. Recalling *Death Mills'* own grim roll call of victims, this taxonomy is now mobilized as evidence of American heterogeneity. Each group performs a traditional dance dressed in the regalia of the old country while Tom explains each group's signatory features. "You can always tell the Armenians," he remarks from the car. How? "By the priests and the kids. That's what they believe in: God and children." Typical of Hollywood's melting-pot sentimentality, *The Human Comedy* strains to showcase the immigrant heritage of American citizenry and, just as important, this citizen's mastery and ebullient celebration of American variety.

Complementing *The Human Comedy*'s portrait of national typicality, *The Town* (Sternberg, 1944), an Office of War Information documentary also selected for the reeducation program, contributes an even more varied repertoire of spaces and activities of American life as practiced in Madison, Indiana.[17] The film describes first the town's European architecture and then the lineage of its European immigrant population. In the spirit of ethnography, it takes us through typical days and explores the workings of this town's civic institutions, such as the public school, the public library, the corner drugstore, the free press, and open elections. Named after James Madison, the "fourth president who is known as the father of the American constitution," the town is a quintessential example of an ethnically diverse community that engages in fair and equitable self-governance. The film's final shots feature second- and third-generation immigrant children heading back to Europe in U.S. military uniforms to liberate the people from whom they are descended.

Just as *Death Mills* condemns Nazi cinema in its quotation of *Triumph*, Hollywood features shown in Germany thematize filmgoing as central to the politics of the American experience. In *The Town* we are told that citizens go to the movies as one of their favorite pastimes. But it is *Human Comedy* that most explicitly connects filmgoing to national feeling. Three GIs who are killing time on Main Street meet two of the film's main characters, Mary (Dorothy Morris) and Bess (Donna Reed), who invite the soldiers to join them at the movies. In Ithaca's packed local theater we catch glimpses not of a Hollywood film but the opening shot of a newsreel. As the American flag is superimposed over a close-up of FDR's stalwart face, we cut back to the audience where a GI remarks to Mary, "There are my lucky stars and stripes." "I guess you don't really get to understand your country until it's in trouble," comments another soldier to Bess. "All the rest of the time, well, you just take it for granted, like your family." With tears in her eyes, Bess chimes in, "I get a lump in my throat every time I see the flag. It used to make me think of Washington and Lincoln. But now it reminds me of my brother Marcus. He's a soldier too." Though the American flag waves prominently in Ithaca's town square, it is the flag represented in the newsreel (which no doubt precedes a Hollywood film) that prompts Bess to articulate the deeply felt connection between the flag and her own imperiled brother. Given the film's emphasis on Ithaca's immigrant community and on the diversity of the soldiers we see training by Marcus's side in other scenes, we can only assume that the town's Greeks, Armenians, Russians, and Mexicans similarly cathect the highly individuated and culturally nuanced sentiments of familial love onto the filmically reproduced icons of the state.

Yet in occupied Germany, movies would hardly have summoned such sentimental patriotism. *Human Comedy* in many ways staged the stark contrast between the American and postwar German filmgoing experience. In occupied Germany all feature films were preceded by the U.S./UK jointly produced newsreel *Welt im Film* (hereafter *World in Film*), compulsory for all exhibitors in the U.S. and British zones until January 1950.[18] In the first years of the occupation especially, *World in Film* was devoted to depicting Allied reconstruction efforts in Germany and reporting on the various war crimes tribunals so as to continually remind audiences of the fallen status of the once omnipotent Nazi leadership and the inhumanity of Hitler's regime. Where Mary and Bess tear up at the sight of Roosevelt, Germans might be differently moved by episode 55 of

World in Film, in which Nazi authorities, such as SS doctor Josef Mengele, are shown awaiting trial in dank prison cells. In this episode, we cut from the prison to a trial where American prisoners of war finger their Nazi torturers, while the judges who will sentence the offenders sit beneath an enormous American flag. Whether the affective politics of the flag—"my lucky stars and stripes"—can be redirected in the service of judgment is just one of the dilemmas of cinematic reeducation.

In the United States, Hollywood motion pictures were an unofficial entertainment form, first and foremost, that served to affirm America's self-image as a strong and vital melting pot whose political and social unity was achieved and maintained by a shared sense of the national community. Importantly, Hollywood produced not a single feature film specifically for German reeducation. The military government initially selected from a list of about thirty-five features that were made during the war to entertain and, in some cases, patriotically galvanize American audiences in the United States. As the occupation progressed, the U.S. government shipped postwar films that were still tethered to the American experience of nationhood and history, such as westerns and films about the United States during the war. Thus films made in the United States for the predominantly American market were exhibited in Germany to perform a pedagogical function far afield from the production's original intent. This transnational shift produced a new set of reading protocols and meanings as these films were now part of an official platform of racial and political education.

Several of the films selected for Germany manifest the ethnographic logic discussed in chapter 1, which was designed to contrast American multiculturalism to Nazi racialism but which always threatened to collapse the distinction between the two. For example, Tom Spangler's Valley Festival commentary (complemented by Brown's exhibitionary gaze) reduces immigrants to typologies such that the ethnically designated individual is categorically subsumed. According to this scene, one can always *tell* an immigrant just by looking. The omission of Asian Americans, African Americans, and Native Americans in Brown's film, moreover, signals that American citizenship is multiple only to the point of what Carrie Tirado Bramen calls "variegated whiteness."[19] Even *Death Mills,* made for German audiences, evinces this problematic in its efforts to condemn the dehumanization of Nazi victims. The film's graphic illustration of abject, evidentiary bodies does not restore their humanity but rather reproduces a fascist racial aesthetic according to which non-Aryan "animal-like creatures" inescapably signify their own, less-than-human status. As we will see in the following examples, Hollywood ethnology tutored audiences to scrutinize the faces and bodies of ethnic others to discern the good immigrants from the bad foreigners. In efforts to reeducate the Germans by showing them what, according to Hollywood, American democracy looked like, Americans unwittingly exported not only their unbridled nationalism but their own racial notions of statehood and justification for exclusionary violence. This is especially true of films about American history and the history of immigration.

In a manner of speaking, German audiences took Hollywood films at the military government's word insofar as they interpreted these less as pure entertainment and more as educational texts screened by a foreign, once enemy government to tutor them in their political rehabilitation. At a time in German history when the availability of food, fuel, and water were construed as reflective of U.S. policy, when film studios housed refugees, and when movie theaters distributed food ration cards on the condition that viewers watch sobering images of starved bodies, every film experience signified through the conditions of defeat, occupation, and the tenuousness of daily life. Further, accused of false consciousness and historical denial, guilty of having made and seen films that fostered a fascist public sphere, Germans were primed to read American films in terms of their occupiers' founding and foundering democratic logic.

Fixing German Guilt

What, exactly, did the Americans hope Germans would learn from the film program and how did they select films for this purpose? Initially, the OWI's German Subcommittee thought that Hollywood films, mostly "escapist" in nature, would—and the choice of words here is fitting—"assist the military in keeping people occupied."[20] Germans would be lured off the streets and into theaters where "more serious informational material is to be given to them." Thus a feature film with "pure entertainment value" would be programmed with a documentary "in which such a propaganda line as the inevitability of German defeat . . . is given."[21] The OWI determined in 1945 that a balanced film program of newsreels, documentaries, and feature films could "implant" "certain attitudes" in the German audience that would make them more open to Allied occupation and resocialization, such as "the variety, attractiveness, and general decency of life in the democracies" and "the healthy unfolding of individual personality in a free society."[22] As one OWI German specialist explained, feature films could trigger the audience's imaginative engagement with a more hopeful, democratic future, not least because Germans would arrive in the theaters psychically fatigued from war and its devastating aftermath: "Exhaustion will be in the early stages our greatest ally." In their enervated mental state, akin to slumber, Germans would be "more open to suggestion" while watching Hollywood's inspiring tales about "American pioneers," "the building of Alaska," and the "thousand and one scientific achievements (discoveries, improvements, etc.) of recent years." "It is a well known fact," he asserts in reference to this hypnotic pedagogy, "that communication whispered to a person [when] asleep will influence his behavior far more than the same communication given him when he is wide awake."[23]

The OWI felt that Germans should watch Hollywood films that dramatize "everyday situations" in the United States, particularly those that "project the themes of individual resourcefulness, civic courage and democracy of man to man in a free society." Films whose heroes were scientists, artists, and advocates of human rights, those "who have pitted themselves against the forces of ignorance," would steer audiences toward new models of public virtue and "help wean the Germans from the notion that heroism is synonymous with making war." At the same time, dramas concerning the merchant marines and Allied fighting in the Pacific could acquaint audiences with less familiar aspects of the war.[24] While films should not be shown "that devote their main emphasis . . . to criticism of British and American institutions, or which have the effect of denigrating democratic ways of life" (one memo specifies "champagne and plutocracy on a large scale are to be avoided!"),[25] another OWI document notes that "this does not mean that the picture presented must invariably be a rosy one. On the contrary, a picture showing that America too has its troubles and its problems may very well be included, as long as the effort . . . to solve such problems is presented at the same time."[26] Independent of narrative content, high-budget, prestige films would demonstrate the artistic advances of "free people" in contrast to the comparatively feeble creative efforts under Nazism.[27] And films featuring "stars once famous in Germany whom the policy of the Third Reich has prevented the Germans from seeing—Gary Cooper, Chaplin, Clark Gable, Mickey Mouse, etc."—might rekindle Hollywood's German fan culture.[28]

In 1945, the U.S. military government's Information Control Division streamlined and formalized the criteria for selecting feature films for occupied Germany, and I quote these criteria as they appear in the archive:

A. Wish to fix German guilt and truth of Nazi exploitation of Europe.
B. Indicate unfavorable global attitudes toward Fascism and Nazism.
C. Offset efforts of Nazi propaganda about the USA and correct German misconception of modern history.
D. Demonstrate great values and strength of democratic living.
E. Indicate the U.S. as a strong democratic society striving for full realization of the 4 freedoms.
F. Motion Pictures should be best of cinematographic art, with some Technicolor included.[29]

I dwell on these objectives to show that it would have been difficult to find an American feature film in the 1940s that did not, in some way, fulfill at least one of the U.S. military's criteria, particularly in light of Hollywood's narrative conventions and its wartime cooperation with the OWI.

Choosing films to fulfill these six pillars of reeducation was initially under the jurisdiction of the OWI, which carried out scientific research to calculate the effects of Hollywood films in Germany. To begin with, the OWI selected nineteen features for pretesting on German POWs held in England. After each program, the Survey Branch asked a select group of "anti-Nazi" and "Nazi" POWs to complete questionnaires about the film and its suitability for German audiences.[30] Though hardly representative of the home front population, the OWI presumed that these prisoners, who had lived and served in Nazi Germany, could engage these films from the perspective of an audience member dubious of a foreign democracy.

These initial tests are interesting because they reveal how Germans, no doubt prompted by the questionnaires, read and assessed these films as reflective of American values. For example, Hitchcock's *Shadow of a Doubt* (1942) received positive marks from only 16 percent of the respondents. According to the Survey Branch, the majority were appalled "that the leading actor portrayed a murderer in a highly sympathetic fashion." *Christmas in July* (Sturges, 1940) was overwhelmingly condemned by the prisoners who gleaned from the film "that America was money-mad and that greed and business dominate American thinking."[31] According to a later report, *My Sister Eileen* (Hall, 1942) "was one of the most unpopular and most unsuitable films yet shown to this group of prisoners." "Trite, superficial, exaggerated and trashy," *My Sister Eileen* "conveyed to the prisoners of war . . . the over-importance of economic success and the existence of low living standards in America." The report concluded, "This is a film which not only would be disliked, but which might even do some actual harm if it were exhibited in Germany." Though less problematic, *The Human Comedy*'s wartime sentimentality was deemed too anachronistic for any postwar audience. And Sonja Henie's star vehicle *Sun Valley Serenade* (Humberstone, 1941) suggested to POWs that war refugees live an excessively luxurious life in the United States, thus not only minimizing German accountability to its victims but leaving the impression that Hitler may have done his victims a favor by forcing them into exile.[32]

These surveys, however, seemed to have little impact, since all of the films noted above were among the first to reach the film-hungry Germans. Tracking the film program's early failure, a 1946 *New York Times* story titled "Our Movies Leave Germans Hostile" reported that, according to U.S. officials, "the thirty-five American films shown to Germans since the end of the war have, with only a few exceptions, had no observable effect in the political and psychological re-education of the Germans." On the contrary, these films had "reduced American cultural prestige and probably damaged the future market for American films in Germany."[33] This misfire was not just a consequence of an ill-conceived information program. The vetting process was time consuming and involved a complicated relay of information between Washington, London, Frankfurt, Berlin, and Hollywood—a massive bureaucracy often at odds with itself.

Once the occupation commenced, the film program was in the hands of a complicated military administration. Though most of the thirty-five films initially chosen played through 1949, additional selections and deletions were made by the Civil Affairs Division of the military government in cooperation with the Information Control Division.[34] New films were chosen from a list provided by the Motion Picture Export Association, a cartel formed in 1945 representing U.S. film distributors who gave the MPEA exclusive right to distribute their wares in several European countries and U.S.-occupied territories.[35] Recognizing the volatility of some themes in foreign contexts and the importance of international relations for Hollywood's economic future, the MPEA explained to Congress that it undertook to export films that portrayed the United States only in a positive light without offending foreign audiences. And these assessments were based on the research of the MPEA's parent company, the Motion Picture Association of America, whose foreign representatives reported on the market conditions and cultural sensibilities of native populations. The final decision of which films to export rested with the host country except in the occupied territories, where the military government made final selections.[36] Unable to anticipate German reactions to the film program, General McClure, head of the Civil Affairs Division, at one point recommended banning any Hollywood film that evoked unfavorable comment from German authorities.[37] But Hollywood was loath to comply with this reactive policy. The companies agreed to absorb the cost of striking prints, subtitling, and dubbing films for the occupied territory and suffer short-term net losses, with the presumption that they would have unregulated access to the German market and influence over policy governing the structure of the postwar film industry as Germany transitioned from a military to commercial enterprise. Though the profit potential was huge in the long term, the Hollywood companies were reluctant to release new films and incur more debt in the service of confused policy and for the sake of a still uncertain and volatile market.

Yet even if these structural problems had been resolved, the film program would still have likely failed to convey to Germans exactly what they had to learn and unlearn. The reason is that American officials, guided by specific ideas about democracy and Hollywood's share in the American character structure, could easily read these feature films as narrowly fulfilling the reeducation mandate. For example, *Shadow of a Doubt* was directed by one of Hollywood's premier European émigré directors, Alfred Hitchcock, garnered Academy Award nominations, and starred Hollywood's A-list actors. Its technical sophistication and use of on-location shooting in a real California town would surely enhance the reputation of American cinema, especially in light of the critical success of Hitchcock's *Rebecca* (1940) and *Sabotage* (1936). But as a reeducation film, *Shadow of a Doubt* is troubling not only because it features a sympathetic murderer, as the POWs noted, but because it reveals that just beneath the surface of American wholesomeness lurks a sinister, murderous pathology.

Re-Nazification?

American officials programmed these Hollywood films overlooking how these films could signify otherwise. Germans, however—denied access to the numerous lists and plans determining their precarious future—tacitly constructed an occupation policy of their own through the films and film culture they encountered. These two modes of reading were most at odds with regard to war films. As one German specialist explained, this American genre would teach audiences that "German Nazi blood and iron was crushed in the end by the flame and spirit of the democracies."[38] Rather than convince Germans that they really had been defeated by superior democratic forces (as if the air raids and subsequent occupation alone were not proof enough), these war films reignited in some filmgoers the "flame and spirit" of militarism. One year into operations a schoolteacher complained to the Motion Picture Branch that the children in her class, apt pupils of America's mimetic campaign, started enacting war scenes after watching *Corvette K-225* (Rosson, 1943), Universal's epic tale about the captain of a Canadian naval vessel who hazards a mission against bestial Germans and their lethal U-boats.[39] Film critic Gunter Groll sounded another mimetic register when he ironically noted that the battle scenes from *Corvette* so reminded him of Nazi propaganda that he momentarily feared that "the last year (of occupation) had been a dream." "But then through the cacophony," he explains with mock relief, "we heard the sound of human voices. They spoke English, and that set my mind to rest." The tactless display of militarism puzzled him as it did the others in the theater who sat "mouths agape," wondering why the Americans would authorize a movie that resurrects the very heroic ideal of the Nazi war film. "What does one call all of this? My neighbor calls it: renazification."[40] We find a different response to Warner Bros.' *Action in the North Atlantic* (Bacon, 1943), which gave rise to a near riot in Bremen when former members of the German navy in the audience walked out in protest of a scene in which a German U-boat commander ruthlessly guns down survivors of a torpedoed U.S. merchant ship.[41] In this scene, it is not only the captain's violation of the codes of honorable warfare that disturb, but the almost pathological pleasure he takes in filming the survivors on the raft with his handheld camera before mowing them down with his sub. Had the boys from the navy stuck around, however, they might also have protested the payback scene at the end of the film when the merchant marines, under Humphrey Bogart's command, do the same to the German U-boat. In this film at least, Americans are just as ruthless and sadistic, just as given over to schadenfreude, as their Nazi adversaries. Responding to these and other disturbances, a Professor Van de Well, on behalf of the German Quakers, queried in a letter to the U.S. authorities if the military government had reflected in the least on its decision to release such films in demilitarized Germany:

> Are the men of the military government aware that they are dangerously counteracting their own efforts at education by the release of such war films, which are not even particularly good? . . . [T]he naïve youth (especially girls) are first of all enthusiastic for the hero of such war films . . . and details, like the pictures of the social life in the barracks and the sound of the accordion, awaken nostalgic memories of the former German soldiers of their own military service. In the end, these young people are all the more completely enmeshed in the militaristic ideology. . . . The question which comes to mind is: Why is militarism for victorious powers considered justifiable while for us it is a crime?[42]

In contrast to the protest in Bremen, these German boys transnationally identify with the American enemy as fellow combatants while Hollywood soldiers make fräuleins swoon. These four examples represent a wide range of reading practices (not one of which the military government intended). These responses also show that German audiences recognized that these films were supposed to serve some reeducation purpose but could not construe the military government's specific rationale. Indeed, as the Information Control Division reported, for the majority of German filmgoers war films were merely indicative of the very militarism and nationalism in the United States that the film program was meant to expunge in Germany.[43]

Likewise, the majority of Germans surveyed in 1945 found the newsreel World in Film to be tendentious and biased. Rather than convincing them of the evils of Nazism, the newsreel was, for many Germans, evidence that one form of state-sponsored propaganda had merely replaced another. In particular they found the unrelenting representations of Axis defeat to be humiliating and depressing. As one German put it in an admiringly simple and telling formulation, "I dislike [World in Film] because I am German." At the time, Information Control Division reasoned that German defeat was unpalatable to German nationalistic and patriotic sensibilities and therefore dismissed such criticism.[44] In 1946, the Motion Picture Branch stated that, during news clips that reported on the Nuremberg trials, Nazi generals in captivity, or anything having to do with war, Germans either left the theater or timed their entrance so as to avoid the newsreel altogether.[45] An American correspondent writing in 1947 was struck by World in Film's emphasis on Allied military ceremonies, each segment of which was "replete with men marching, tanks rolling, and all the military pomp we deplored when Goebbels presented it."[46]

Eventually the military government withdrew the troublesome war films and recalibrated the tenor of World in Film, especially as the postwar gave way to the cold war. Yet given the vagaries of the film selection criteria and Hollywood's reluctance to give its best films over to an unstable and as yet unprofitable market, feature films that were withdrawn were not always replaced and films the military requested were not always provided.[47] Due to shortages and mismanagement, even the controversial Corvette K-225, which aroused hostility at most every screening, remained in circulation along with a number of other war films for the first two years of the occupation.[48] When Action in the North Atlantic was deemed inappropriate for Germany, Warner Bros. asked that it be reimbursed for its out-of-pocket expenses. In rejecting the request, the Information Control Division's film section explained:

It is true that the industry supplies all of those films in conformity
with the choice made by a responsible government department and
that the industry should not be penalized because another arm of
the government has withdrawn some of them. However, are these
not the risks of the game? Does not the industry stand to gain so
much from the Army's keeping its channels open that it should take
the bitter and the sweet?[49]

This statement reflects not just the quid pro quo of the occupation
economy, it confirms that all films selected, however strange and
inappropriate, were—at some point and by someone in the military
government—thought to say something positive about "the great
values and strength of democratic living." Given that Hollywood
films were vetted at every stage, the film program was arguably
overdetermined in its representation of American ideals but accidental in what it revealed to German audiences.

An Elusive Text

That these films produced a range of unanticipated responses is
hardly surprising given that the censorship codes by which all of
Hollywood abided intentionally produced narrative ambiguities
and obscurities open to interpretation. What Hollywood films reflected was not democracy but a consensus, a majoritarian commitment to myths of American history and habits, many of which
were predicated on decidedly undemocratic, illiberal practices.
The Production Code Administration, Hollywood's self-regulatory
censorship body in place but subject to substantial revisions from
1930 to 1966, begins to explain Hollywood's approach to race,
ethnicity, sex, and politics. Ruth Vasey shows that Hollywood studios catered to the presumed tastes of both the corporate American
and lucrative foreign markets by minimizing offensive film content
rather than by maximizing appeal.[50] By the late 1930s, the code
eliminated controversial plots in favor of benign love stories and
effectively foreclosed any room for opposing political views and
debate (195). The national cinema of this so-called vibrant democracy was "uniform [in its] ideological outlook" and committed to
representing a "homogenized picture of the social and racial characteristics of urban America and the world beyond" (227). At the
same time, this strategy of avoidance meant that controversial material related to labor, revolution, race relations, and sexuality was

either eliminated or presented with intentional indeterminacy, such that audiences would have to creatively interpret subtle cues a film offered. Vasey argues that Hollywood produced "open," "ambiguous," even "cryptic" texts that signaled without explicitly signifying contentious content—or films displaced politics onto the fictional obscurities of romance:

> Indeed, Hollywood constituted its audiences as "American" in a remarkably literal fashion. By involving audiences in its particular vision, which was characterized by bourgeois and consumerist behavior, it influenced attitudes and behavior both inside the United States and abroad. At the same time, as a result of the "openness" of its texts, Hollywood invited individual audience members to complete or interpret the action on the screen according to their own imaginative desires. (228)

This interpretative invitation most intrigues me in the context of occupation, where Germans were expected to extract arguments about the strength of American liberalism but might just as well have decoded these films as indictments of this very system.

Of course, many of the feature films and documentaries brought to Germany were made during World War II, when Hollywood was beholden to the political mandates set forth by the Office of War Information, whose own "common law" supplemented the Production Code. As Clayton R. Koppes and Gregory D. Black explain, where the code tried to avoid explicit politics the OWI requested that studios produce films that supported the war effort by promoting American democracy and the Allied battle against the enemy forces. Yet, recognizing the diffuse, multivalent nature of democracy, the OWI "retreated to a world of symbolism designed to evoke the desired responses." Citing the work of social theorist Robert Merton, Koppes and Black argue that even under far more exacting political pressure, "concepts such as 'democracy,' 'fascism' and 'unity'" conformed to what Merton designated as "sacred and sentimental symbols," "beliefs and opinions grounded in emotion, as is characteristic of patriotic and religious feeling." Koppes and Black conclude that the OWI and Hollywood colluded "to manipulate opinion by denying or clouding relevant information."[51] In addition, and against the OWI's wishes, Hollywood, enticed by the incendiary dimensions of war, began to articulate a racialized notion of ideology, especially with regard to the Japanese and Japanese Americans who in numerous films were depicted as atavistically prone to deception and uncivil violence.

The American films sent over to teach the circumscribed lessons of reeducation were thus made under the official code of political obfuscation and structures of national feeling that either left wide room for interpretation or failed to address a foreign, defeated audience. Worse, some of these films appealed to white American viewers' shared sense of racial superiority. Occupation authorities were befuddled by the German response to the film program because they were blind to the promiscuity of their own visual culture. While the film program may have failed as calculated propaganda, it succeeded in producing the unruly image world of America's democratic unconscious. This world, palatable to most American viewers and lauded by American officials, revealed in its fissures, obscurities, and curious asides a darker side of American politics to those audiences open to alternative readings, as indeed Germans were. America's German film program was itself symptomatic of what Sigmund Freud calls parapraxis, or what one might call the psychopathology of occupation life, whereby these errors, "bungled" choices, slips, and, as I elaborate below, forms of political forgetting become readable and politically significant accidents of communication.[52]

Hollywood's Democratic Unconscious

The second part of this chapter reads a selection of Hollywood films brought to Germany through the horizon of spectatorship and historical optics that "reeducation" produced. I organize this discussion around the trope of immigrant assimilation and Hollywood's ambivalent relation to the foreigner because it was not only that Germans had to learn from these films how to regard others, but that immigrant assimilation was itself the master trope for reeducation. The failure or success of immigration to restore people to their better selves in these narratives tells us something about occupation policy and, just as important, exposes the myths underwriting America's own democratic fantasies.

The Myth of Immigrant America

Immigration to the United States has served as the basis of the "neutrality" of an idealized American citizenship. This position is evident in Michael Walzer's assertion that "the adjective 'American' named, and still names, a politics that is relatively unqualified by religion or nationality, or alternatively, that is qualified by so many religions and nationalities as to be free from any one of them." Because its citizens all have roots elsewhere, America's politics have been "universally accessible," and thus by this logic, we may extrapolate, infinitely exportable.[53] That millions have immigrated to the United States reinforces this universality and constructs what Bonnie Honig designates as the "choiceworthiness" of American citizenship. Honig explains that the myth of immigrant America "recuperates foreignness, en masse, for a national project":

> It does so by drawing on and shoring up the popular exceptionalist belief that America is a distinctively consent-based regime, based on a choice, not on inheritance, on civic not ethnic ties. The exceptionalists' America is anchored by rational, voluntarist faith in a creed, not ascriptive bloodlines, individualism, not organicism, mobility, not landedness. The people who live here are people who once chose to come here, and in this, America is supposedly unique. In short, the exceptionalist accounts normatively privileges one particular trajectory to citizen: from immigrant . . . to citizen.[54]

The willing, eager immigrant reinvigorates the often unrealized promises of liberal democracy, class mobility, communitarianism, and capitalist plentitude. As Ali Behdad elaborates, immigrant America supports the myth of national hospitality (this despite, or perhaps to negate, America's record of deportation, immigration restrictions, and the fact that immigrants were welcome as cheap labor and as participants in America's colonialist westward expansion).[55] Against the claim of equal accessibility, however, there is a cultural (often corporal) price to pay for American citizenship, as non-European newcomers especially are expected to "shed their old skins" and disavow or erase visible signs of their foreign nativity. *Tomorrow—the World!* demonstrates Behdad's observation that "national identity in the United States is a linear narrative that begins with difference but ends in sameness" (13). This also describes the narrative of reeducation as Americans attempted to have Germans undergo an acculturation to democratic citizenship but without undertaking the transatlantic journey.

For Behdad the myth of immigrant America does something more: it underwrites a willful collective amnesia in the United States that "simultaneously denies certain historical facts and produces a pseudo-historical consciousness of the present" (4). Through this consciousness Americans may acknowledge and intellectually accept as fact the violence of national founding and the ongoing repressive means by which the community maintains and reinvents itself as a liberal state while refusing to assume any responsibility for this violence: "The project of democratic founding . . . is a forgetful narrative, producing the retrospective illusion that freedom and equality, not brutality and conquest, were the principles upon which the nation was founded, principles whose repetitive invocation in the official discourse of founding continues to support the imaginary singularity of national culture in the United States" (7).

Behdad theorizes this phenomenon of intentional forgetting through Freud's concept of "negation," which Behdad, quoting Freud, explains is "a repudiation by means of projection of an association which has just emerged." I want to unpack Freud's essay in more detail here, not only because he mobilizes a visual (even cinematic) vocabulary of "image," "perception," and "projection," but because negation operates through an associative logic, a logic that Hollywood spectatorship in particular evokes.[56] In psychoanalysis, negation requires an uncoding of the patient's own associative interpretation. Freud offers the following exchange, which begins with the patient's statement of denial:

> "You ask who this person in the dream can have been. It was *not* my mother." We amend this: so it *was* his mother. In our interpretation we take the liberty of disregarding the negation and of simply picking out the subject-matter of the association. It is just as though the patient has said: "It is true that I thought of my mother in connection with this person, but I don't feel at all inclined to allow the association to count." (213)

The negative judgment is not repression per se. It is an intellectual assessment of the associations an image summons that an individual, or, in the case of Behdad's usage, a national collective, would rather not accept. This judgment turns on two kinds of decisions. Writes Freud, "It may assert or deny that a thing has a particular property; or it may affirm or dispute that a particular image exists in reality" (214). Both of these decisions revolve around the distinction between the *inside,* the ego's desire to incorporate all that is good, and the *outside,* the ego's rejection of what is judged as bad or "alien" to it. In the individual patient, negation is a matter of incorporating or rejecting a taboo pleasure. For the national conscious, negation is not only a question of civic inclusion and exclusion, but, as Behdad argues, drawing on the work of John Steiner, a penchant to "turn a blind eye" or to "retreat from truth to omnipotence," such that citizens know about the violence but do not admit guilt for being complicit with the brutality carried out in their name (6).

Hollywood has borne the signatures and strains of American exceptionalism in ways that both acknowledge the cruelty of that history while helping viewers to justify, ignore, or forget it all the same. Put differently, in providing the images and implicit associative logic of America's "democratic" injustice, Hollywood gives a certain truth to the lies about U.S. citizenship most Americans know but would rather not avow. This truth emerges in the slippages and elusiveness of representation inherent in Hollywood's adherence to the Production Code discussed earlier but also through the intertextuality of the star image and the historicity encoded in film genre formulas, especially when these films are forced onto another nation that does not share America's collective ego formation. Tracking an associative and historical logic across the Atlantic, I am interested in how films brought to Germany construct and dismantle the ethnic origins of American democracy in ways that became fully resonate in the context of "democratic" reeducation.

White Ethnicity

Films selected for the reeducation program in Germany, like *I Remember Mama* (Stevens, 1948), *The Sullivans* (Bacon, 1944), and *Sun Valley Serenade,* prop up American exceptionalism by showcasing European—and especially Scandinavian—immigration to the United States. The themes of these films are encapsulated in the OWI documentary *Swedes in America* (Lerner, 1943). With Ingrid Bergman as our guide, we tour the United States in search of those aspects "that so appeal to the Swedish Character." In New York we encounter, whirling around the Rockefeller rink, the figure skating star Carrie Lynne, who has found the United States to be most hospitable to skating and skiing enthusiasts. Swedish American statesmen in Minneapolis are attracted to the American promise of equal opportunity "and with it the right, if they choose, to retain the customs and the language they had brought with them." "And this freedom holds true," Bergman explains, "not only for the Swedes, but for all the people of the world who have made America their home. To these freedoms there was a response: a devotion to country." From a Swedish American schoolteacher the film cuts to the munitions factory where Swedes work alongside other immigrants toiling to defeat the Axis powers, their sons already fighting on the front. It is not only the ecumenical citizenship that attracts but the landscape itself. Traveling through the Upper Midwest, Bergman comments on the way that Sweden's romantic clear lakes, valleys, and plains are mirrored in the spaces of this new chosen home. But the most fundamental attraction to the United States is the sense of cooperative industry and community that Swedes share among themselves and with the rest of the country's citizenry. Assimilation is effortless because everything in the United States is so much like home, and these immigrants, we might add, are so much like other, predominantly white Americans.

In this respect, the musical *Sun Valley Serenade,* which played for the duration of the occupation, is particularly interesting for its star, Sonja Henie, the Norwegian Olympic figure skating champion turned Hollywood leading lady and American citizen (in fact, *Sun Valley Serenade* was released the same year Henie became a naturalized American). Diane Negra notes that though Henie's foreignness was always a feature of her on-screen roles, her association with whiteness—of skin, of clothes, houses, cars, even a lucky white rabbit's foot—was marshaled in the United States as evidence of her physical and civic fitness for citizenship. As a romantic lead, Henie is "emphatically costumed and lit to bring out her superior whiteness" in contrast to her female rivals.[57] In *Sun Valley,* Henie's Karen woos her love interest, Ted, away from the dark-eyed brunette Vivian Dawn (Lynn Bari), whose smoldering vocals, the film implies, are no match for Henie's athletic "ice capades," particularly once the film shifts from New York to the Nordic setting of Idaho's winter resort. Nor can Vivian compete with Karen's ethnic charm when, for example, Karen entreats Ted to dance the "Kiss Polka," which just happens to be playing at the mountaintop café. Though it is clear that Karen will stop at nothing to win Ted as her husband and replace Vivian as the lead in the show, we have little sympathy for Vivian, who lashes out against Karen not woman to woman but xenophobe to immigrant. When she catches her fiancé Ted in Karen's embrace, Vivian calls the wily ingénue a "Scandinavian hillbilly" and demands that she be deported. Talented, tenacious, and conspicuously Teutonic in looks, Karen is sentimentalized and vigorously defended. Though she is in her thirties, she comes to the United States as an orphan because her parents have been killed by Nazi strategic bombing. Henie's character is thus a victim first of German militarism and then American xenophobia. But the film enacts, then quickly redresses, the problem of hostility toward refugees and reasserts American hospitality by displacing antagonism to foreigners onto Henie's darker, less engaging competition, Vivian (who is duly banished from the show). The film's grand finale features Henie skating to a medley of Jerome Kern songs in her signature white dress and white feathered tiara surrounded by the snow-covered banks of the Sun Valley rink and complemented by her synchronized white-sequined chorus. It is not just that her whiteness is fully assimilated into this Idaho winter mise-en-scène; as the lead, Henie has become the feminine standard to which other women should (and in this scene do) conform.

Sonja Henie's grand finale in *Sun Valley Serenade* (Humberstone, 20th Century Fox, 1942). Production still courtesy of Photofest.

Thus in just a few weeks in the United States, Karen is cata-
pulted from refugee to citizen-starlet, surpassing all of the local talent, including the Nicholas Brothers, whose own athletic virtuosity
is featured in one of the film's "rehearsal" numbers (the award-
winning "Chattanooga Choo Choo"). These African American
performers, segregated from both the rest of the Sun Valley troop
and from the film's diegetic world, hint at another narrative of
American founding and a history of ethnic variety that has little
to do with choice, hospitality, or equal opportunity. Indeed, Negra
argues that Henie's "strenuous whiteness" and Olympic-winning
athleticism functioned in the United States as a "shadow character
for a Germanness" that both confirmed but comfortably displaced
American wartime racism "that the culture [did] not quite want
to speak" (95). According to Negra, Henie's victory in the 1936
Winter Olympics earned Hitler's approbation as it confirmed Nazi
racial science (despite Jesse Owens's achievements to the contrary).
Not only did photos of Henie greeting Hitler circulate throughout Europe and the United States in the 1930s, it was well known
(contra her war-besieged character in *Sun Valley*) that Henie's
Norwegian house was spared Nazi pillage because she prominently
displayed on her mantel an autographed photo of the führer (95).
In Germany, these Nordic immigrants, and Henie's star persona
in particular, were the proof that America too attracted the blond-
haired specimens of other racially pristine nations who could, upon
their arrival, be held up as better, or at least more successful, than
their darker compatriots.

Democracy Noir: *The Maltese Falcon* and *Across the Pacific*

Henie's "benign ethnicity" makes her a prime candidate for citizenship and a poster child for American hospitality both on and off
the screen. We find a counternarrative in two of John Huston's noir
thrillers, *The Maltese Falcon* (1941) and *Across the Pacific* (1942),
which played with *Sun Valley* simultaneously in Germany during
those film-hunger years of 1945 and 1946, when Germans watched
the same film several times over (at least until the Huston films
were withdrawn). Taken together, the films are shot through with
national and racial substitutions that were animated by America's
pernicious orientalism. Both films pit Humphrey Bogart's street-
wise American masculinity against Sydney Greenstreet's western
European cunning and criminality, and both stage curious scenes

The Nicholas Brothers (Fayard Nicholas and Harold Nicholas) perform "Chattanooga Choo Choo" in *Sun Valley Serenade*. Production still courtesy of Photofest.

in which Bogart encounters Greenstreet's foreign, ethnically marked coconspirators. In *Maltese Falcon*, Greenstreet's sidekick is Joel Cairo, played by the Austro-Hungarian Jewish émigré Peter Lorre, who, like Henie, became a naturalized American citizen in 1941, the year of *Falcon*'s release. Though Henie, not herself a victim of Nazi aggression, could use her foreignness to play a sympathetic, easily assimilated refugee, Lorre (who fled Hitler's ethnic pogrom) always bore the marks of foreign inassimilability and undecidability. For example, we are first introduced to Cairo when Effie, the secretary, presents his gardenia-scented calling card to her boss, Sam Spade (played by Bogart, in his first starring role). Cairo's entrance into the office is accompanied on the sound track by a vaguely Egyptian leitmotif, announcing a foreignness whose origins will remain unclear. In this scene, well known for its homoerotic overtones and sadomasochistic reversals, Joel is the effeminate aesthete adorned in a tuxedo, bow tie, and white gloves. The flirtatious inquiry takes a turn when Cairo pulls a gun on Spade in order to the search the office. No sooner does Spade raise his hands above his head than he knocks out Cairo with a deft punch to the chin, smirking all the while. With Cairo prone on the sofa, Spade searches for clues of his identity. And though there is a proliferation of evidence, Cairo's nationality is impossible to pin down. In his wallet are passports from Greece, Britain, and France, tickets to a San Francisco theater, and a handkerchief smelling, of course, of gardenia. Named after both Egypt's capital city and the Old Testament prophet, Joel's nationality and ethnicity are far more obscure than his sexuality, which finally comes to define his otherness and perhaps also explain his criminality. As the film unfolds it becomes clear that Cairo is working with Greenstreet's Kasper Gutman and Mary Astor's Brigid O'Shaughnessy, who in the film's first scene makes a rhyming entrance to Cairo's but uses her feminine charm to seduce Spade. As befitting the genre, this dysfunctional, feminized, and decidedly foreign family is arrested,

Joel Cairo (Peter Lorre) tidies himself after a tussle with Sam Spade (Humphrey Bogart) in *The Maltese Falcon* (John Huston, Warner Bros., 1941). Production still courtesy of Wisconsin Center for Film and Theater Research, University of Wisconsin, Madison.

and Brigid, who earlier kills Spade's partner, is bound for death by hanging. The gang, though rehearsed in the affect of cosmopolitan refinery, will stop at nothing, kill anyone, to retrieve the mythical, jewel-encrusted artifact, which, in the end and like those who pursue it, proves to be a fake.

For German film audiences Peter Lorre would have been well-known for his starring role in Fritz Lang's *M* (1931), in which he plays Hans Beckert, a child-murdering sex offender. As Anton Kaes describes him—"effeminate, childlike and diminutive, given to oral fixation . . . and with an intense fascination with objects in store windows"—Beckert bears some affinity to Joel Cairo.[58] Kaes analyzes the scene in which we see Beckert's face for the first time as he confronts his own mirror image searching for and, in the process, performing the grimaces that make visible his pathology. This scene is set against the investigation that calls on all of the resources of modern police surveillance and technologies of detection, including "scientific" typologies of graphology and physiognomy. In this mirror scene, the sciences used to profile the sex offender collapse onto the face of the actor who now bares the prototypical visage of the psychopathic murderer. Queries Kaes, "It is Lorre or Beckert, played by Lorre, who is mirrored in the film?" (54). The face of an Austro-Hungarian Jew became the signpost for the serial murderer, and the serial murderer in turn became the face of the Jew, particularly when scenes from *M* were later used in Hippler's viciously anti-Semitic Nazi propaganda film *The Eternal Jew (Der ewige Jude,* Hippler, 1940), promoted as a "documentary about world Judaism."[59] The final scene, in which Beckert pleads clemency because of his mental derangement, was cited in Hippler's film as an example of how "Jew Lorre" subverted the law by making a sexually deviant criminal sympathetic.[60]

However, for American audiences, Lorre's Cairo would likely have summoned a different mode of seriality and racial substitution. From 1937 to 1939, Lorre was featured in no fewer than eight of the *Mr. Moto* films as the eponymous character, a refined Japanese sleuth who works undercover to protect international peace. Though no film from this series played in occupied Germany, Lorre's role as Moto speaks to how his star image was ethnically constructed in his newly adopted country. If in Germany Joel Cairo could be connected to sex murderers and anti-Semitic propaganda, in the United States Lorre's star image connected him to Japan.

Peter Lorre poses as Mr. Moto. Publicity photograph courtesy of Wisconsin Center for Film and Theater Research, University of Wisconsin, Madison.

In fact, the transition from Mr. Moto to Mr. Cairo is somewhat anticipated in the last film in the series, *Mr. Moto's Last Warning* (Foster, 1939), which takes place in Port Said, Egypt. Here Moto thwarts a plot to blow up the Suez Canal and a fleet of French ships.[61] He manages this feat through a series of substitutions. As the film opens, his undercover decoy, played by the Japanese actor Teru Shimada, is mistakenly abducted by the saboteurs. Then later in the film Moto escapes detection by pretending to be the Japanese proprietor H. Kuroki, owner of the Oriental Treasures souvenir shop. Like the iconic objects he sells to tourists, Kuroki embodies Hollywood's stereotype of the Japanese man. As Kuroki, Moto wears horn-rimmed glasses, black burlap pants, and matching coat. Through his fake gapped teeth, he speaks halting pidgin English. In contrast, Moto dons wire-rimmed glasses and double-breasted white suit, and his continental English is marked by a hint of a Hungarian (but coded here as Japanese) accent. If we parse this film's ethnic representations, we may conclude that the authentic Japanese man is, finally, European. Hollywood thus manages to substitute the Hungarian Jew for a Japanese agent and the Japanese agent for a stereotyped Japanese merchant. In this way *Mr. Moto's Last Warning* established the substitutions that would take place in Huston's quasi-sequel to *The Maltese Falcon, Across the Pacific* (which played in Germany in 1945 and 1946 along with *Maltese Falcon*). In this second film Greenstreet, Bogart, and Astor are reunited, this time in the Panama Canal. Lorre, as the criminal sidekick, however, is replaced by Victor Sen Yung, a Chinese American actor who plays a Japanese American spy.

Promoted by Warner Bros. in the United States as a "Jap-slapping story sensation," *Across the Pacific* aimed to capitalize on the success of *Maltese Falcon* and to place the drama squarely within American wartime policies. Working as an agent of the army Secret Service, Rick Leland (Bogart) boards a Japanese freighter posing as a dishonorably discharged gun for hire. On this ship he encounters the alluring Alberta Marlow (Astor), a big-city girl pretending to be an unworldly midwesterner, and the European Dr. Lorenz (Greenstreet), a sociologist of the Philippines by trade but an unabashed Japanophile by disposition. Having spent more than thirty years in Asia, Lorenz is convinced that the Japanese— these "wonderful little people"—are "greatly misunderstood" and underestimated. As we later learn, he is the mastermind behind the Japanese plan to bomb the Panama Canal on December 7, until Rick single-handedly takes down the entire operation. Lorenz is in league with Joe Totsuiko (Sen Yung), by far the film's most treacherous pretender. A self-described "second-generation Japanese . . . born in the good old USA," Joe is a fully assimilated "live wire." He dresses in a smart double-breasted suit, plays shuffleboard, and

In this poster for *Across the Pacific* (John Huston, Warner Bros., 1942), Rick Leland (Humphrey Bogart) punches Joe Totsuiko (Sen Young), who is now exposed as a Japanese spy. Courtesy of Wisconsin Center for Film and Theater Research, University of Wisconsin, Madison.

exploits every opportunity to flaunt his unaccented street English. "Finally," he declares upon meeting Rick, "there's someone around that speaks my language." Yet Joe's mastery of Japanese literary and martial arts, combined with his foreign features, makes us wonder if he is really an American or just acting like one. Early in the film, Huston offers us a clue.

As Rick, Alberta, and Lorenz join the others to watch a judo match on the ship, Rick wonders aloud if these Asian moves are any match for a good right cross. In response, the suspiciously affable Joe proposes a friendly challenge: Rick should punch Joe as hard as he can. We cut from a medium shot of Rick over Joe's shoulder as he delivers the blow to an overhead long shot as Rick, and not Joe, lands flat on his back (this scene, of course, sets up Rick's payback when, at the end of the film, he disposes of Joe with a hard right cross). When we return to the deck, Huston frames Joe in a close-up. Readjusting his thick horn-rimmed glasses by moving them right and left across his face, Joe appears grotesquely distorted, his eyes monstrously magnified until his glasses finally rest on his nose. The shot lasts only a few seconds but is accompanied by mocking laughter so that we may perceive, with our own eyes, the villainy concealed by Joe's Western affect and apparent pacifism. Though he walks, talks, and dresses like an American, anyone who looks closely can see that Joe is a Japanese and thus a traitor. *Across the Pacific* thus reverses the ethnic coding of *Mr. Moto*. In the latter, the stereotyped Japanese man Kuroki is merely an act to evade being captured by Western bad guys; in the former, Joe's performance of Americanization is the cover for his authentic and criminal Japanese character.

Joe's mimetic slippage is a version of what Katrin Sieg calls "fascist drag," wherein the "dupe's conflation of appearance and essence" is "both false and 'natural.'"[62] That Joe does not convince Rick (or the film's audience) of his Americanness is explained in the film by his foreign features that always betray his racial otherness and "natural" origins, even as it speaks to the failures of the Japanese to become fully Americanized. That Joe is played by a Chinese and not a Japanese American actor would seem to shore up but also complicate this assessment. In describing fascist drag's origins, Sieg offers the example of the German stage actor Albert Wurm imitating a Jewish aristocratic lady attempting (unconvincingly) to pass as German. As Sieg explains, "Ethnic difference here is presented in terms of mimetic register and proficiency: one impersonation fails, becomes recognizable as superficial masquerade, and is hence coded Jewish. . . . The other stays unmarked and cements the equation of 'Germanness' with mimetic competence" (42). Such competence is not only founded in the penchant to imitate the failure of mimesis, it suggests that even this nineteenth-century performance is predicated on a certain kind of ethnographic acuity.

In *Across the Pacific,* however, we have a Chinese American playing the part of Joe, a casting that would seem to play on Americans' inability to differentiate Asian populations or to collapse willfully Japanese and Chinese features. In fact, on December 22, 1941, *Time* magazine published a quasi-anthropological guide titled "How to Tell Your Friends from the Japs." Recalling the "science" that Lang subtly critiques in *M,* the one-page checklist delineated in head shots and bullet points the physiognomic, expressive, and even gestural differences of the Japanese and Chinese (significantly, we learn that "most Chinese avoid horn-rimmed spectacles").[63] The truly vigilant American might see that Sen Yung is a Chinese American playing a Japanese posing as an American. But with no mirror to signal this duality, such a reading is unlikely. Those who had seen *The Maltese Falcon* (presumably the very audience the film aims to attract) would correlate Joe to Joel, two foreigners played by immigrant Americans whose traces of ethnicity make them suspect as citizens. The film thus finds other ways of showcasing the false but natural failures of Japanese identity, which begins to explain one of the film's stranger scenes.

Following a tip from his Chinese comrades, Rick enters a Japanese movie theater in Cristobal, Panama, where he hopes to find information that will lead him to Lorenz. In the darkened theater we catch a few moments of what appears to be an old-fashioned Japanese comedy concerning a woman who attracts the amorous attention of men as she walks with her boyfriend through the gardens of a rustic Japanese village. As cued by the audience's laughter, the film's salient action is conveyed through body language in the spirit of silent cinema. But the sound track of the film, combined with the ambient sound of the theater, produces a series of off-putting disjunctures. Though the film is a comedy, the traditional Japanese music track is slow, somber, and amelodic to Western ears. The dialogue, which is neither translated nor subtitled and which seems to be incidental to the action that elicits the audience's response, is awkwardly postsynchronized so that the speech does not quite match the lips and, in longer shots, the actors sound closer to the camera than they appear. Though the audience laughs at the film's physical humor, its ebullience is undercut by a baby who cries in the theater. These tonal mismatches eventually take on narrative significance when Rick meets with his Chinese contact and is ambushed by the Japanese henchman. Hearing gunshots, the audience flees. But the film comedy, at complete odds with the violent action in the theater, plays on as Rick runs behind the screen, dodging daggers and bullets. Now the grave sound track and images of smiling characters are retrospectively not so much childishly ironic as threatening.

As a film within a film this Japanese comedy would seem to attest to the comparative superiority and sophistication of 1940s Hollywood and of *Across the Pacific* in particular. The sound track alone suggests that the Japanese have yet to surmount the challenges of sound cinema or master more complicated techniques of Western storytelling. But as a statement about the Japanese, this film, like the eyeglasses that magnify Joe's sinister character, makes even the familiar genre of comedy unintelligible and even menacing. Given that U.S. officials presumed that national cinema correlated with national character (as demonstrated by *Death Mills'* quotation of *Triumph of the Will* and *Human Comedy's* citation of an American newsreel), this illegible film about Japanese characters walking in a preindustrial townscape proved their foreign, less developed, and unassimilable nature.

Hollywood's ethnopoesis provided the visual registers for Washington's own shameful wartime persecution of Japanese Americans. Huston's film demonstrated what Secretary of War Harry Stimson declared of this group in 1942, namely, that "their racial characteristics are such that we cannot understand or trust even the citizen Japanese."[64] *Across the Pacific* premiered in the United States in September 1942, nine months after Franklin Roosevelt signed Executive Order 9066 authorizing the internment of Japanese aliens and American citizens of Japanese descent in what Roosevelt himself described as "concentration camps" on the grounds that they might conspire with the enemy (as Joe does) through sabotage or espionage.[65] John Dower notes that there were several of Roosevelt's advisers who felt that only the extermination of the Japanese race would sufficiently remove them as a threat to national security.[66] This internment order was in place through March 1946, when *Across the Pacific* continued to play on German screens until it was belatedly banned.

What is interesting about the film in the German context is that its representation of Japanese otherness bears comparison to the stereotypes of Jewish culture in Veit Harlan's *Jud Süß* (*Jew Süss,* 1940), a Nazi-era film that likewise dramatizes the danger of assimilating the ethnic minority. Stylistically we find the cacophony of Harlan's synagogue sonorous with the Japanese theater, at once exotic and threatening. Both films also trade on the audience's recognition of mimetic detection in these dramas of passing in which characters pretend to be assimilated into the dominant national culture. Katrin Sieg argues that *Jud Süß*'s narrative enables a "consent to genocide" because despite Faber's (Malte Jäger's) ability to recognize the Jew, he is powerless to stop Süß's corrupting influence (52–53). In *Across the Pacific* Joe is prevented from carrying out his Panama campaign, though, significantly on this same day, the Japanese assault on Pearl Harbor succeeds. *Across the Pacific* foments a consent to internment by showing that the Japanese can be stopped only if they are detected and detained in advance of their attack. Further, just as Lorre's Beckert became the face of the Jew in Hippler's anti-Semitic "documentary," Sen Yung's Joe is a dead ringer for the caricatured Nippon man from Frank Capra's U.S. War Department propaganda film *Know Your Enemy, Japan* (1945), which also, not incidentally, manufactures a case against the Japanese through excerpts of untranslated samurai films and historic melodramas comprehensible to American viewers only as artifacts of Japan's violent and uncivilized history.[67] Betraying its own mimetic tautology, *Know Your Enemy* remarks that "all Japanese look like prints from the same negative." Though Germans did not have access to *Across the Pacific*'s backstory, the history this film encodes signals an intersection of state-sanctioned racial persecution on both sides of the Atlantic abetted through the filmic imputation of racial difference.

The Hollywood Western and Parables of Democratic Founding

While *Across the Pacific* only hints at the logic of internment, the brutality of U.S. history was pointedly staged for German audiences through the genre most associated with America's self-image:

westerns. Shown in occupied Germany under the aegis of the re-education program were John Ford's *Drums along the Mohawk* and *Stagecoach* (both from 1939) and Fritz Lang's *Western Union* (1941). These films take us to pivotal moments and romantic spaces in America's westward expansion where the pioneers clash with Native Americans in their efforts to tame the land and bring legal order. While each film pits "savage Indians" against the white settlers so as to authorize the genocide that made possible America's democratic founding, these films also argue for the ethnographic proposition that culture and not blood determines one's access to citizenship. These westerns, made by directors who personally experienced the force of America's (and Hollywood's) assimilationist creed, implicitly question the costs of cultural conformity by working through the outsider's relationship to America's civilizing mission.

Drums along the Mohawk taunts us with its ethnographic thesis when we are first introduced to Blue Back (Chief John Big Tree). Our newlywed pioneer protagonists Gilbert (Henry Fonda) and Lana Martin (Claudette Colbert) arrive at their rustic homestead in 1776 at night and in a torrential downpour. Lana is drying herself by the fire while Gil tends to the horse outside when, out of nowhere, a menacing-looking Indian appears in the doorway. Illuminated only from the light of the fire below, his stoic and foreign features betray no sign of civilized sociality. As he slowly approaches the now hysterical Lana, who screams as she retreats to the far corner of the cabin, we can only assume he intends to violate her. Yet when Gil finally comes, it is not to Lana's but the Indian's rescue. He slaps Lana to her senses and introduces her to his friend. "Blue Back wouldn't hurt you. Why, he's as good a Christian as you or me, maybe better." Indeed, throughout the film, Blue Back helps the settlers protect the land they've claimed against attack from the generic Indian marauders who have sided with the British Royalists in exchange for vague promises and a generous supply of liquor. In Mohawk Valley, these barely clothed savages seem to be, like the liquor they drink, in endless supply and more than willing to die for the cause of American subjugation to British rule. Blue Back, on the other hand, given to almost Tourettic outbursts of "Hallelujah!" and fluent in "Hollywood Indian English," has forsaken his tribal ways and thus is poised to benefit from the promises of the American Revolution.[68]

Lana (Claudette Colbert) defends the fortress from warring Indians in *Drums along the Mohawk* (John Ford, 20th Century Fox, 1939). Production still courtesy of Photofest.

After a harrowing final battle in which two of the settlers and scores of warring male Indians are slain, Blue Back stands in the fort with Gil, Lana, and the other pioneers, including the African American maid Daisy (Beulah Hall Jones), and gazes at the new flag of the state he helped to defend. Daisy and Blue Back prove the educability of all ethnic minorities, and the good Americans' acceptance of them proves the genuine openness of U.S. citizenship to all like-minded people. Yet, perhaps because of his cultural conversion, Blue Back is the sole surviving Native American without a mate or offspring. But this film does not draw our attention to Blue Back as the lone tribesman. We focus instead on Gil's son, who, though only now a toddler, will inherit the country his father and Blue Back helped to found. Read in this way, assimilation for the Native American is only a temporary solution to inevitable dispossession from a society over which the white sons and daughters of the Revolution will preside.

Also produced in 1939 and in circulation in Germany at the time with *Drums*, *Stagecoach* takes us one hundred years after the

American Revolution at a time, we soon realize, when the fighting with the Indians is far from over and American civilization far from civil. In this well-known film, Dallas (Claire Trevor), the prostitute with the heart of gold, and Doc Boone (Thomas Mitchell), the town's drunken but well-meaning physician, are forced by the vicious ladies of the Tonto Law and Order League onto the outbound stagecoach, where they are brought into close riding quarters with what constitutes a cross section of nineteenth-century (white) America. Though the passengers are starkly divided by class and codes of honor, as they travel deeper into Apache territory and witness not just the burning of settlements but the slain white bodies of the settlers themselves, the group puts their differences aside and begins to act together. They vote on their course of action, later ferry the coach across the river, and finally shoot at the Apaches who attack them. Thanks to a last-minute rescue by the cavalry that saves those who survive the onslaught, the carriage makes its way to Lordsberg, where the passengers permanently disband. In contrast to Mohawk Valley's united citizens, who manage to build a community despite Indian attacks, the people of the stagecoach

Indians attack the fortress in *Drums along the Mohawk.* Production still courtesy of Photofest.

can muster only an impermanent détente under such a threat. That is, the Apaches of *Stagecoach* do not impede westward expansion or disrupt the formation of political sovereignty; now they are necessary to create "civil" bonds by giving Americans of all walks of life a fear and hatred in common. In Ford's version of history, as told in these two films, genocide is not just the founding violence of American statehood, it is constitutive of its sustainability.

This reading of Ford's treatment of America's "Indian problem" is closely connected to his ongoing critique of U.S. mainstream culture. Charles Ramírez Berg argues that Ford's racial politics were inflected by his own status as a second-generation Irish American who, having come of age in a culture denigrating to Irish immigrants, was critical of the assimilation process, in particular the expectation that ethnic minorities had to conform to the "rigid, intolerant, and merciless" standards of WASP culture or be exiled to the margins of American social and economic life.[69] For Berg, Ford's frontier is a space where the stakes of assimilation are most pronounced. Sandwiched between the "ever-advancing colonizing Mainstream" and the inscrutable, sometimes hostile Native Americans are the ethnic minorities—the misfits, outcasts, immigrants, refugees, and poor—who have come to the West to find property and to live, if not prosper, in the spirit of their ethnic heritage or cultural otherness. Berg argues that Native Americans function in these films to demarcate the "cultural limits" of these errant ethnics: "If the Mainstream represents Ford's fear of what the Margin ethnics will likely become via assimilation, the Native American is what they can't become—another race. . . . Though they struggle to maintain an ethnic identity separate from both, Ford's immigrant pioneers discover that the effort is hopeless. They must choose between assimilation or life among the native Americans, both of which are viewed as a cultural death" (80–81). While we can see these tensions worked out in *Drums,* where Blue Back's assimilation is the source of his isolation, and in *Stagecoach,* where the mainstream is represented by vicious hypocritical ladies of law who banish to almost certain death the town's well-meaning misfits, it is Lang's *Western Union* that is most preoccupied with cultural circumscription.

Of Viennese Jewish descent (raised as a Roman Catholic), Lang immigrated to Hollywood after his illustrious career at UFA was cut short by Goebbels's proposition that Lang put his directorial skills to work for the Nazi Party. Rather than prop up Hitler's regime, Lang fled Germany and eventually landed himself a contract with MGM.[70] As his filmography suggests, Lang shared Ford's distrust of America's cultural conscription, and, as we know from *M,* Lang was sympathetic to the plight of those whose uncontrollable impulses and desires make them susceptible to mob violence and prone to self-imposed seclusion. While Lang's early western casts the forces of civilization in far more charitable terms than does *Stagecoach,* the film is nonetheless acutely aware of the barriers to entering this civil society. *Western Union* is Lang's Civil War–era tale of the company's cross-continental journey to erect the telegraph wire. In this film it is not Indians but a gang of white, southern, Civil War–profiteering bandits *dressed* like Indians who thwart the company's progress by raiding the livestock and setting fire to the camp. One of the reformed members of the gang, Vance (Randolph Scott), works for the company and sets out to retrieve the stolen goods. In a scene that recalls Blue Back's introduction to Lana, Vance spies the men around a campfire, draped in blankets and adorned in feathers and war paint; the Hollywood Indian theme music suggests that he has come across thieving natives. The sound track crescendos and then abruptly stops when the "Indian," framed now in a medium close-up, smiles and calls out to his brother, "Vance!" "Jack!" Vance affably returns. When we cut back to Jack, his blue-eyed friendly face and five o'clock shadow make him a poor candidate for Native impersonation.

Though he initially maintains his allegiance to his brother, Vance eventually exposes the cross-dressing charade when the gang sets fire to the company campground and nearly ignites a war between the company men and the Indians. Rather than betray his brother and his own family lineage to the company, Vance decides to take matters into his own hands. He leaves the job that promised to deliver him respectable prosperity, rides into town, and kills the bandits (including his own brother). In the process, Vance himself is killed. His position in the company as the CEO's right-hand man and suitor to the boss's sister points to both Vance's ability and opportunity to transcend his birthright and criminal past. It is his sacrifice, however, that makes him worthy of corporate and thus American citizenship, neither of which he lives to enjoy.

Western Union distinguishes the savage from the civilized in terms of acculturation and not race, and like *Drums* it suggests

that those who convert to either mainstream norms *or* Indian dress
are not likely to reap the benefits they seek. Thus, this story avoids
the genocidal logic of the other two films by displacing Native
American slaughter onto criminals dressed in native garb, who, the
film assures us, deserve to die. This displacement of genocide, then,
may also be read as its denial. The tragic figure is Vance, who, despite his patriotism, hard work, and gentle ways, is caught between
the Confederacy and the Union, between civil and savage culture,
and thus can find no place for himself in either.

A Shared Denial?

Most of the Hollywood films brought to Germany under the aegis
of reeducation, especially those concerned with American westward expansion and the history of immigration, did little to teach
Germans about democracy or assure them that assimilating to the
customs of their occupiers would restore them to a more enlightened, liberal way of being. Some audiences might have interpreted
the film program in a manner consistent with the reeducation
policy by focusing on how these filmic scenarios contrasted with
Nazi racial and military culture. There is, however, one popular
phenomenon that suggests, at least where westerns are concerned,
audiences had the very opposite response. In *Ethnic Drag,* Katrin
Sieg explores how in the years following the occupation Germans
mapped the experiences of defeat and collective guilt onto
indigenously produced fantasies of the American Wild West.[71] As
Sieg notes, German cast themselves not as American settlers and
pioneers but as Indian victims of colonial expansion—an identification enfleshed through Indian masquerade. This impersonation,
or "ethnic drag," was performed in western stage plays and in
"Indian Village" theme parks where the German hobbyist, dressed
in authentic costuming, enacted Native American rituals as other
Germans looked on. In these scenarios, Indians are not the warring simpletons of Mohawk Valley and *Stagecoach,* but are rather
idealized, peaceable nobles under siege by white American capitalists who savagely kill or encamp them in reservations. Rejecting
Hollywood's western formula, Germans refused identification with
their occupiers and thus resisted both the Americanization of their
culture during the occupation and the explicit assimilationist mandate of reeducation. Ethnic drag was also, as Sieg explains, a means
of evading, even forgetting, the genocidal legacy of Nazi Germany:

Indian impersonation . . . provided postwar Germans with a way to both mourn the vacancies left by the Holocaust and refuse the role of perpetrator in racial aggression. Hobbyism allowed Germans to explore alternative notions of ethnicity that supplanted prior concepts of Aryan supremacy. Postwar Germans' identification with the victims of foreign invasion reflected (and displaced) the historical experience of Allied occupation, but also constituted a form of historical denial. (24)

Especially for those who might have seen the curious and likely pairing of Hollywood westerns about the slaughter of Indians (shown to teach Germans the truth about culture) on the same program as the *World in Film* newsreel reporting on the judgment of Nazi mass killings (shown to teach Germans about the extent and shared responsibility of Hitler's genocide), such a critical rewriting of the American West makes very good sense. Germans refused to adopt the role of American pioneers and cowboys because it would doubly inscribe their genocidal guilt. This phenomenon thus intimates that to recover from the Nazi era, Germans did not need to become *more* like Americans but to find new paradigms of "ethnological correctness" and ethnographic sympathy.

And yet we should be mindful that, however much Indian impersonation was a *post*war, *post*occupation phenomenon, it recalled and perhaps updated in important ways the Nazi fascination with American Indians and the money-lusting (read Jewish) settlers who threatened them. As Lutz Koepnick reminds us, Hitler "apotheosize[d] himself as a double of the last of the Mohicans, a representative of a race of heroically dying, yet morally infallible, warriors," an identity that Emil in *Tomorrow—the World!* mimics when he announces to the class his admiration for the pure-blooded Sioux.[72] The Nazi western perpetuated a mythos of immigration but with an important twist. Contra the trope of the fully Americanized German immigrant touted in U.S. reeducation policy, these westerns celebrated "the image of the German as the good American immigrant resisting Jewish American greed, functional abstraction, cultural hybridization, and racial miscegenation" (115). As Koepnick argues, in these films, the German maintains his connection to homeland and blood. Impervious to the sullying effects of assimilation, the German immigrant "reminds multicultural Americans that ethnic difference matters" (115).

The film program also suggests that even the American occupiers sensed a disturbing similarity between themselves and their Nazi-era German wards. In chapter 1, I argued that American anthropology and psychoculturalism metonymically primitivized the Germans (by comparing them to the Japanese and indigenous tribal people, including the Plains Indians) so as to authorize a reeducation program that would be marked as successful in part when the problem of race was erased. The primitivist alibi was necessary but not only because Germans (especially those assimilated in the United States) may look and act like white Americans. As Hollywood films alone suggest, this alibi may also be an anxious disavowal or accidental admission of the ways that Americans, in their history of racial violence and exclusion, look and act quite a bit like them.

3. Garbo Laughs
and Germans Eat

The benchmarks of America's occupation policy in post–World War II Germany are well known. In the first years, its directives were to strip Germans of their war-making capacity by demilitarizing the culture, deindustrializing the economy, and de-Nazifying the population. By ferreting out and, through the war-crimes tribunal, bringing to justice high-ranking Nazis, the Americans hoped to discredit Hitler's regime and minimize Nazi influence over postwar reconstruction. But the breakdown of the Soviet–American alliance, the spectacular Berlin airlift, and the ensuing cold war brought about a significant policy shift that manifested itself in the occupation's filmic rhetoric. This chapter explores the new model of citizenship promoted in America's cold war film campaign. Where in the first years reeducation emphasized America's melting pot democracy as the ethical contrast to Nazism, beginning in 1947 the contest was now between American democratic capitalism and Soviet communism.[1] I am particularly interested in how films at the center of America's cold war propaganda—such as *Ninotchka* (Lubitsch, 1939) and the German-language newsreel *Welt im Film (World in Film)*—celebrate American capitalism as a form of embodied, even satiric citizenship in contrast to communism's austere and increasingly perverse ideals. Helmut Käutner's own failed satire *Der Apfel ist ab (The Apple Fell,* 1948) undercuts this binary logic and sensual appeal and in so doing makes a radical but elusive statement about the limits of Germany's democratic agency.

Ninotchka Laughs

By far the most celebrated scene in *Ninotchka* takes places in a working-class bistro in pre–World War I Paris. The film's eponymous character, the Soviet special envoy extraordinary played by stoic Greta Garbo, joylessly sips her fish soup as her aristocratic seducer, Leon (Melvyn Douglas), plies her with clichéd jokes, hoping to elicit some sign of conviviality that bolshevism has apparently suppressed. While his deliberate attempts to humor her fail, he unwittingly succeeds when he pushes away from the table in exasperation and falls backward out of his chair. Lubitsch cuts from Leon collapsed on the floor to the bistro's guffawing working-class patrons, to Ninotchka, who, like Garbo herself (so the publicity

Poster for *Ninotchka* (Ernst Lubitsch, MGM, 1942). Courtesy of Photofest.

goes), laughs robustly for the first time on screen. Like Emil in *Tomorrow—the World!* in this scene Ninotchka undergoes a conversion from a dispassionate, affectless communist to a fully embodied, consuming capitalist who not only laughs but eats, drinks, and finds romance. Once stripped of her political pretensions and sensual repressions, she is, we are led to believe, really just like us.

For some American reviewers in 1939, Ninotchka's sensual turn attested to the film's generous humanism. Writing for the *New Republic,* for example, Otis Ferguson found that the "meeting-of-East-and-West" humor marked *Ninotchka* as "the first movie with any airiness at all to discover that communists are people and may be treated as such in a story."[2] Yet precisely when these communists reveal their humanity, they stray from the austerity of Moscow's belt-tightening regime. In a sly reversal of Marxist causality, the sensate body deprived under communism is naturally drawn back to capitalism's abundance. In the film's final scene, Stalin's model citizen, awakened to capitalism's carnal allure and amorous freedoms, defects, joining Leon and her three corrupted (defected) comrades in Istanbul. Recalling reeducation's immigrant trope, *Ninotchka*'s final act is new confirmation of capitalist hospitality. She immigrates not to the United States but to Turkey, which by 1948 is under the American sphere of influence and Marshall Plan affluence.

In the United States, *Ninotchka* was greeted with enthusiastic notices for Garbo's comic reinvention under Lubitsch's elusive touch, and the *New York Times* alone ran two features specifically on the film's *audiences,* whose laughter so overwhelmed the theater that the dialogue was nearly inaudible.[3] The Hearst-owned *New York Daily Mirror* declared that "Garbo does more in one line to debunk Soviet Russia than we have been able to do in a hundred editorials!"[4] It is perhaps, then, little wonder that this satire of communism, made on the eve of World War II, became the centerpiece of America's official cold war campaign—not in the United States, but in Europe, where, the Americans feared, communism vied as a postwar alternative to Nazism and fascism and seemed to offer quick solutions to the many privations of the war-torn region. At the state department's request the film made its controversial Italian debut during the 1948 national election.[5] In occupied Germany that same year *Nintochka* was the U.S. military government's antidote to communism and Soviet anti-American propaganda.

Moscow's reeducation campaign was designed to promote its own political and social system of Marxist-Leninist Communism as a democratic model for the postwar order. The Soviets sponsored a host of musical, theatrical, and artistic events to tutor the Germans in a new brand of politicized culture.[6] As the U.S.-Soviet conflict escalated, Moscow's promotion of communism consequently went hand in hand with its attacks on American capitalism and Hollywood's debased film culture. For instance, film director Ilia S. Trauberg publicly denounced American cinema for its pornographic, overly romantic, and profit-oriented narratives; such films appealed to the people's "lowest instincts" compared to Russian films that aimed to "serve the people and show them natural life."[7] An editorial in the Soviet-controlled *Tägliche Rundschau* sums up the paper's tongue-in-cheek criticism of capitalist film culture, particularly as it was used as an instrument of reeducation and political modeling. The editor reasons: "For I think I am right in assuming that films sent over to Berlin are likely not chosen randomly, but only the best, most carefully selected ones are sent. . . . These films are true heralds of English and American culture." Noting the numerous instances of violence, greed, and depravity in American and British features, he concludes: "They are—all of them—harbingers of the free, progressive and unique culture of Western democracy. If these films do not convince you, nothing else will."[8]

Soviet control of German theaters also proved to be an outlet for political maneuvering. Beginning in 1947, a series of plays critiquing the United States premiered in the Soviet zone. For instance, Konstantin Simonov's *The Russian Question (Russkiy vopros)* tells the story of an American journalist who uncovers the repressive and monopolistic spirit of the United States when he tries to publish the truth about life in the more enlightened Soviet Union. In its revision of American history, the play asserts that Franklin Roosevelt had been assassinated by greedy capitalists and that the U.S. War Department had been created with the express purpose of stifling international communism.[9] In May 1948, a film version of *The Russian Question* premiered in East Berlin and the Soviet zone of Germany that augmented the play with newsreel footage from the United States, including the persecution of African Americans, unemployment lines, brutal strike breaking, and jarring scenes of urban poverty. Two additional theatrical productions underscored the Soviets' anti-American position: *Deep Roots* depicted the oppression

and exploitation of African Americans at the hands of racist capitalists, and the Sheinin brothers' *Colonel Kuz'min* staged scenes
in which American soldiers disclose the American plan to colonize
postwar Germany for commercial exploitation.[10]

In response to this cultural offensive, U.S. authorities rushed
prints of *Ninotchka* to Berlin and then to the rest of the Western
zone of Germany. Noting that even France and Britain were
more inclined toward socialism and were increasingly critical of
American designs for living, the New York Office of the Civil
Affairs Division proposed a new, unabashedly propagandistic campaign that emphasized capitalism as the most distinct and least
understood feature of American political life:

> We should get rid of the concept of information as it was visualized
> when reorientation represented the only source by which informa-
> tion could reach the Occupied Areas and admit frankly that we
> are now in the business of propaganda. . . . When everybody else
> is criticizing this country and emphasizing its shortcomings, it has
> become our task to seek out the points which make the American
> system appear good, sound and the best possible of all systems. . . .
> To give an example: Few things are more controversial than the
> capitalistic system. It is not official policy to "sell" the capitalistic
> system under which this country prospered, but the fact remains
> that it is the only system which has been able, up to this minute, to
> guarantee the greatest number of individual freedoms which sur-
> vive anywhere. . . . [C]apitalism is basic to the American way of life
> as it is known today, and secondly, it is attacked from all sides.
> Therefore, it should be our task to emphasize the good points of
> capitalism wherever possible. . . . America has become the most
> misinterpreted and calumniated country on earth.[11]

Reflecting what Victoria de Grazia has identified as America's
uniquely formulated "democracy of consumption," this statement begins to articulate the logic of American "Market Empire,"
whose global ascendancy was coincident with the onset of the cold
war in Germany.[12] Even Ninotchka's transformation confirms that
the freedom to consume may foment an acquired will to choose a
liberal economic and political model.

In occupied Germany, however, the connection between choice
making in the civic and consumer sphere had yet to solidify in the
popular imagination, at least insofar as the pubic opinion surveys

conducted by the military government evinced.[13] According to a 1947 report, there was little question that Germans living in the Western zones were hospitable to American capitalism, particularly when communism was the alternative. Yet the same survey concluded that less than half of these residents felt that Germans were capable of democratic self-rule. Moreover, four of ten respondents could not fathom how democracy would benefit Germany. Overwhelmingly those questioned claimed to know very little about politics, expressed little desire to learn more, and felt that such matters should be left to "others" to decide.[14] To be responsive to such findings, propaganda needed above all to galvanize Germans by linking their faith in capitalist consumerism to confidence in political democracy and, conversely, needed to naturalize the culture of American consumer capitalism as *the* culture of democracy. But what exactly is the culture of democratic capitalism? How is it practiced? How and according to what myths and narratives could Germans in the Western zones become convinced of the "choice-worthiness" of (American) capitalism and their own readiness to assume democratic self-rule?[15] The films under discussion in this chapter respond to the cold war crises by staging and delimiting political choices. As I will read them in conjunction with U.S. information policy, these films are typological narratives of sense and sense making that both question and reinscribe reeducation's mimetic imperative in cold war terms. With propaganda front and center, this chapter begins and ends, appropriately enough, with satire.

The Best of All Possible Systems

The policy statement quoted above is nothing if not earnest. Still, one can detect echoes of Candide's unbridled optimism in the assertion that America's is "the best of all possible systems" and that capitalism is the best guarantee of all personal freedoms. This bald assertion, however, is undercut by the possibility that Germans, either misinformed or persuaded by hostile propaganda, might choose otherwise. Earlier in the memo this officer notes that objections directed against the American system, written for and by Americans, are acceptable because these readers "may be able to judge [these assessments] as they are meant: namely, as detailed criticism of something that as such is being accepted." "Foreign audiences," on the other hand, "do not accept the American system as such and will, therefore, misinterpret the criticisms of details as criticism of the American system."[16] In other words, commentary intended to change the system is acceptable only when the system is accepted "as such." Or we may more cynically observe that America's is the best system because even dissenting American voices agree that it is the *only* possible system. There is, then, an unwitting irony, worthy of satire, in the American proposition to "sell" democratic capitalism to a population unsure of its readiness and desire for self-rule and who, once democratically empowered, may not buy it.

Given the gravity of Soviet anti-American attacks and the geopolitical stakes of this opportune moment in German history, *Ninotchka* is a curious but, as a satire, perhaps apt choice to promote the American/democratic/capitalistic way of life. This is curious given that our European characters never reach America's borders in the film. And, far from shoring up the political commitments of its adherents, the free market seems to foster—at least in Ninotchka and her three comrades—material indulgence and a forsaking of higher ideals. Yet the film's geographic dislocation speaks to the cosmopolitan nature of capitalism as it is practiced, not in the United States but in Paris, where, in this film, it comes to represent a natural, depoliticized, and universal state of sensuous being that communism has perverted. The film's satiric mode, moreover, points to the gaps between communist ideology and the capitalist world it purports to correct. In Paris, for example, White Russians work as bellhops and waiters serving the Soviet envoys who have come to sell off White Russian jewels "legally confiscated" during the revolution. This sale is necessary to buy food and farm equipment for the hungry Soviet masses. Not only must the envoys resort to capitalist exchange to feed their starving proletariats, they exploit the formerly aristocratic working class to do so. Similarly, Leon's butler, who opposes the principle of collectively shared wealth, has more in personal savings than his noble but completely bankrupt employer. In Paris class is a veneer unreflective of material wealth; in Moscow, on the other hand, all citizens are equally impoverished. The economy of communist community is summed up in culinary terms on the occasion of Ninotchka's Moscow dinner party. She has invited her three comrades over for an omelet and each must bring his own rationed egg. Her roommate surmises, "Stand alone and it means a boiled egg. But if you are true

Ninotchka (Greta Garbo) refuses to indulge Leon's (Melvyn Douglas) jokes.
Production still courtesy of Wisconsin Center for Film and Theater Research,
University of Wisconsin, Madison.

to the collective spirit and stick together, you have an omelet." True
enough. But the difference between a boiled egg and a four-egg
omelet shared four ways is still only one egg apiece.

Rather than condemn these wayward bolsheviks, capitalism
converts and absorbs its critics into the system; it enables them to
transform gastronomic longings into satisfying, enterprising ventures. In Istanbul, comrades Iranoff, Buljanoff, and Kopalski have
opened a Russian bistro of their own, featuring not the anemic omelets of the Soviet collective but the beef Stroganoff, borscht, and
blini of a more plenitudinous, prerevolutionary era. For Germans
suffering during the occupation's lean years, the appeal to full bellies was a politics unto itself. For as one Dresden resident remarked
of the Soviet play, "The real 'Russian Question' has to do with dismantling and the shortage of potatoes."[17]

Ninotchka is effective as propaganda because it so clearly sim-
plifies the choice between capitalism and communism as one be-

tween embodied enjoyment and the suppression of desire, affect, and appetite. Who would not choose as she does? And the choice to eat well or not eat was almost as easy as the choice Berliners faced in their selection of entertainment. They could pay to watch the Soviet Union's humorless and didactic *The Russian Question* or the Hollywood comedy featuring UFA's own Jewish émigré talent (director Ernst Lubitsch and screenwriter Billy Wilder), whose biographies attested to the choiceworthiness of the American system even as they signaled the Nazi brutality that forced their immigration in the first place. When *Ninotchka* opened in Berlin, the demand for tickets was so great that screenings were sold out three days in advance; on the black market, tickets traded for more than double the box office price, making *Ninotchka* "the biggest money maker" in Berlin since the currency reform.[18] The great triumph of America's procapitalist information campaign is that it actually turned a profit. Or, to refer to the policy statement above, the U.S. military government was indeed in the business of propaganda.

The U.S. deployment of satire was also consistent with the genre that would help to found and sustain West Germany's liberal republic and distinguish it from the communist East. In his

Ninotchka finally succumbs to laughing at and with Leon. Production still courtesy of Photofest.

anthropological study of cold war Berlin, John Borneman argues that, despite their close proximity and once-shared cultural heritage, East and West Berliners developed radically different interpretations of the law and policy. These state-inscribed narratives functioned much like genre to control "the range of meanings" citizens import to the law and to shape their experiences of it. As a result, Borneman writes, "even when the content of law or policy in the two [German] states [was] nearly identical, it [would] be read differently."[19] East German citizens would learn to relate to the state through "romantic emplotment," a genre "intrinsic to socialist republics." Referencing Northrop Frye's classic study of genre, Borneman finds that the East German policy revolved around a forward-looking utopian fantasy aimed "at the transfiguration of the everyday to restore some lost Eden or to anticipate some future one." The language of the law was crafted "toward a future communist destiny . . . its meaning was less practical than visionary." On the other hand, citizens in West Germany would come to experience the law through a "satiric emplotment," a genre "intrinsic to liberal republics with constitutions." This mode "presupposes homogeneous, transcendental moral standards in order to ridicule vice in a supposedly stable society." Borneman turns to Theodor W. Adorno's critique of the genre when he claims that the satiric form, in contrast to the visionary romantic, disparages those present-day practices that fail to fulfill the promise of the constitution as the almost biblical text of the people's origins. As such, satire is an inherently backward-looking, conservative genre that aligns itself with authority "to maintain its vision of humanity as invariant" and, in the case of West Germany, to protect citizens "from a fallen or degraded world (e.g., Nazism or communism)." Like the criticism of the American system discussed in the preceding policy statement, the satiric state aims to return citizens to their constitutional ideal but never proposes to change the system itself. Similarly in *Ninotchka,* it is less the case that the heroine is converted from communism to capitalism than she is *restored* to her senses. In West Germany in particular, satire was "convenient" for the people and leaders who, as liberal democrats, identified themselves as victims of fascism "while simultaneously incorporating former Nazis into a number of prominent positions in government and industry."[20] While he does not refer to the genre of satire, Jeffrey Herf remarks on the irony of democratic founding in the

Western zones of occupation that was at odds with justice and public memory accountable to Nazi genocide: "For democrats in the West, their own ideology and experience of the Nazi era were at cross-purposes as they sought to establish rule by and for a people who had fought for Nazism to the bitter end."[21]

In his study of German occupation cinema, Robert Shandley finds the seeds of a similar generic divide: films made in the Western zones responded to defeat and foreign occupation more often through comedy in pointed contrast to the moralizing melodramas made in the East under Soviet supervision.[22] Germans, who up until 1945 shared a sense of nationhood in ethnocultural terms, now found themselves on opposite sides of a geopolitical divide. These new narrative affiliations, derived from the political ideologies of their respective foreign military forces, became *the* touchstones for postwar citizenship. Unique to European statehood, notes Borneman, the two Germanys that emerged out of the occupation "were artificial products, fictions of an international order given a kind of virgin birth by their superpower patrons: they were in no way indigenous creations, although their legitimacy was often dependent on their passing as such."[23] On both sides of the iron curtain, propaganda had to ease Germans into this new political identification with sovereignty that, while constructed from above, could be embraced as if emanating from below. *Ninotchka* may have demonstrated the ease of choice making, but it did little to address German readiness for democracy or to convince Germans themselves of the nativity of the new emerging state. In my reading, these twin crises are satirized in Helmut Käutner's 1948 surrealist cabaret musical *Der Apfel ist ab,* a film that stages the limitations and futility of political choice under foreign military rule.

Democracy, or Taking Sides in an Earthquake

Upon returning from her extended stay in occupied Germany, Hannah Arendt observed that, in the face of destruction and the horrors of the Nazi genocide, Germans were listless and indifferent to the crises surrounding them. Dispossessed of their cities and nation, and unwilling to accept responsibility for the current state of affairs, "the average German looks for the causes of the last war not in the acts of the Nazi regime, but in the events that led to the expulsion of Adam and Eve from Paradise." What Arendt finds most threatening to the creation of a democratic state is that

Germans, "denied the power to rule the world," have "fallen in love with impotence as such, and now find positive pleasure in contemplating international tensions and the unavoidable mistakes that occur in the business of governing, regardless of the possible consequences for themselves."[24] Despite Soviet aggression to coerce East Germans into political supplication, Germans are not unequivocally pro-American but determined to remain neutral, "as though it were as absurd to take sides in the conflict as it would be to take sides in an earthquake" (342–43). Arendt describes a population who has forsaken its own political agency and the laws of men in favor of a fate and history determined by natural, even messianic law over which they have no control. German suffering, even when it is a consequence of the lost war or, as she notes, "outside the will and control of the Western powers," is interpreted by the occupied as a "careful scheme of [Allied] revenge" demonstrating "the equal sinfulness of all men" (343).

I turn to Arendt not because her description necessarily captures a truth of German despondency, but because her imagery describes both the problems of democratic founding and the very representation of German complacency Käutner parodies in *Der Apfel ist ab*. As if taken from the pages of Arendt's essay, Käutner's film journeys through the story of creation to allegorize German politics and indecision in this presovereign moment of the nation's history. Because *Apfel* is so odd and, as it turned out upon its release, so inscrutable, it requires a brief summary.

The plot centers on Adam (Bobby Todd), a doleful apple juice manufacturer who cannot choose between his vampish wife Lilly (Joana Maria Gorvin) and his virginal mistress Eva (Bettina Moissi). Indecisive and inept at suicide, Adam seeks professional counsel in the White Hills psychiatric resort. Even here, however, Adam is inadequate to the minimal self-discipline of therapy because he refuses to accept responsibility for his love life. He is, in the words of his psychiatrist, Professor Petri (played by Käutner), a self-avowed *OdZ (Opfer der Zeit),* or victim of the times. Discharged and uncured, Adam falls asleep in the psychiatrist's lobby and dreams he is the original Adam forced to wait with Eve (also played by Moissi) in paradise until Earth—under *re*construction—is ready for human habitation. Fashioned as a sanitized military outpost, Eden, as administered by the angel Petrus (also played by Käutner), is a disorganized and highly dysfunctional bureaucracy. While

Petrus and Lucifer—meant to represent some configuration of the occupation forces—fight over the rearing of Earth's first children, Adam and Eve are torn between the safe boredom of an artificial, sterile paradise and the sensual decadence of hell as variety theater, where all manner of delicacies and diversions are offered. Upon his visit to hell, Adam cannot choose his poison and Lucifer punishes this indecision by forcing Adam and Eve to watch all of the variety acts simultaneously. Sitting on a revolving platform they are witness to a phantasmagoria of entertainments: a boxing match, jazz music, and a fashion show collide with the cancan, which bleeds into an SS rally and a performance of Wagner's *Lohengrin*. High and low, democratic and fascist, the culture mix is dizzying and cacophonous. Shell-shocked back in paradise, Adam is once again triangulated between the heavenly Eve and the serpentine Lillith (Gorvin) until, after picking the bewormed apple for Lillith's breakfast, Adam finds himself exiled to the unfinished Earth, where he is again joined by Lilly and Eva. Petrus, feeling that mankind deserves another chance, calls the administrators of heaven and hell to a summit meeting, which fails to produce any resolution to Adam's predicament. He cannot have both women nor can he choose between them, so Adam leaves the negotiating table by rejecting both. In a sense, he is right back where the film began. The future of the human race looks bleak until, from the upper right-hand corner of the screen, the papier-mâché hand of God intervenes and combines both women into one ideal bride. Upon awakening back in the lobby, Adam encounters this very woman while waiting for the tram back to town.

Even before *Apfel*'s premiere, the Catholic Church, fearful that Käutner's irreverent, even pornographic vision of heaven (where Adam and Eve wear only cellophane clothing) would offend filmgoers' religious sensibilities, denounced the film at the production stage and vigorously pleaded with U.S. occupation forces to implement more stringent, spiritually sensitive, and locally responsive film censorship.[25] As a result of advanced publicity, this comedy was understood upon its release not as a parable of German politics, but as an undecipherable satire of original sin and thus a *serious* problem. For example, the *Westfälische Nachrichten* attacked Käutner for appropriating biblical material for pointedly un-Christian ends. For this anonymous reviewer Adam's solution to break it off with his wife and mistress in favor of a third woman is

Adam (Bobby Todd) and Eve (Bettina Moissi) investigate the forbidden apple in *Der Apfel ist ab* (Helmut Käutner, Camera, 1948). Production still courtesy of Filmmuseum Berlin—Deutsche Kinemathek.

hardly the solution a Christian god would sanction, let alone fashion.[26] Though praising the film's technical flair and sophisticated comedy, the *Hamburger Echo* could not make heads or tails of the satire: the film "invited many interpretations and makes several insinuations. Maybe too many." For this critic the film was "too literary and complex to be accessible to the masses."[27] Robert Shandley, assessing the film's reception from some historical distance, writes that *Apfel* "uses allegory as an excuse for ambiguity" that "opens the gate for any possible reading."[28] Called upon for clarification at the time of the film's initial release, Käutner explained the central conflict in secular, political, and humanist terms:

> At the forefront there is simply the fate of humankind, of any man. I intentionally chose the most lucid symbol: a man between two women. It is not just this problem that interests me. It is every private trouble that a person can make for himself when he cannot choose between two things. You can take it politically, but you can also take it purely as human nature in reference to all things which we come across today in these uncertain times.[29]

For Käutner, *Apfel* was not about religion but indecision. And we might note that where Käutner's film features a man who cannot choose, at the heart of the church's intervention in film culture was the concern that audiences, without proper guidance, might choose badly. While the campaign against *Apfel* was an attempt to keep it from theaters, the Catholic and Protestant churches were finally less interested in curbing film expression and more in channeling entertainment through Germany's cultural custodians in resistance to Market Empire's direct appeal to sensual, pleasure-seeking consumers.[30] Moreover, the *Evangelischer Film-Beobachter* shrewdly (and with irony) defended the church's position by mapping out the logic of market censorship. Written as an absurd skit whose circularity mirrors Käutner's bizarre film, this editorial merits quotation at length:

> The public is constantly complaining about how bad most films are. We spoke to a theater owner: "Why, week after week, can you not book one good film?" "Oh, if it were up to me, I would only book good films . . . but I can't because I am beholden to play whatever the distributor brings me." We went to the distributor: "Why out of the ten films you rent to our theaters is there not even one good film?" "You have a good point. What should I do? I must rent what the producers give me." We wrote to the producer: "Why do you make such awful films? Couldn't you for the same amount of money make an occasional good film?" "We don't make these decisions, the financiers order us to make these movies." We spoke to the financiers: "You alone are responsible for the hundreds of bad films made every year in the United States. You have the money and no one gives you orders. Why do you finance such bad movies?" "Films are expensive to make. We have to give the people what they want. We take our orders from the people and the people pay us." So there we were right back where we started from.[31]

Though the public complains bitterly about the quality of films, the *Beobachter* quipped that, according to the logic of an American consumer-oriented industry, only the public is to blame. The theme of Käutner's film and the tenor of the church's objections to it are equally skeptical of the people's preparation for and opportunities to make good choices under the postwar pressures of democratic capitalism. This skepticism may be understood as both a critique of the free market's responsiveness to the public interest as well as a symptom of democratic anxiety (though Käutner's satire may cut deeper still).

The Democratic Paradox

As a parody of origins, *Apfel* is dubious that there can be any new beginnings and it raises serious doubt that humankind will ever be capable of self-rule. Only by the grace of God does Adam find any resolution. We can understand this plot as also concerned with the paradox of democratic beginnings and, as such, an origin story of the liberal republic. In his reading of Rousseau's *Social Contract*, Alan Keenan summarizes the paradox on which democracy is both founded and founders:

> The paradox concerns how the people, in the process of self-foundation, can find or create the laws that would guarantee the equal treatment and general norms necessary to their legitimate authority (and thus their existence as a people). Rousseau's answer is that they would be able to create, or recognize, such general laws only if they had already developed the social spirit—the orientation toward generality and attachment to the common good—which it is precisely the job of general laws to create.[32]

If the people are not yet capable of creating the laws that will call them into being, then Rousseau, Keenan explains, proposes the necessity of a lawgiver or founding legislator who "invokes the powers and authority of 'the gods' in order to persuade and threaten the people into accepting his laws for their own good."[33] As Keenan notes, Rousseau's democracy is brought into existence through a nondemocratic, authoritarian dictum. But this paradox is an important reminder that democracy is always in the process of formation and that a people must sometimes appeal to undemocratic means to enact democratic ends. For Bonnie Honig it is significant that Rousseau appeals not just to a founding legislator but to a *foreign* legislator, whose outsider status enables him to *know* the people and form laws in their best interest while not being *of* the people.[34] As Honig explains, in Rousseau's founding scenario it is the task of the foreign founder to change human nature by denying the people their own force and giving them laws that are alien to them—laws, moreover, that they are not able to use without some assistance. But once the law is given, this foreign founder must make a timely departure. As long as he remains, the foreignness of the law he gives will always undermine the legitimacy of the native democratic community.

This reading of democratic founding via Rousseau explains the paradoxical circumstances under which a republic comes into being, circumstances that a foreign occupation inevitably puts into bold relief. For what are the nearly interchangeable terms of reeducation, reorientation, and democratization if not designs to alter German nature after twelve years of totalitarian rule? The Allies would permit German democratic self-determination only when Germans were sufficiently reoriented and predetermined. Alarm bells went off when a 1948 survey indicated that more than 50 percent of those living in the Western zones *still* believed that Nazism "was a good idea poorly carried out" and that "a plurality" of Germans *still* "appeared doubtful of their ability to carry on democratic self-government."[35] Only a constitution made by the people could guarantee democratic rights and principles, but the people in 1948, as far as the U.S. military government was concerned, were not ready to call themselves into being.

We can reread this scenario from the position of the occupied through Käutner's film. As a satire of democratic choice, the film does not just poke fun at Adam's indecision but continually draws attention to the limited range of choices he confronts. Between the virgin and the vamp, heaven and hell, the manna and the *Sahne,* Adam must choose between two extreme, unsatisfying, and already constituted options. There are traces of this quandary in the public opinion surveys the U.S. military government commissioned. For example, Report No. 74 (cited earlier) states, "Despite the claimed preference for democracy, when forced to choose between a government guaranteeing liberty and one providing economic security, 62 percent selected the later and 26 percent the former." It is striking that liberty without stability cannot survive, and yet those questioned are hypothetically, like Adam, *forced* to choose.[36] As if responding to a similarly oxymoronic choice, Käutner constructs a brilliant ambivalence at the film's end. On the one hand, we may say that Adam gets the woman of his dreams, when in his dream, he asserts his will at the negotiating table. Heide Fehrenbach argues:

> [Adam] ultimately learns that he must, as an individual, think, decide, and act for himself and that he must accept the consequences and responsibilities of those actions rather than attribute blame

to rule, laws, or higher authority. Thus, the political and ethical lesson for postwar Germans was manifest. And all who claimed to have merely "gone along" with national socialism in order to weather the fascist storm, or would complain of the victimization by the Allied bombing or occupation politics, were prescribed a dose of honest self-scrutiny.[37]

For Fehrenbach, *Apfel* is a morality play of responsibility for the past and current conditions of Germany. But read as a satire of democratic freedom, Käutner's film is a radical critique of Germany's imagined political future. At the summit meeting, when Adam refuses to choose either Lilly or Eva, he chooses *not* to choose. In other words, he rejects the binary limitation of his democratic dilemma. To bring him back to the table, God offers Adam the amalgamated bride, a compromise we assume Adam accepts. Perhaps Adam's brinkmanship forces the law to bend more to his desire. Or perhaps, like Rousseau's lawgiver, this God instills Adam's faith in him by eliminating choice altogether, and, knowing Adam well, gives him a solution that, upon wakening,

The representatives of heaven and hell call a summit meeting to resolve Adam's indecision. Production still from *Der Apfel ist ab* courtesy of Filmmuseum Berlin—Deutsche Kinemathek.

Adam may claim as his own. The film respects the ambiguity of Adam's agency.

Read in the context of the cold war, *Apfel* shows that democracy under occupation is hardly an act of political freedom or a creative initiative of the people; it is a matter of choosing between two things or accepting a compromise handed down from on high. This allegory also makes clear how little faith Germans should have in these foreign lawgivers. Again surveys show that in 1948 only 8 percent of Germans living in the Western zone believed the Allies would rebuild their country. The majority of the population feared that Germany would be torn apart in a game of tug-of-war between two superpowers, and 73 percent of Berliners felt that Germany would be at the center of another world war.[38] In *Der Apfel,* Petrus and Lucifer are far too consumed with bickering and the operation of the universe to attend to Adam and Eve's best interest, and still there is little hope these incompetent immortals will ever withdraw from Earth's affairs. Käutner's film not only gives expression to German skepticism of Allied intentions, it rejects Rousseau's founding narrative or at least exposes the undemocratic machinations that empower the *demos.*

The very fact that *Apfel* failed to produce critical agreement over its satiric object reinforces this reading. In his postwar aphorism on satire, Adorno observes that while the genre seems to be "on the crest of progress," satire in fact upholds "whatever is endangered by progress" and stages a consensual return to an ideal state or truth. Thus, for Adorno, satire is always on the side of authority (and, in Borneman's study, on the side of the constitution).[39] Because it shields its subjects from the forces of progress, moreover, satire for Adorno actually forecloses future possibilities, debate, and political choice and "dispatches each of its victims" through a "transcendental agreement" of "that's-how-it-is" (212). Where in an earlier age irony might point to the gaps between ideology and reality, irony in the age of fascism "resigns itself to confirmation of reality by its mere duplication" (211). *Ninotchka* could be read as demonstrating Adorno's caution. As a restoration narrative the film brings Ninotchka back to her truer self and better nature (to use the phrasing of the German committee quoted in chapter 2), which, in this film, is an apolitical mode of capitalist subjecthood. In the world of Lubitsch's film, there is only one viable choice between the failed social experiment of communism and the tried and true capitalism that recalls only the very best of Russia's aristocratic past. *Apfel,* on the other hand, looks all the way back to the origins of man and finds ambiguity and illegibility in place of immutable standards. Even heaven fails to provide the moral authority through which Adam may be regenerated. Unable to find an origin to which he would want to return, Adam keeps finding himself in the same place where he began. In precisely the ways that *Apfel* fails as satire, it succeeds as political critique by exposing the crippling binarism of the propaganda campaign at which *Ninotchka* was the center. Where *Ninotchka* propels us back to capitalism's authority, *Der Apfel* refuses to cast its future lot with any one system. Such plotting is a disaster for good satire, but it may well be a recipe for a more genuine and radically open democracy "in these uncertain times."

The World in Film As It Is in Heaven

Where *Ninotchka* makes choosing easy, *Der Apfel* complicates the very terms of indecision. But both of these films functioned in the occupied territory as lures to what the military government held as the most important instrument for reorientation, the newsreel *Welt im Film (World in Film)*, introduced in chapter 1.[40] Despite its generic label, by 1947 it became clear that *World in Film* was not really a source of current news; in the time it took to shoot and process the film and strike and distribute prints to theaters, the events depicted were typically weeks, often months old.[41] Instead, the newsreel served to establish, and then compulsively reiterate, the cold war's central visual themes and images, thus building a mnemonic repertoire of associations that distinguished the Western (increasingly American) vision for and of Germany from the Soviet in distinctly binary terms.

Take, for example, issue 161, "Währungsreform!" ("Currency Reform!") on the currency reform in the Western zones of occupation, an economic measure that produced the first signs of West German economic revival but also sealed the division of Germany. As the newsreel begins, a pile of tattered reichsmarks littering the frame are blown offscreen. A dissolve presents a sheet of crisp new deutsche marks symmetrically arranged, almost decoratively, behind the title.[42] The film then takes us through a short history of this conversion from disorder to order. Under cloudy skies in cold, wet city streets, Germans stand in long lines to buy goods that are quickly disappearing from local shops. But desperate spending leads only to shortages and outrageous inflation, a circumstance reinforced by images of barren storefronts where Sold Out signs are displayed in place of bread and canned goods. At the black market the *World in Film* camera captures a furtive exchange: the last portion of cherries trades for an astronomical one hundred reichsmarks. Mass starvation is imminent. Then, the voice-over exclaims, the Western Allies announce a new currency and with it the hope of economic recovery. Germans flock to newsstands to learn of the proposal to break the economic cycle. A montage revealing how the new bills are packaged and dispersed concludes with shots of a new Germany: bustling, sunbathed streets are lined with stores selling everything from meat and vegetables to confections and fashionable handbags. American economic policy delivers not simply a tidy plenitude of consumable goods; somehow this currency buys clear skies and cheerful weather as well. When subsequent *World in Film* episodes refer to Moscow's protestation over the currency reform, the iconography would suggest that the Soviets would have Germans living in the cold, damp despair of the prereform era. The rhetorical strategies here are rather transparent. The newsreel qua news is not announcing the currency reform or showing Germans what steps they must take to exchange their old marks for new ones, as the film obviously was made after the currency reform was implemented. Instead it provides an interpretative (though not particularly subtle) framework justifying American policy as the best and only course for postwar recovery.

Claiming (rightly) that the currency reform was a violation of the four-power Potsdam Agreement, the Soviet Union responded with the blockade of Berlin.[43] Beginning in April 1948, the Soviets blocked mail transport from Berlin to the west. In June, the Soviets suspended all rail activity in and out of Berlin, including passenger and freight traffic, and interrupted the delivery of coal, food, and medical aid to the Western zones of the city.[44] Though the Soviets initially claimed that the transportation restrictions were due to technical difficulties, by July Moscow stated outright that the Berlin situation was in retaliation for the economic and industrial policies carried out by the Western Allies in their zones of occupation. The Soviets reasoned that in violating the Potsdam accord, the Western Allies had compromised all tenets of the agreement, including their claim to four-power control of Berlin. The

Western powers could allow Moscow by its own means to supply for all of Berlin, and thus grant the Soviet Union control of the entire eastern half of Germany or reverse the economic policies already implemented in the Western zones.[45] Rather than cave to Soviet demands, the United States and Britain parried with the Berlin airlift. From June 1948 to May 1949, the Western Allies succeeded in flying sufficient food, fuel, and supplies to the beleaguered region so that West Berliners could subsist independent of Moscow's support.

For *World in Film* the blockade occasioned a comparative study of communist and capitalist mise-en-scène. Despite the privations of the blockade, West Berlin is represented as a politically vital, improbably sunny, and active city. Issue 163, which offers a history of the events leading to the airlift, features the besieged population buzzing around Berlin's central shopping mile, Kurfürstendamm— hungry for news of their fate, fearful of hunger itself. We then cut to a rally of the Social Democratic Party held in a soccer field in the American sector where West Berlin mayor Ernst Reuter addresses ten thousand supporters. The next sequence takes us to another anti-Soviet demonstration at Fehrbelliner Platz, as if such events have become an almost daily occurrence. After these rallies we cut to Allied headquarters, where U.S. and British forces, unable to broker on Berlin's behalf a humane détente with Russian general Alexander Kotikov, organize the airlift. According to the chronology of this newsreel, the airlift is less an American initiative than an Allied response to German grassroots activism. While it is not surprising that a newsreel pointedly addressing a select German audience might foster a powerful identification with the local terms of history, it is important to realize that this strategy was also intended to proffer a political alibi for U.S. intervention while buttressing the ordinary Berliners' sense of effectuation. We are first introduced to the conditions of the blockade and then to the imperiled Berliners. From here we witness German political rallies of protest, and only then do we see the Western Allied countermeasures being planned and implemented.

If West Berliners wondered about their fate under Soviet rule, the issue titled "Die Krise dauert an" ("The Crisis Continues") provides glimpses of life on the other side of the Brandenburg Gate. A close-up of the border sign "You Are Now Leaving the British Sector" announces a new destination. But in place of live action footage the camera scans a photograph of East Berliners waiting in long lines in overcast weather to exchange their currency for the *second* Soviet reform. In issue 170 cameras visit General Kotikov's now abandoned office at Allied headquarters, where there remains only a desk and a stodgy yet menacing portrait of Stalin who, like the citizens in the photograph of East Berlin, is frozen on the canvas. Elsewhere the Soviet Union is represented as a looming but increasingly figurative presence. Shots of roads at the border between the East and West sectors of Berlin are empty; train tracks overgrown with weeds are inactive except for the railcars full of industrial equipment shipped to Moscow as war reparations. In contrast to scenes of vibrant West Berlin, the newsreel reveals "life" in the Soviet zone as stultifying, inanimate, and joyless. For Berliners the veracity of these representations might be tested by crossing the border, provided they secure the right paperwork. For the rest of West Germany, the other half of their country, including half of their former capital, could now be imagined as a distinctly different, even opposite place.

In West Berlin citizens attend rallies, make sacrifices, and endure hardships to preserve their freedom. Issue 176, made one hundred days into the blockade, registers the almost seamless adaptations Berliners make in their workaday lives as the effects of the blockade become routine. As the voice-over explains, the Soviet plan to starve Berlin did not take into account the Allied commitment to the airlift, nor the unwavering pluck of West Berliners: "The Russian blockade means that industry has less power"—a claim reinforced visually by a generic shot of a factory meter falling to zero—"but Berlin industry has adopted new methods and nine out of ten workers are still employed." To save electricity during the day, Berliners work at night, visit the dentist at night, go to the beauty salon at night. Cutting first to the locked entrance of the U-bahn and then to a street filled with pedestrians, the voice-over explains, "The Russian blockade forces public transportation to shorten its operational hours, so Berliners go by foot." As the Russian blockade brings darkness to the city at night, "the spirit in Berlin remains bright nonetheless." At this prompt we move into the parlor of an industrious couple who have fashioned their own printing press by rigging the duplicator to a stationary bicycle. Such creative alternatives to shortages and the uniformly good nature of West Berliners as depicted here create a nostalgia for the present, each episode a

sentimental reminder of West Germany's rebirth into the democratic world. That this rebirth takes place in the domestic spaces
of cramped kitchens and living rooms or along the city's sidewalks
and side streets reinforces *World in Film*'s ascription of historical
will to the city's common and collective efforts. Just as important,
Berliners are featured taking part in "democratic" activities—such
as campaigning, voting, debating, and shopping—that the documentaries in the first years of the occupation had associated with
immigrant American life. Through such repeated representations,
the newsreel finds paradigms for expressing the nativity of democratic capitalism, now not a uniquely American phenomenon but
a German enterprise requiring neither immigrants nor multiethnic
nationals to legitimate its populism.

Political Reconditioning

In December 1948, the U.S. Information Control reported that a
Soviet-licensed magazine published a thirty-two-page photo essay
titled "Berlin: Worth a New War?" The photographs depicted the
postwar suffering and destruction in Berlin and other German
cities as a result of the American and British air raids during the
war. The spread also connected the Berlin airlift to an escala-
tion of Western military aggression. One especially incendiary
page offered the following chain of associative logic: "Yesterday
Phosphorus, Today Raisins, Tomorrow Atom Bombs."[46] To dispel
German fears of Allied planes overhead, *World in Film* developed
an optic visual regime intended to recondition the occupied gaze.
In 1945, Allied planes triggered deafening air raid sirens and sent
Berliners on a mad scramble to bomb shelters where they might be
stranded all day and night, only to reemerge to the rubble of their
homes. In 1948 this formerly hostile fleet was working on behalf of
the same civilians it once attacked. Germans, habituated by war to
fear these crafts, were now supposed to look upon them not with
horror but relief and even pride. The final sequence of "Berlin in
Crisis" constructs a series of Kuleshov-inspired eye-line matches
intended to promote a new, affective relationship to Allied aircraft.
From a low-angle medium close-up of two smiling German women
looking up offscreen left, we cut to a long shot of an American
plane flying overhead. We then switch from a low-angle long shot
of a group of German workers standing in silhouette on a preci-
pice gazing offscreen right to an extreme long shot of the cargo

plane soaring over the city. The next pairing connects a close-up profile of a decidedly proletarian German worker glancing off-screen right to a high-angle long shot of the runway at Tempelhof Airport, where American and British planes are queued for take-off. The Germans in this series of shots not only smile at the sight of the planes, they remain peaceably immobile. The imaginary geography of the last eye-line match, moreover, suggests a kind of mastery over the operation as the German worker appears to be looking down at and visually presiding over Tempelhof Airport. So that Germans in the theater may learn to mimic those on the screen, this reconditioning is reinforced in subsequent episodes. "Berlin Blockade" concludes with an eye-line match of another German worker looking skyward as an American plane flies over-head, and this same eye-line match sequence, now stock footage at the *World in Film* editing room, begins the issue "The Crisis Continues," shot some weeks later. Framing Germans in this way, *World in Film* not only memorializes the events and the ordinary German participants made extraordinary under siege, it also tutors spectators in the appropriate emotional and political response to the sight of these planes through filmic techniques first systemati-cally developed and deployed by Soviet montage theorists. It was Sergei Eisenstein who in the 1920s proposed that cinematic spec-tacles could create "a new chain of conditioned reflexes by asso-ciating certain phenomenon with the unconditioned reflexes they produce."[47] For Eisenstein, this physical reconditioning was the elemental basis for the Soviet film propaganda that could penetrate and politicize the spectator's mind by first carefully controlling the body. Thus reflexively or not, *World in Film* adopts Soviet methods in its anti-Soviet cause.

In fact, U.S. policy stressed to Germans the particularly em-bodied stakes of their political sympathies. For as the newsreel persistently titled it, the Soviet measure was not a political stand against the Western Allies but a "hunger blockade" intended to starve West Berliners into political submission, suggesting that a population would accept communism only as an alternative to death.[48] The buying, cooking, and eating of food, activities essen-tial to survival but never taken for granted, are enacted in some form in every episode dealing with the airlift. Because hunger is linked with Soviet oppression, eating functions as a form of po-litical resistance against a new totalitarian threat and as a sign that

West Germans are politically rehabilitated. But more to the point of reconditioning, scenes of eating serve as fetishistic reminders of American aid and airplanes. Issue 166 takes us from operations at Tempelhof Airport to a West Berlin preschool where toddlers, framed in close-up, look into the camera and smile while spooning an Allied-supplied hot lunch into their little mouths. Taking *World in Film*'s cue, Germans, like their Pavlovian counterparts, should salivate when they hear the buzzing airplanes overhead.

Within the newsreels themselves, however, hunger looms as an invisible threat, a corporeal specter too volatile to make manifest. Images of the emaciated bodies of Holocaust victims made familiar to German moviegoers through *Death Mills* and the various *World in Film* issues covering the war crimes tribunals were the most graphic symbols of Nazi inhumanity. West Berliners are now themselves prey to state-sponsored starvation, victims in a new drama of persecution. The hunger trope thus emphasizes the links between the Soviet and Nazi tactics and yokes threats to the German body via starvation to communist assaults on the German body politic. Rather than threaten Berliners with starvation directly through images of empty stores and thin bodies, *World in Film* exposes the fragility of the airlift and the status quo it sustains.

Issue 166, discussed previously, marks a day that an American plane crashes into a Berlin building. Shots of the still smoldering fuselage signify the tragic loss of the five-man crew and the precious load of supplies. In honor of the pilots, the locals erect a memorial on a nearby tree thanking the pilots and the West Allies for their sacrifices. This small disaster and the many crashes that followed are ongoing reminders that starvation and political disorder are potentially only a few plane crashes away. The image of the plane wreck itself, a dramatic display of mangled metal crushed against the brick of an apartment building, is an emblem of military combat. Though the crash is a result of mechanical error, it is *as if* the American plane had been shot down by Soviet fire. Though the air raids are over, people in the neighborhood witness the destruction of their home from above. This iconography then frames the ideological war between the United States and the Soviet Union in conventional military terms while still teaching Germans to welcome the Allied fleet. In this issue's final shot, an American flag framed in a low angle fills the frame as it billows in the wind, recalling a similar shot described in chapter 2 from the

newsreel that makes Bess cry in *Human Comedy*. This flag now
symbolizes West German–American unity, and as long as it hangs
outside the Allied control headquarters, Berliners can be assured
· of U.S. protection. Or to put it in *Human Comedy*'s words, these
are now West Berliners' "lucky stars and stripes." Where *Der Apfel*
intimates a concern that the Allies will never leave, *World in Film*
produces a fear that they might not stay.

Bridges and Borders

Deploying much of *Ninotchka*'s sensual iconography, the newsreel
makes the case that just by virtue of eating, smiling, and speaking
on a regular basis, West Germans are already making and reap-
ing the benefits of sound political choices and are thus capable
of democratic self-rule. While assuring viewers that the momentum for statehood and political action originate from the people
of West Berlin, *World in Film* not only domesticates global politics, it also, like *Ninotchka*, universalizes this democratic, capitalist citizenship. As the Social Democratic leader Luise Schröder
proclaims in issue 166: "Berlin fights for Germany and Germany
does not forsake Berlin. For together, Berlin and Germany fight
for democracy all over the world." Schröder's "democratic citizen
of the world" sentiment is pinned down in a *World in Film* special
featurette titled *Die Brücke* (*The Bridge*, 1948), produced by the
Information Services Division of the U.S. military government.[49]
Co-narrated by real-life American pilot Lieutenant Lewis Droll and
Berlin-Tempelhof worker Joseph Müller, the film provides an official history of the airlift through the supposedly lived experience
of these two men who, over the course of their many Tempelhof
interactions, come to appreciate the parallels between their countries and the similarities they as individuals share: they both smoke
pipes, are married with children, and embrace the political spirit
of the airlift. As Droll reflects: "We're not feeding a city. It sounds
kind of corny to say we're feeding a spirit of freedom, but I'll go
ahead and say it anyway." At the end of the film Müller rejoins that
the air bridge "is not an air bridge at all. It is a human bridge linking together people who like to be free." The language of Müller's
last observation (presumably "people" refers to Americans and
Germans) suggests that the bridge between Frankfurt and Berlin is
in fact between Germany and the United States. The film supports
this supposition by limiting shots of Frankfurt to the American

air base and to the neighborhood where our American pilot lives with his wife and family. Constructing the similarities between Americans and Berliners, the newsreel attempted to foster a new kind of West German "official nationalism," to use Benedict Anderson's category, predicated not on the populism of shared cultural, linguistic, or historical experience with Germans in the East but on a commitment to a capitalist, democratic, American-oriented ideology. West Germans could now imagine themselves as more like Americans than like East Germans living under communist rule, and Americanism in turn could appear "attractive in [West German] national drag."[50]

At the same time, this air bridge opening the border to the west seals off West Germany to the east. The Berlin blockade was, in this sense, paradigmatic of how nations are formed by international allegiances and threats. Foreign policy, writes David Campbell, is an "integral part of the discourses of danger which serve to discipline the state" and "needs to be understood as giving rise to a boundary rather than acting as a bridge."[51] Accompanied by a map of a divided Germany where the west is white and the east a dark gray, Droll advises the spectators thusly: "Think of Berlin as an island. That's what it really is, an island in the Russia zone sea. You couldn't cross that sea by train or truck anymore, but you could fly over it." Indeed, what cements the American and West Berlin bond is a mutual understanding of this postwar geography of danger.

By suturing the personal memory of these two men to the official visual record, moreover, *The Bridge* demonstrates the newsreel as a prosthetic memory. Specifically, the documentary recycles images from *World in Film* (I estimate that three-fourths of the shots come from the *World in Film* archive) and, through techniques of editing and voice-over narration, places these men at the center of airlift history. Müller in his recollection describes the effects of the blockade as the exact images from episode 177 flash across the screen: the factory power meter falling to zero, a Berlin thoroughfare cast in darkness, a light going out in an apartment window. His memory of the food rations motivates a shot of the same grocery store featured in episode 176, where a shopkeeper measures a portion of canned meat on a scale, as if these are his visual memories. On his way home from work, in a *Forrest Gump*–like eye-line match sequence, Müller is eyewitness to the Skymaster crash dramatized in episode 169. At Tempelhof, he is among those anonymous German workers who unload the sacks of flour. In his voice-over narration, Droll recalls the plane crash in "The Crisis Continues" and notes, as the tree memorial appears on-screen, "They even made a memorial for the guys." He and his wife reenact history when they come up with the idea, now known as the legendary Operation Little Vittles, of sharing their candy bars with the children of Berlin. From the plane where Lieutenant Droll dispatches his rations in handkerchiefs, we cut to the ground where laughing Berlin children run after the little chocolate satchels of American goodwill.[52] Müller and Droll's personal narrative confirms the newsreel's representation of everyday life as historical in significance, and they construct a synecdochical connection between the individuals and their respective nations so that the division of Germany, which this alliance in effect produces, is nothing more than a friendship between people who like to be free.

When the blockade ended on May 12, 1949, the division of Germany was not a temporary measure but a permanent feature of Germany's postwar geography. For the crew of *World in Film*, however, Berlin—still divided and soon to be barricaded—could not have been a brighter, more jubilant city. Tote bags that were full of bread during the blockade now runneth over with potatoes. Berliners sunbathe by the Spree and picnic on fresh egg omelets and leafy green vegetables. Here a West Berlin baby, born during the blockade, seems born again in a close-up as it samples fresh citrus for the first time. On a bench close to the market, a solitary little girl devours an apple, transforming the fruit of original sin into the manna of political freedom and national regeneration (by contrast, when Adam finally picks the apple for Lillith's breakfast in Käutner's film, it is already home to a worm and decidedly unappetizing). The next segment brings us to Bonn and to the end of the American military government (though not to the end of occupation). The German Basic Law is ratified, and in the final shot of this episode West Germans gaze, bellies full, at their own flag billowing in the wind. The end of the blockade and the creation of the West German state evacuate not only the threat of hunger but the darkness, disorder, and emptiness that haunted West Berlin, and thus the Western zones of Germany, for the eleven-month siege.

You Are What You Consume

Taken together, what do these narratives tell us about West Germany's founding and America's designs for German cold war citizenship? Despite its appeal to the senses, this campaign aimed to politicize and even reenchant democratic capitalism as the natural, popular choice, a choice most Germans were already inclined to make. Ninotchka's enthrallment with capitalism reinvigorates an appreciation for the system that its jaded members (such as Leon) take for granted or, in the case of the White Russians, have corrupted. Given its address to West Germans, the film presumes a free-spirited, capitalist spectator whose consumerist identification the film's humor reinforces. Likewise, World in Film's West Berliners not only risk starvation for capitalism's preservation, they demonstrate that the consumption underwriting the system is really a matter of physical and political survival. Buying a handbag or a new suit is not a market dalliance (and it may not be an indicator of political savvy); rather it is connected to the consuming necessary to subsist. Ninotchka and the West Berliners of World in Film, in choosing capitalism over communism, prove without irony that it is the best of all possible systems. For the Americans this is the good news.

On the other hand, as a tool of democratic pedagogy, World in Film's representation of political choice is, in the spirit of Der Apfel ist ab, completely absurd: between pleasure and unpleasure, survival and starvation, freedom and unfreedom, is there really a choice to make? U.S. propaganda dulls the political senses, enhances sensual desire, and reduces democratic openness to a closed binary system. Or, to rephrase an earlier point: capitalism is best because, in this choice between two, it is the only possible system. Further, the newsreel itself was an example of consumer unfreedom. Harold Zink, a former historian for the military government, wrote that the newsreel "enjoyed considerable popularity among the German movie-goers because of its good technical and interest-holding qualities." Reports from the field, however, tell a different story.[53] One exhibitor wrote to the Film Section in Bavaria that because prints were old and out-of-date, "the public does not come into the cinema until after World in Film has played." And when he put the newsreel at the end of the film program, audiences left early.[54] In 1949, exhibitors in the British zone organized a boycott of *World in Film* in part because their patrons complained that the strip offered little more than political speeches, conferences, and handshakes. It was not news, audiences claimed, but Allied propaganda.[55] Because it was mandatory in theaters until 1949—to the exclusion of all other commercial newsreels—audiences could not compare *World in Film* coverage to that of other newsreels, nor could exhibitors select among competing productions.[56] The overtly anticommunist position, while consistent with West German attitudes, undermined the newsreel as an objective source of information and, one could argue, did not hold itself to the standards of market competition.

The best propaganda by far was Lubitsch's satire. *Die Welt* reported on the occasion of *Ninotchka*'s 1955 rerelease, however, that Goebbels himself had circulated censored versions of the film, hoping to undermine Bolshevism's political self-righteousness. But he failed to realize the performative nature of totalitarianism and the promiscuousness of satire. As *Die Welt* explained, one cannot censor a film that mocks totalitarian censorship without drawing upon oneself the same critique. In fact, in *Die Welt*'s analysis, Lubitsch does not attack communism per se but "splendidly denounces the absence of humor in all ideologues," including the Nazis themselves, even when they use satire as a political weapon.[57] The Americans too may have unwittingly released a film that could be taken as a parody of the very reductive anticommunist campaign it was supposed to anchor, one that, moreover, exposed sensual humanism as a retreat from politics and (recalling Käutner's infernal nightclub) revealed the curious affinity between "democratic" and totalitarian propaganda. That Goebbels also celebrated *Ninotchka*, moreover, raises the possibility that in choosing as Ninotchka does, Germans may in fact restore themselves to ideals of Nazi citizenship. Where *Der Apfel* failed to register with audiences as a satire of democratic choice, *Ninotchka* succeeded in consolidating, even reviving an anticommunist consensus that would become the basis of West Germany's satiric liberal state.

4. That's Jazz Made in Germany

Rudolf Jugert's occupation-era musical *Hallo, Fräulein!*
(1949) is a curious cultural artifact made during the transition to
West German sovereignty. The film anxiously, and to some degree ironically, enacts the cultural stakes of political rehabilitation
and provides a German twist on the culture of American democracy and its "melting pot" sociality. If *Der Apfel ist ab* implicitly
satirizes the limits of political choice under occupation, *Hallo,
Fräulein!* uses the genre of the musical to refigure the terms of these
choices. And this film realizes the imitative logic of reeducation
by foregrounding the politics of performance. Fittingly, Jugert's
film marks this moment of national formation by combining the
conventions of the Hollywood backstage musical (and its persistent celebration of American folk culture over highbrow European
culture) with those of the German musical revue of the 1930s and
1940s, which features German folk music and light operetta, invoking a nostalgia for Old Vienna.[1] The dialogue moves between
English and German and the music alternates between American
jazz numbers and German dance music, melding at times into a
strange mixture of the two. As if the German–American culture
contest alone were not sufficient, the female lead, Maria (played by
real jazz songstress Margot Hielscher) must, like Kräutner's Adam,
choose between two suitors: Tom Keller, a jazz-crazed German
American officer and band leader (played by Peter van Eyck, a
real U.S. military officer), and Walter Reinhardt (Hans Söhnker),
an American-educated German engineer and devotee of classical

music. In contrast to Adam, however, Maria proves herself capable of making choices when at the end of the film she settles on Walter, the German engineer. What is most striking, however, is the film's rhetoric concerning the connections between jazz and democracy and the depth of German national culture, which, in the American imagination at least, tethers all Germans to Hitler.

Consider a pivotal moment in which Maria and Tom first meet. The war has just ended, the occupation is newly under way, and de-Nazification is the order of the day. Our scene opens in U.S. military headquarters as German women rounded up by the U.S. authorities stand in line awaiting their hearings, the outcomes of which will send several women to labor camps and others to resume their pre-war careers. Those affiliated with Wehrmacht and Luftwaffe stand in front of one door as the women of the SS assemble across the hall. Just as the final group, "the artists," queue for their hearing, a comically suspicious and rather plump SS woman defects to this group in hopes of performing—literally singing and dancing—her way out of punishment. Presiding over her audition is American officer Tom Keller, who we know from an earlier scene uses the de-Nazification vetting as a means of both identifying the guilty as well as scouting local talent for his jazz band. Without the benefit of a questionnaire, official documents, or an interrogation, Tom quickly exposes the Nazi pretender. Unlike the first woman who breaks into a vigorous tap dance accompanied by Tom's jazz riffs played on the piano, or the two sisters who harmonize in English to "Home, Home on the Range," the SS woman will not, or cannot, perform to American music. It is only when Tom hits upon a Chopin waltz that she awkwardly sashays around the room, striking mock-balletic poses. In a wider shot, Jugert reveals this space to be the well-appointed music room of a commandeered chateau in which the heirloom piano on which Tom plays is complemented by portraits of the former aristocratic residents, the true custodians of German high culture. Against this mise-en-scène, the woman's political and cultural guilt is doubly inscribed. Not only is she a Nazi, she makes a joke of high culture in hopes of dodging justice. Tom stops the charade and gets down to business. "You call yourself a dancer? . . . Maybe you play the drums?" he inquires, spying her unkempt uniform. On Tom's order, the woman is dispatched to a labor camp amid the muffled laughter of the other women. Her inept dance reveals that she is no artist. But it is her intransigence toward American jazz and her preference for the waltz that mark her as a Nazi. In this military outpost German women are either talented performers or camp-bound combatants. The stakes of performing one's politics could not be more explicit.

When Maria approaches the piano she announces that she sings Strauss, Brahms, and Schubert. Disappointed, Tom casts his eyes to the floor. Maria continues, "And modern American music." "So," Tom confirms, "you like jazz? . . . Where have you heard *real* jazz?" In broken English, Maria explains that she has surreptitiously defied Nazi culture code by listening to BBC shortwave broadcasts. Thanks to this "Schwarzhören," as she puts it (literally translated "black listening"), she is able to corroborate her allegiance to antifascism by singing in English the following lyrics:

> I like concerts and opera
> I think they're all mighty fine
> But the swing, swing, swing
> Yes, the swing, swing, swing
> Oh, the swing is music divine.
> Mozart's, Wagner's, and Verdi's
> Music's all very smart . . .

The words and sentiment are right but the tempo and temperament are off. Tom's diagnosis: "That's jazz made in Germany!" Here Maria, played by Hielscher, whose career stalled under Hitler because her mouth looked "too American" and her singing sounded too hot, is told that, in fact, she's neither American nor hot *enough*.[2] Tom proceeds to demonstrate the American way by playing his own upbeat rendition of the song as another gum-chewing officer impulsively joins in on double bass. Impressed with this display of spontaneity and rhythm, Maria claims that she could never make that kind of music. But Tom avers, "You can do anything! And what you can't do, you can learn." Jazz, explains Tom now in German, is not a particular kind of music so much as a posture, a feeling, a way of life—"ein Lebensgefühl." To facilitate this musical feeling, Tom adjusts Maria's stance, eases the position of her shoulders, and unclenches her hands. Thus Maria, clearly not a Nazi and ripe for democratic tutoring, begins her jazz reeducation and, at Tom's initiative, the couple's innocent flirtation.

This scene of de-Nazification establishes an instinctual and politically consequential link between jazz (and a talent for performance) and quasidemocratic commitments. Consistent with Margaret Mead's definition of American democracy as "a type of behavior and an attitude of mind," Tom's explanation and demonstration of jazz as a *Lebensgefühl* is likewise couched in ethnography's totalizing but elusive, gestural rhetoric.[3] The lyrics to "Swing, Swing, Swing," which we hear throughout the film, not only celebrate jazz over opera and Wagner but explain its instrumental bodily effects:

> Dieser tolle Rhythmus
> Packt mich, daß ich mit muß.
> Und die dummen Beine
> Tanzen von alleine

Awkwardly translated: "This wonderful rhythm thrills me that I must (participate). And my stupid legs dance all by themselves." Jazz then works through the body to produce the American *Lebensgefühl*, which, as we know, is the foundation for American (and thus German) democracy. Walter later offers another reading of jazz that likewise connects it to involuntary (but not democratic) convulsion when he refers to it as "rhythmic epilepsy."[4]

As the scene concludes, however, it is significant that Maria's flirtation with jazz and the American officer occur under the sign of the foreign/racial other. No sooner does Tom embrace Maria under the pretense of teaching her how to comport herself for jazz singing than an African American GI interrupts them to report a "bad case of fraternization." This "case," which we earlier spied in the hallway, involves a German woman and a white American GI. The black soldier who announces the violation and interrupts Tom's similar indiscretion serves as a reminder that jazz and even democracy may threaten the racial purity of the German woman and thus the integrity of the not yet sovereign German state. When Tom and Maria leave the room, the black soldier stands in the shadow behind and (rather ominously) between them.

Premiering after four years of American reeducation, the problem *Hallo, Fräulein!* tacitly addresses and attempts to solve is whether democratization must come at the price of Americanization and, if so, what the racial implications of this process might be. The film connects these dual threats through parallel plotlines: Maria's flirtation with jazz and her flirtation with the American officer. The German American hybrid identities that subtend both

Tom (Peter van Eyck) escorts Maria (Margot Hielscher) out of the audition room to investigate a "bad case of fraternization" in *Hallo, Fräulein!* (Rudolf Jugert, Camera, 1949). An uncredited African American GI stands between and behind them. Production still courtesy of Filmmuseum Berlin—Deutsche Kinemathek.

plotlines resolve by film's end to produce sameness out of national, racial, and cultural difference in order, finally, to reauthenticate German culture and reassert the primacy of German masculinity. If American cold war propaganda represents Germans as becoming more like Americans, Jugert's film suggests that, at the very least, this mimesis cuts both ways. In representing German American similitude, *Hallo, Fräulein!* offers a uniquely German response to America's melting pot ethos, especially as the film works through the so-designated *democratic* idiom of jazz. Moreover, Jugert's emphasis on performance as politics may be read as a metacritique of an American desire for Germans to adopt American cultural and consumptive practices (including watching Hollywood films and listening to jazz music) as a means of achieving, or perhaps even in place of a demonstrable commitment to, democracy.

But more troubling, this film reflects some of the lessons learned from the U.S. occupation, in particular America's troubling racial politics. For jazz is not simply the sound and *Lebensgefühl* of

American democracy; it signifies racially as the culture of African Americans whose experience in the United States did not originate in the voluntary choice of European immigration and whose assimilation was problematically limited by visible difference. I want to track how race and blackness figure in this narrative of national regeneration. In keeping with Hollywood norms, white America's appropriation of black song and dance, especially as it is enacted in the American film musical, gets restaged in Jugert's film when Germans appropriate and then discard jazz. Which is to say, this film replicates America's cultural guilt and historical amnesia toward African Americans and slavery in order to work obliquely through Germany's genocidal past. If German cinema develops an obfuscating relationship to racial violence, this impulse may be learned from Hollywood. In a perverse way, reeducation facilitates a mode of historical reckoning in which a film genre is used to produce a discourse about democratic culture that is politically obscure and, perhaps by its very nature, haunted by disenfranchisement.[5] By connecting *Hallo, Fräulein!* to the racial and sexual disquiet of the occupation and to the aims of U.S. reeducation, I hope to demonstrate how the film uses American logic to defuse the Americanizing crises that lay at the heart of Germany's stateless citizenship.

A Racial Preoccupation

Foreign military occupation in Germany has historically animated fears of racial contagion. Germans first came into intimate contact with Africans following World War I, when the French sent colonial troops to occupy the Rhineland. A mythic propaganda soon spread about the "Black Horror on the Rhine": African men raping, infecting, and, worse to some, engaging in consensual sexual relations with German women as their husbands and countrymen could do little more than watch in revulsion.[6] For the Nazis, the progeny of these interracial encounters, referred to as the "Rhineland bastards," seemed to attest to the conspiracy between blacks and Jews to undermine German purity, and their offspring were among the first groups to be sterilized during the Third Reich. "Jews," wrote Hitler in *Mein Kampf,* "brought the Negroes into the Rhineland" with the "clear aim of ruining the hated white race by the necessarily resulting bastardization."[7] Writers like Artur Dinter predicted that the offspring of these sexually compromised women would bear the features of these racial others even if the biological fathers were Aryan.[8] The occupation following World War II produced similar paroxysms. African Americans comprised approximately 15 percent of the U.S. occupation army but were disproportionately blamed for incidents of rape, the spread of venereal disease, and the moral decay of Germany in the postwar era.[9]

In both periods, these were less local reaction to Africans and African Americans and more hysteria generated from the offices of German and (after World War II) American officials who were united in their stand against interracial sex.[10] Upon their return from occupied Germany, a group of black American journalists urged the secretary of war to amend the U.S. Army's policy of physically restraining black GIs who flirted with fräuleins: "Strong arm tactics are employed at the mere sight of a Negro soldier and a white girl, regardless of her character. The natives reflect seriously on this racial distinction in our army."[11] Black soldiers, who continued to serve in Germany in segregated units as they did during the war, were stationed in remote areas, far from major cities, and were excluded from social events where they might have come in contact with German women after the ban on fraternization was lifted.[12] Thus, through its policies, the army in effect imported American Jim Crow laws to the "liberated" territory, while U.S. information preached the virtues of American ethnic difference. Recognizing this irony, Secretary of War Robert P. Patterson admitted that "to accept the racial prejudices of the German people as a reason for the nonutilization of the American soldier who happens to be nonwhite is to negate the very ideals we have made a part of our reeducation program in Germany."[13] Even U.S. officials recognized that the segregation of black GIs in Germany gave lie to the democracy promoted by Hollywood, and it seemed to confirm Soviet anti-American propaganda.

While African Americans were the source of the anxiety about miscegenation, it was the German *Ami-liebchen* ("Yanks' sweetheart," or female fraternizer) who shouldered the blame for its potential. A New German Woman, a fraternizer, was an independent, entrepreneurial-minded, English-speaking sophisticate, conversant with jazz and friendly to both white and black U.S. soldiers. To those who perceived her relations with occupation soldiers as a gesture of national betrayal, she was the embodiment of a femininity in desperate need of disciplining. Within the conser-

vative narratives of reconstruction, she was the most potent symbol of German national enfeeblement. While the Nuremberg trials
officially evinced how Germany had experienced an unprecedented
moral decline under National Socialism, unofficially the occupation and fraternization for many "symbolized a larger degradation of Germany brought about by loss of sovereignty."[14] German
women who offered themselves to occupation soldiers in exchange
for candy bars, nylons, and Lucky Strikes (or political lenience, in
the previously mentioned case of the failed audition) were metaphors for the prostitution of Germany itself—a defeated country
in need of U.S. economic aid, machine goods, and consumer products whose citizens wanted to see Hollywood films, drink Coca-
Cola, and listen to popular American music. Elizabeth Heineman
concludes:

> With fraternization and mass prostitution, the occupation became,
> in the popular imagination, not only the material and political but
> also the moral nadir of recent German history. . . . When focusing
> on issues they described as moral, the ruling [West Germany po
> litical] parties referred to the legacy of the occupation era by work
> ing hard to "reconstruct the family" and to reinforce conservative
> sexual mores. The tasks of "reconstructing the family" and "recon
> structing [West] Germany" were linked.[15]

Hallo, Fräulien!—whose production was coterminous with the
creation of the German Federal Republic—attempts to bridge
these official and unofficial discourses. The film playfully dramatizes Maria's flirtation with Tom and jazz only to return her to her
German suitor, whom she will marry, seemingly untainted by her
postwar dalliance. To achieve this union, the film sanitizes the connections among democratization, Americanization, and the threat
of racial impurity by etiolating both the racial composition of the
American military and the racial roots of jazz. This process is enacted on several levels but is most visible in the appearance and
disappearance of African Americans in the film and in the construction of Tom as an appropriate and sufficiently Germanized
suitor for Maria.

For example, in the beginning of the film, Walter, whose journey on foot to the U.S. camp we initially follow, comes into fleeting
contact with American troops as they drive by in tanks. A black GI
spies Walter carrying a clarinet case (which he is using as a lunch

box) along the road. The GI subsequently shows Walter to a seat in the wind section of Tom's jazz orchestra and stands by as Walter sits with the case, unable to explain that, despite all appearances, he cannot participate in the rehearsal. When Walter displays a sandwich where the clarinet should be, the black GI escorts Walter out of the room and into the back of a truck as another soldier calls from offscreen, "Here's another Nazi for you!" (Unable to perform, Walter's war guilt is presumed.) The next day, a black GI is among Tom's assistants as the women line up for questioning. Once the black soldier mentions the incident of fraternization, however, African Americans vanish from the film.

The disappearance of African Americans is particularly important when, in the film, the military ban on fraternization is lifted and Tom can openly court Maria. By this point in the narrative, fraternization is an international affair to be sure, but one between white Americans and Germans or, in this case, between Germans and their congenial American counterparts. Tom Keller not only has a German name, but he is fluent in German and, frankly, looks

Walter (Hans Söhnker) reveals to Tom that his clarinet case contains only his lunch as the African American GI watches. Production still courtesy of Filmmuseum Berlin—Deutsche Kinemathek.

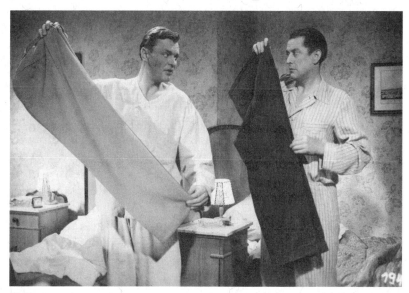

Walter and Tom undress for bed after their rhyming courtship scenes with Maria. Production still courtesy of Deutsches Filmmuseum/Deutsches Institut für Filmkunde, Frankfurt.

more stereotypically German, with his light brown hair and light eyes, than his German competitor, Walter. Tom's German likeness is reinforced in the hotel room that he and Walter share on tour: here, the two men prepare for bed by going through similar routines, humming the same tune and even splitting the one cigarette that remains between them. Just before they extinguish the light, Tom peels off his U.S. Army uniform and Walter his ordinary suit coat. As they stand next to each other in their matching underclothes, one could hardly guess that these men were on opposite sides of the world's most devastating war.

The differences between Tom and Walter are further minimized through narrative parallels. Both, we come to learn, attended Harvard in 1936 and studied with "old Professor Brumby"; both preside over the administration of displaced persons, Tom as an army captain, Walter as the interim *Bürgermeister* (appointed by Tom, until the town can hold democratic elections). But the two characters are most bound in their open competition for Maria's affection, as each has an almost identical courting scene with her while they are in the hotel. Tom is clearly interested in launching

Maria's career in the United States and in delivering her from the material privations of the postwar period. Walter, it seems, has a double motive: quite apart from his attraction to Maria, he wants to shield her from the corrupting forces of jazz and America's military culture, particularly now that Tom is the leader of Maria's newly formed jazz ensemble. When Maria first asks Walter to serve as the band's manager on tour, Walter declines so he may stay at his appointed post. He changes his mind, however, when he observes Maria leaving his office to a chorus of catcalls from American GIs. As Jugert cuts from Walter to Maria and back again, the sound track alternates between a baroque rendition of "Swing, Swing, Swing" and its jazzy original, thus connecting Walter's romantic agenda to the preservation of the German woman and German high culture. Though Maria suspects she shares more in common with Walter than Tom, she cannot decide which man to marry and so stubbornly resolves to stay single. Recognizing that he has come between Maria and Walter, Tom orchestrates the German couple's reunion just before the band's final performance and the film's final scene. The rapprochement between the rivals for Maria, between Germany and the United States, occurs when Maria and Germany are finally returned to German male control.

Censoring Race and Reconciliation

The very idea that Tom and Walter are both viable contenders for Maria is an important indicator that Maria, having embraced Tom, has also embraced the United States, its culture, and thus, perhaps, democracy, though democratic politics never explicitly come up. The film makes clear, however, that Tom and Maria's flirtation never advances beyond a kiss so that Maria may return to Walter edified but unsullied. Walter, in his acceptance of Maria and her music, is likewise rehabilitated, although he was never a Nazi to begin with. The stability of this love triangle depends on the erasure of the imminent racial threat. African Americans must be eliminated from the film so that Americanization is no longer represented as a racial compromise. In deciding to marry Walter, Maria is not choosing a German over an ethnic other. Racial tolerance, simply put, is no longer an issue.

Jugert was not alone in hitting upon this solution to Germany's postwar racial appeasement. Films explicitly about German Jews (and directed by German Jewish exiles) such as Herbert B.

Frederdorf and Market Goldstein's *Lang ist der Weg* (*Long Is the Way*, 1949) and Fritz Kortner's *Der Ruf* (*The Summons*, 1949) avert the question of Jewish reintegration altogether.[16] In *Der Ruf*, the Jewish professor dies in Germany of a broken heart but succeeds on his deathbed, through the melodrama of sheer suffering and last-minute recognition, to rehabilitate his Nazi son. In a manner worthy of a Douglas Sirk weepy, Kortner has the confused boy accept his half-Jewish status only with his father's death, a resolution that produces pathos in place of a political solution to lingering anti-Semitism. *Lang ist der Weg* tracks the fate of a Jewish family who suffers (and succumbs) in concentration camps during the war and who finds little relief in refugee camps after Allied liberation. Achieving a stark realism by combining archival footage of the camps with fictionalized scenes, the film concludes when the two surviving Jewish characters resolve to immigrate to Israel rather than rebuild a life for themselves in inhospitable Europe. Fearful that German audiences would interpret the film as an endorsement of Jewish exile and postwar displacement, the U.S. military government limited the film's distribution. One U.S. officer explained:

> This picture may be good Zionist propaganda, but it is entirely the wrong line for German—and European—consumption generally. When David [the son] says, "Nach Hause—Nach Israel" [To home—to Israel], he is voicing a passionate nostalgia which will strike a very warm responsive note among many Jews and will be regarded with understanding sympathy by many liberal Americans. But it will have a very different meaning to all but an enlightened and highly sophisticated German minority. To the average German, this is European Jewry's concession that the last 1000 years have been a fraud forced upon the Jews against their will. A handful of Berlin or Munich intellectuals will understand this plea in its proper context; most Germans will say: by all means ship the bastards to Palestine, as long as you clear them out of our poor country where they are now living as black market parasites. That this reaction is eminently pathological does not alter the fact that it is the probable reaction of most Germans.[17]

I quote this statement at length because it reveals the degree to which film censorship was predicated on an American presumption of German anti-Semitism, which, when articulated as such, often reproduced its logic. And it suggests that Americans were perhaps just as skeptical of Jewish reintegration and German multiculturalism. Thus, while we could easily interpret *Hallo, Fräulein!*'s treatment of race and romance as a native response to occupation, another possibility is that censors in the American military were even more invested in controlling the representation of relations between American military and German civilians and those between Germans and ethnic minorities.

Further, the U.S. military government held little truck with any film explicitly critiquing American culture or its occupation policy. Consider another censorship case of Fritz Andelfinger's 1949 comedy *Zwölf Herzen für Charly (Twelve Hearts for Charly)*, a film, like *Hallo, Fräulein!* that pits American jazz against German classical culture. The plot focuses on twin brothers (played by German actor Willy Fritsch) who are separated at birth. One is raised in the United States, the other in Germany. The brothers are reunited after the war when the American brother, Karl Maria (called Charly for short), returns to Germany as an occupation soldier and leader of a jazz band. The German brother, Dr. Wolfgang Amadeus Wagenbichler, teaches music and composition at a local school for girls whose twelve graduates are looking for husbands. When the two brothers happen upon each other in the small town, they decide to switch roles and, inadvertently, romantic interests. The film's madcap antics involve several cases of mistaken identity and paternity.[18] In its review, *Die Neue Zeitung* noted that Andelfinger avoided the perils of a boring musical revue by spicing up this German–American comedy with "an American bride-to-be" who harbors "a secret baby and jazz-crazed *(Jazzneger)*" love interest "[This film] entertains and, at moments, is really funny."[19] After the film's Hamburg premiere, the U.S. military censors temporarily banned the film from the U.S. zone "because it depicts the American soldier as a skirt-chaser, gum-chewer, and jazz-hound in unfavorable contrast to his twin brother raised in Germany who is a serious and honorable musician." According to the censorship record, Wolfgang displays great restraint and composure and, in keeping with his namesake, is devoted to the study of the classical arts, while the American drunkenly flaunts his rations so he may court hungry German schoolgirls, one of whom he seduces. "Particularly offensive," the report concluded, "are the scenes in which the American's alleged illegitimate German baby appears as a cause for great merriment."[20] Against the wisdom of the psycho-culturalists, the immigrated German in this film has been corrupted by American culture and thus must travel back to *Germany* to be restored to a *better* self or truer nature.

Also rejected for German exhibition was Billy Wilder's 1948 famous send-up of occupied Germany, *A Foreign Affair,* which stars Marlene Dietrich as the double-crossing fraternizing cabaret singer Erika von Schlütow, who seduces American captain John Pringle (John Lund) to evade punishment for her wartime collaboration and to protect her Nazi lover. What so offended the U.S. military government was not just the film's treatment of fraternization, in which army rations serve as the currency for amorous exchange; it was also the way the film comically undercut and complicated the sincerity of U.S. reeducation and democratization efforts in Germany. Stuart Schulberg, who served in the Motion Picture Branch of the military, opined, "Berlin's trials and tribulations are not the stuff of cheap comedy, and rubble makes lousy custard pies."[21]

While *Hallo, Fräulein!* was in production, the German film industry was converting from U.S. military censorship to industry self-regulation (*Freiwillige Selbstkontrolle der Filmwirtshaft,* or FSK). The former mandated that all German films condemn National Socialist doctrine and demonstrably promote "democratic thinking."[22] The new code, however, was designed to prevent films ("primarily a means of entertainment," not political education) from exercising a "negative influence in the field of morals, religions, and politics." With special clauses for the unique problems of German society, the code stated that "no motion picture will be produced, distributed or shown in public that treats subjects, plots or situations which":

a. [Offend] ethnic and religious feeling, and especially have a brutalizing or demoralizing effect;

b. Promote and abet National Socialist, militaristic, imperialistic, or nationalistic tendencies, and racial discrimination;

c. Prejudice the relations between Germany and other nations and especially deprecate their governments; official representatives, and institutions;

d. Distort historic facts by grossly biased and propagandistic treatment. (This provision will not be construed to apply to the adaptation of historic subjects for reason of the liberty of artistic creation.)[23]

In the spirit of the Hollywood Production Code Administration, on which the FSK was modeled, producers should simply learn to offend the fewest people possible while attracting patrons to the theater with interesting content. Indeed, according to the U.S. military government, film industry self-regulation "modified to suit the German mentality" was "one of the most important steps towards the democratization of the German film industry," not least because now that Germans were presumed to be democratically reeducated they could be trusted, as American audiences were, to support democratic films.[24] The industry trade journal *Filmwoche* explained: "In Germany, no one is forced to see what he doesn't want to see. In a country with freedom of opinion, bad films will fail to make money and the public will decide."[25] This marketplace of democratic consumerism, however, presumed that Germans were sufficiently reeducated to support the right kinds of films. American censors were themselves not so sure the public could be trusted to decide well. Thus *Twelve Hearts* was initially withheld, *Lang ist der Weg* had only a limited distribution in Germany, and *Foreign Affair* was banned altogether.

At the same time, this market sensibility brought new pressures on German producers. Hollywood films imported to Germany under the auspices of the U.S. reorientation program dominated the Western zones and set the commercial standards against which local productions would have to compete.[26] Like his American counterparts, Jugert's financier wanted him to push the envelope of acceptable content under Germany's new censorship regime. Film attendance had declined since the 1948 currency reform and German producers had to redouble their efforts to attract audiences away from Hollywood films. Despite its comparatively low budget, a musical dealing with verboten themes of fraternization and jazz would surely lure Germans to theaters.[27] After submitting the *Hallo, Fräulein!* script for American approval, Jugert was forced to cut scenes depicting intoxicated American officers and to excise all dialogue suggesting that Tom gives Maria nylons and cigarettes in exchange for kisses. The film's treatment of fraternization, however, passed military muster.[28] *Hallo, Fräulein!* was approved and widely released (in the Western zones, at least) because it bridged the national and cultural divide so prominent in *Twelve Hearts for Charly,* eliminated (literally) the real racial and ethnic tensions of occupation, and tempered the sexual bartering so explicit in *Foreign Affair.* It also propped up, however elusively and problematically, the connection between American culture and democratic politics.

An Infectious but Democratic Culture

Although the American military government did not elaborate on what made American music democratic, the Nazi ban on jazz bolstered its status as an oppositional art form after the war. Michael Kater has shown that the Nazis believed jazz threatened both the regimentation and sexual purity of Aryan bodies. The syncopation and individual improvisatory freedom in jazz were problematic to a regime founded on a rigidly structured military culture and fraternal nationalism. Practically, it was hard to march to jazz music or to use it in propaganda messages. But it was the racial origins of jazz that made it not simply impractical but degenerate. Because it was associated with African American culture and taken up by Jewish jazz legends such as Benny Goodman, Irving Berlin, George Gershwin, and the many German Jewish jazz musicians performing in the metropolitan centers of Germany, Nazis denounced the musical form as "Nigger-Jew jazz."[29] Imbued with the presumed rapacious sexuality of both black and Jewish cultures, jazz, the Nazis claimed, encouraged wild dancing and promoted promiscuity such that even comported German audiences were compelled to behave like blacks and Jews.[30] In Paul Gilroy's words, the "coding of biology as culture and the coding of culture as biology" yoked antiblack racism to anti-Semitism, whereby both groups could be reduced by racially deterministic theory.[31] This homology between black and Jewish culture and biological impurity continued to energize debates in Germany over jazz, and later rock and roll, well into the 1950s.[32] According to this paradigm, performing, listening, or dancing to jazz was potentially as infective as sex itself.[33] But it also betrays Hitler's own belief in the instrumentality of culture and the power of gestures. Even German blood could be overwhelmed and undone by the wild dancing associated with jazz, and this was, in fact, the stratagem of American reeducation. Despite the Nazi ban on the music, jazz proved too popular to be eradicated completely. Joseph Goebbels, in response, commissioned

German musicians to create an indigenous alternative, free of the Jewish and black influences. The outcome was the "new German dance music," which, according to Kater's characterization, was "melodically and harmonically simplistic and employed crudely conventional instrumentation and intonation."[34]

It is little surprise then that *Hallo, Fräulein!* presumes to celebrate American jazz as the idiom of democratic rehabilitation and the vehicle for the cultural repudiation of Nazism. Having learned from her initial lesson with Tom, Maria creates her own jazz band by auditioning refugees who file through the camp—a project whereby Hitler's victims and enemies rally around the very music he denounced and embrace the very people he persecuted. At the conclusion of the band's triumphant opening night, even classical-music-loving Walter recognizes the ethnic melting pot possibilities of jazz. "Tonight," Walter says in his toast to the musicians,

> as I watched the orchestra play, I observed you all sitting happily next to one other: the French next to the German, the Hungarian next to the Czech, the American and the German, the Greek with the Italian and the French. . . . I witnessed how this music can serve the highest purpose of bringing people together, of making friends out of enemies, and of taking many diverse voices and producing a melody—a very modern melody.

Indeed, as Walter looks around the table, the band's multinational character is self-evident. Its tour is threatened, however, when one show after another is canceled because German audiences, initially so enthusiastic over Maria's show, have turned sour on this modern music. When their final concert is canceled, Walter offers his still-unfinished auditorium for the show. And the band, in turn, changes its program to include more German dance music. The entire band works with the German crew to install the seats before the final performance that brings German and American audiences together and unites Maria and Walter. Uta Poiger writes that upon release the film was celebrated for its musical politics:

> West German reviewers applauded the band as a symbol of speedy reconciliation between former enemies, ignoring the question of who had been the aggressors. The movie helped make jazz music, though as one reviewer complained only in its tamer version, into a symbol of a new West German beginning, in which Germans,

DPs [displaced persons], and Americans alike had been victims of National Socialism.[35]

This celebrated reconciliation, as we shall see, is orchestrated through a recognition of racial differences—differences the film subsequently labors to eliminate.

Far from challenging Nazi doctrine, the scenes above commemorate jazz in National Socialist terms. Walter's index of the various nationalities in the band is accompanied by a montage of head shots held just long enough for viewers to register the visual rhymes and ethnic differences. The first band member, a Frenchman, is presented in a proud profile, his head tilted upward. The lighting emphasizes his chiseled, even features. We then cut to a close-up of a light-eyed German, frontal to us, in even, three-point lighting, his head cocked slightly to the left while he smiles and gazes just past the camera. The melancholic Hungarian of the next shot looks down, screen left. The top lighting gives prominence to his brow line and worry wrinkles at the forehead. His nose casts a shadow

Maria leads her jazz band in rehearsal. Production still courtesy of Filmmuseum Berlin—Deutsche Kinemathek.

over his lower lip, accentuating the comparatively bulbous shape of his nose. The next shot, of a Czech, rhymes with the first shot in the sequence; he is framed like the Frenchman, only with more fill light. And the American, Tom Keller, is framed, like the German before him, frontal to the camera in conventional three-point lighting. Not only his physical characteristics but the composition of the shot reinforce Tom's Germanness. The greatest contrast comes in the next two shots. A blond, exuberantly grinning German looking directly into the camera gives way to a close-up of the Greek musician, the darkest and, in this series, the least animated member of the band, who gazes listlessly screen left. At the moment when the film most explicitly heralds the power of jazz to make friends out of enemies and to forge harmony out of desperate voices, it emphatically reinscribes a physiognomy of national difference.

There is nothing about the musical form itself, however, as it is described or practiced in *Hallo, Fräulein!* that ties jazz to a democratic sensibility. But it does allow the band to experience the anti-American, antijazz backlash when, later in the film, the German public begins to boycott Maria's show. In this way, the entire band is constituted, however indirectly, as a casualty of German chauvinism. Why else would a film whose mission is to preach the exigencies of tolerance enact a widespread outcry against American jazz music? One explanation is that the film is a call for tolerance or an attempt to represent a balance between democratization and Americanization. However, more likely, *Hallo, Fräulein!* is part of a discourse that increasingly resonated in the formation of cold war identity politics and a West German orientation toward American ideology.

At the time *Hallo, Fräulein!* was released, the "multiple restorations" of German public memory were consolidating around the terms of victimization and guilt on the one hand and the perceived continuities and discontinuities between Hitler's Germany and the new postwar order on the other.[36] To embrace the culture of Hitler's victims was to break with the dogma of Nazism and reconnect with Germany's democratic heritage, albeit through a distinctly foreign culture (this restoration is, of course, perfectly in keeping with the satiric mode). One of the most salient traits of National Socialism was its racially intolerant provincialism. Inverting syllogistic logic, denouncing jazz, was akin to supporting National Socialism. However, socialists in the emerging East German state accused the Western powers of cloaking their economic and military imperialist designs in West Germany with forms of cultural cosmopolitanism that undermined both the sovereignty of the state and the ideals of international proletariat unity.[37] Soviet authorities banned jazz in the Soviet Union beginning in 1946 and soon after prohibited this music in the East German state.[38] From an official East German position, anticommunism and capitalism under National Socialism, and later under Konrad Adenauer's administration in West Germany, were evidence of the ideological continuities between the Nazi and West German governments.

In fact, the first German film of the postwar period, *Die Mörder sind unter uns* (*The Murderers Are among Us*, Staudte, 1946), reflects its ties to the Soviet occupation government and presents a new narrative of German suffering. The central character, Dr. Hans Mertens (Ernst Wilhelm Borchert), forced to serve as a military physician during the war, is now debilitated by the trauma of having witnessed the mass executions ordered by his commanding officer, Brueckner (Arno Paulsen). Subsisting through the occupation's lean years, Mertens finds Brueckner comfortably reinstalled in his bourgeois life as owner of an industrial plant that, ironically, converts army helmets into soup bowls—a kind of military industrial complex in reverse. Staudte clearly connects the excesses of bourgeois life and exploitative capitalism when he shows Brueckner and his family gorging at their dinner table (an obscene display of capitalist consumption) after a scene in which we have watched Mertens's girlfriend, Susanne (Hildegard Knef), stave her hunger with stale bread and water. Later in the film, in a flashback, we see Brueckner give orders to kill innocent men, women, and children as he prepares a Christmas feast for his soldiers. The film also implies that Susanne was interned at a concentration camp because of her father's leftist political activism. In this way, Staudte redescribes Nazism as principally bourgeois and anticommunist.

As Jeffrey Herf argues, the logical problem in both Germanys of remembering the Holocaust and the Third Reich was that Nazism exceeded and overlapped the discrete postwar/cold war binaries of fascism and antifascism, communism and anticommunism, cosmopolitanism and nationalism.[39] Historical imaginings on both sides of the iron curtain necessitated that those aspects of Nazism inconsistent with state-crafted national identities had to be suppressed and contained, and that whatever vestiges of Nazism persisted had to remain on the other side of Germany. Just as Soviet-influenced East Germany did not admit to Nazi racism, emphasizing instead the Nazis' capitalist system and political persecution of communists, Americanized West Germany keyed on Hitler's persecution of the Jews, Gypsies, and Catholics and deemphasized the Nazis' anticommunism and the hypertrophic capitalism on which the state war machine rested. Both Germanys looked to the ideological paradigms of their occupiers to try to comprehend the past and forge more ethical identities.[40] Films from this period bring into stark relief the process by which nations consolidate through the act of narration and how the signs of the German self and "other" are renegotiated.

Disembodying Jazz

Returning to a local and discrete example, we can see the paradoxes such negotiations create. Tolerating, even embracing ethnic others and American music in West Germany was potentially to defile German purity, to sacrifice German culture, and to confront what it meant to be occupied by a foreign military. *Hallo, Fräulein!* stages this confrontation but minimizes its potential threat. Conspicuously missing from the national menagerie of Maria's band are African Americans and Jews, whose music this group performs and, by association, whose ethnic identity the band signifies. African Americans, who populate the early scenes of the film, are absent in Tom's band as well, so that while blacks carry out his orders, he and the other white enlisted men rehearse Tom's jazz compositions. When Maria creates her band, it is multiethnic, to be sure. But the shots of the players described earlier make it clear that the band's refugees are not Jewish but French, German, Hungarian, and Greek (based, in part, on the composition of the real band Margot Hielscher formed after the war).[41] Jazz is appropriated first by white Americans in the film and then, after careful study, by Germans. The Germans thus solve their racial crises and stage a reconciliation by way of substitution, a solution itself rooted in the Hollywood musical.

Michael Rogin's analysis of Al Jolson's historic film debut may help us unpack the substitutions so central to Jugert's film. If *Hallo, Fräulein!* was made during the transition to the FKS and German sovereignty, *The Jazz Singer* (Crosland, 1927) returns us to another moment of double transformation: Hollywood's transition to synchronized sound production, spearheaded by a musical about a Jewish immigrant, Jakie Rabinowitz, who metamorphoses into the Broadway sensation Jack Robin. In this mythology of immigrant assimilation, Rogin observes that Jack's blackface minstrelsy functions as his vehicle for social mobility and access to the American gentile dream. Masquerading in blackface, the jazz singer hides one ethnic identity with another so that, in the end, both his Jewishness and ventriloquized blackness give way to a white, middle-class American identity. Significantly, Jack encounters no opposition from mainstream America, for the film offers no evidence of anti-Semitism. Rather, as Rogin astutely notes, Jack's most challenging obstacle to success is his orthodox father, who attempts to block his son's social and economic assent. By "domesticating" the problem of assimilation, the film therefore becomes a family melodrama about Jews whose conflict appears to be resolved with the father's death (a resolution not so different from *Der Ruf*). Wishing away anti-Semitism (and antiblack racism), Rogin argues, requires the disappearance of Jews (and blacks).[42]

In the end, Jack's blackface makes possible the reconciliation between Jews and gentiles as he successfully woos the dancing starlet Mary (May McAvoy) and is reunited with his mother (Eugenie Besserer). Similarly, when German audiences boycott Maria's show to protest the playing of jazz music, the cultural struggle is foremost between Germans and secondarily between Germans and Americans. But always, it is white Americans and gentile Germans who suffer at the hands of other Germans, elsewhere, who are culturally intolerant. So long as blacks and Jews are not the agents of jazz, racism can remain embedded in a postwar nationalist discourse that displaces questions of race onto questions of culture. As Rogin elaborates in his analysis, "Blackface exteriorizes Jewishness, embraces the exteriorized identity as regenerative, and leaves it behind."[43] Similarly in *Hallo, Fräulein!* jazz functions to enable the Germans to shed their Germanness and adopt a democratized, multicultural identity, only to leave blacks, Jews, Americans, and finally even jazz behind. If the Nazis code jazz culture as biology, then postwar Germans code jazz as an ideology in which the principles of democracy remain as elusive as the races the film abandons, a lesson learned from their American occupiers. Despite the generic mandate, Maria does not choose musician Tom but engineer Walter, freeing Tom to depart for the United States.

The orchestra, we assume, will likewise disperse, leaving behind a nation of pure-blooded but democratized Germans.

The film's musical trajectory follows a similar pattern as it moves gradually to replace what the film codes as "authentic American jazz" with a non-Jewish, nonblack, Germanized form. This is evident in the staging of the musical performances: early scenes of spontaneous music making give way to theatrical productions before a nonparticipatory diegetic audience. To pacify both Walter and the general public, Tom tones down what he calls the "hotter" elements of the band's orchestration for its final concert. From the prominently heard brass section in the band's first gig to later arrangements with strings, from English to German lyrics and German torch songs rather than swing, what begins as jazz made in America becomes by the end of the film dance music made in Germany.

But the film plays a trick on us, one that reveals the cultural work the narrative performs. There is no authentic: American jazz in *Hallo, Fräulein!* even according to the film's own logic. From the first scenes, Jugert begins with jazz made in Germany, played by none other than the Deutsche Tanz und Unterhaltungsorchestra, an ensemble founded under Goebbels to record officially sanctioned German dance music (ersatz jazz) during the war. In his assessment of the band's Nazi-era recordings, Kater remarks that, while one could find traces of blue notes and syncopation, "the sound of strings abounded, and improvisation by solo players was all but absent."[44] Like the band in Jugert's film, the Tanz orchestra consisted of Germans vetted by the Nazis and foreign musicians—from Holland, Italy, and Belgium—acceptable to the regime.[45] Beginning with Germanized jazz and then softening this form by progressing to more mainstream German numbers, the film replicates Goebbels's cultural policy (except that Jugert begins with the already tamed, Europeanized template). Not only does the film validate and attempt to authenticate German Nazi-era jazz, it codes this music as American and ushers in an even more conservative instrumentation and performance style. This compromise was, in fact, part of the film's overt advertising. One page of the press book asks a number of critics to weigh in on the question: "Jazz, or not?" The ad then quotes one "jazz commentator" who writes. "Jazz? It is not. But a wonderful modern music."[46] Thus even "jazz" may disappear under the rubric of the more generic "modern."

In this spirit, we might briefly visit one strand of Theodor Adorno's famous critique of jazz in which he attacks the music and its enthusiasts for adhering to formulaic syncopation and rehearsed improvisation—a form "housebroken and scrubbed behind the ears" whose connection to black slave culture has all but vanished with its popularization.[47] The result, to Adorno's ear, is not jazz but "light music . . . dressed up" (270). Most troubling, however, champions of jazz are lulled into a sense of "pseudo-individualization" by the promise that each piece and each performance is a novel and unique exchange between the performer and audience. "Always new and always the same," Adorno contends, jazz in its orchestrated spontaneity "sets up schemes of social behavior to which people must in any case conform" (273). A far cry from a democratic art form, jazz, Adorno insists, is closer to fascist military music but more pernicious because it imposes conformity in the guise of liberation. Lorenzo C. Simpson explains that while Adorno misreads American jazz, he aptly describes what he likely encountered in Berlin when he first wrote his essay—that is, a "peculiarly German interpretation of commercial dance music *(Tanzjazz)*," not unlike the music Goebbels's players recorded.[48] As Simpson emphasizes, central to Adorno's critique is not what jazz *is* but rather the purpose for which it is *used*. Thus, my concern here is not to distinguish authentic from inauthentic jazz so much as to understand how authenticity is constructed and deployed in *Hallo, Fräulein!* and what this deployment tells us about the project of cultural reorientation.

For example, like its Hollywood musical counterparts, *Hallo, Fräulein!* distinguishes between onstage (professional) and offstage (amateur) numbers to validate certain forms of entertainment over others. When the band members make music for their own enjoyment (that is, without Tom or Maria leading them), they play their newly acquired jazz but then switch to European folk and classical music. To understand the significance of this scene, we need to examine how Hollywood typically handles such numbers. In Fred Astaire's comeback vehicle *The Band Wagon* (Minnelli, 1953), the extemporaneous performances of good old-fashioned American singing and dancing are set off against a balletic, modernist stage production of (of all things) *Faust,* which is popular with neither the performers nor the American audience. This pretentious fiasco is subsequently scrapped and replaced with a widely successful vaudeville show called *The Band Wagon* that merely involves putting onstage the kinds of musical numbers the characters have been performing offstage throughout the film. As Jane Feuer remarks, *The Band Wagon* is structured around the contrast between successful mass art and labor-intensive, pompous high art to legitimate the "populist world of musical theater."[49] As Gabrielle (Cyd Charisse) makes the transition from ballet to Broadway, her affections for her choreographer boyfriend Paul (James Mitchell) give way to her romantic interest in the charismatic dancer and singer Tony (Astaire). In Hollywood musicals, "authentic" culture, commercial success, and romance are linked and thus mutually reinforced. *Hallo, Fräulein!* inverts this musical hierarchy so as to denaturalize the authenticity of jazz as a popular (and therefore a democratic) musical expression. Maria's band must work and practice to learn jazz, and this hard work leads to the band's bankruptcy. But European music is effortless, familiar, and, when combined with a lighter strand of American music, popular.

The origins of mass culture are both discovered and buried in its ethnic roots. And the question of origins returns us again to the question of race. In *The Band Wagon,* Jeffrey Cordova (Jack Buchanan) declares, "There is no difference between the magical rhythms of Bill Shakespeare's immortal verse and the magical rhythms of Bill Robinson's immortal feet." Of course, as the film unfolds, there *is* a difference—namely, Bill Robinson's immortal feet produce popular and successful rhythms, even when it is Astaire and not Robinson who is dancing. Shakespeare's verse is no more popular than the Broadway version of Goethe's *Faust.* When Tony first connects with an audience, it is not on a stage but in an arcade, where his tap riffs mingle with those of an African American shoeshine man (Leroy Daniels). Tony, however, goes on to perform these same riffs on stage before a paying audience; the shoeshine man remains in the arcade. Similarly, *Singin' in the Rain* (Donen and Kelly, 1952), as Carol Clover reveals, always returns us to the racial genealogy of genuine talent by anxiously invoking and then masking the African American heritage of dance in the Hollywood musical: "What *Singin' in the Rain* doesn't-but-does know is that the real art of the film musical is dance, that a crucial talent source for that art is African American performance, and that, relative to its contribution, this talent source is undercredited and underpaid."[50]

I am not positing a causal connection or influence between Jugert's film and these later Hollywood productions. Rather, I want to note that the benchmark musicals in American film history are predicated on similar displacements of race and guilt. The ideological resonances of the genre in the American context underscore the process by which romance and populism coalesce into nostalgia for an ethnic culture whose agents have been evacuated from the text or rendered inert by its narrative logic. The appropriation and commodification of black culture by whites is not only a way of enacting and suppressing historical guilt, it is also a means of constructing a national folk tradition around a performative blackness, itself a product of a socially unconscious negotiation of racial difference.[51] And when American culture is exported, the staging of authentic folk traditions becomes the cultural corollary of a larger political discourse of democracy, capitalism, and statecraft.

A Now Familiar Refrain:
Exporting the Democratic Way of Life

In 1949, Secretary of Defense Louis Johnson proclaimed:

> In the face of American motion pictures portraying American life as we live it, no anti-American propaganda can ever succeed. One look at the shows and clothes that we wear, one glimpse at the normal happy American faces on a foreign screen, and harassed peoples of the world take courage in the democratic way of life.[52]

According to this declaration, the representation of capitalism's material promises inure people around the world to anti-American criticism. More important, Johnson collapses the representation of American life in Hollywood films with the democratic way of life, as if cultural products were detachable emissaries of an abstract political and economic system.

Of course, as this book has demonstrated, this same logic undergirded the American reeducation program in Germany, whereby American films were part of an extensive disciplinary program. Of the many Hollywood features approved for their reorientational content in Germany, two were explicitly about American jazz: *Rhapsody in Blue* (Rapper, 1945), dramatizing George Gershwin's rise to fame, and *Night and Day* (Curtiz, 1946), the highly fiction-alized Cole Porter story.[53] As a "white jazz biopic," *Rhapsody in Blue* is particularly invested in placing Gershwin and his refined jazz on the level of Franz Schubert and his symphonic works. To this end, the film emphasizes Gershwin's classical European train-ing and subsequent inspiration to elevate black music to the art-istry of the great European masters. Whereas the American mu-sicals discussed earlier evacuate African Americans while whites appropriate their songs and dances, *Rhapsody in Blue* strives to authenticate white jazz as having some roots in Europe. *Rhapsody in Blue*, as Krin Gabbard reveals, is finally about protecting "white subjectivity from the overwhelming black presence in the history of jazz."[54] White jazz musicians in this subgenre not only master but ultimately tame and transcend black music, thus reassuring white American audiences "that their own cultural rituals could survive the comparison."[55] Hollywood, then, offers variations on the theme of authenticating white culture in reference to a hidden black influ-ence. Consistent with its policy on race relations, the U.S. military government withheld a documentary short about Duke Ellington from German theaters because U.S. officials assumed that the man and the music would ignite German racism and potentially show that black American culture is inferior to European.[56]

When *Rhapsody in Blue* played in Germany, the tension be-tween white and black culture translated as a contest between German and American music. The *Münchner Merker* stridently dismissed the film as "four variations in film trash." "One cannot reeducate us and at the same time bombard us with trash," de-clared the *Süddeutche Zeitung* in its review of the film. "Reeducate us and feed us tortuous films, reeducate us and bore us." It was the comparison between jazz and German classical music that was attacked most bitterly. *Echo der Woche* proclaimed that "to name Beethoven and Mozart in the same breath as Gershwin is more than bad taste—it is impudent."[57] Jugert's film responds to Hollywood's offensive by overturning American genre conventions in ways that both reinstate Germany's cultural dominance and re-veal what appears to be a transnational proclivity to transmute his-torical guilt into a defense of a culture presumed to be under siege. Jugert's film suggests that a willingness to learn a diluted form of "American" (black) music is not only sufficient to overcome racism and anti-Semitism, but it is preferable to entertaining the real consequences of genuine ethnic mixing or the political equality that comes with democracy. Moreover, in deference to Market Empire, *Hallo, Fräulein!* accepts what is popular without probing the tenuous relationship between what is popular and what is democratic. In reverberating with American cultural policies, *Hallo, Fräulein!* exposes but also reproduces the perils of imitation and the limits of democratic pedagogy.

5. A Gothic Occupation

We repeatedly return in this book to the failure of America's cinematic culture to produce a democratic pedagogy in occupied Germany. On one hand, these films may have offered a pleasant distraction from the realities of occupied life, in which case they functioned mostly as entertainment. On the other, however, because many of the Hollywood features encrypted the history of American racism, xenophobia, militarism, and anticommunism, not to mention America's genocidal beginnings, the injunction that Germans imitate Americans and reproduce their popular culture could be interpreted as a terrifying call to reenact the very kinds of violence that prompted the occupation in the first place. Recall from chapter 2 that film critic Gunter Groll, watching Universal's war film *Corvette K-225* in 1946, momentarily felt himself back in Nazi Germany, as if the occupation "had been but a dream."[1] Similarly, in Käutner's 1948 *Der Apfel ist ab,* Adam's dream of the occupation takes him back all the way to the story of creation, where he finds himself a pawn in celestial bickering and slated inevitably to fall from grace. And the screening of *Ninotchka* as the centerpiece of America's cold war campaign eerily recalled Goebbels's own anticommunist propaganda ambitions.[2] Rather than feeling propelled forward into a new political reality, there is a sense that Germans may have experienced the occupation as history's uncanny return or perhaps the return of uncanny history, by which I mean, via Freud quoting Schelling, the return of something gruesome yet secretly familiar, or the involuntary repetition of "something which ought to have remained hidden but has come to light."[3] The uncanny, or *unheimlich,* describes a "quality of feeling" rooted in the familiarity of home and the secret, often sinister past that the home conceals. It manifests itself when this familiar place is experienced as strange through ruination, haunting, and possession. Though the uncanny has its origins in gothic fiction, Anthony Vidler remarks that the "themes of anxiety and dread, provoked by a real or imagined sense of 'unhomeliness,'" as Freud understood it at the end of World War I, were "particularly appropriate to a moment when . . . the entire 'homeland' of Europe, cradle and apparently secure house of western civilization, was in the process of barbaric regression." "The site of the uncanny," Vidler writes, "was no longer confined to the house or the city, but more properly extended to the no man's land between the trenches, or the field of ruins left after bombardment."[4] As Vidler reminds us, the uncanny is not a property of the houses, objects, or ruins beheld, but an affect, a "projected desire," of the beholder.[5] Certainly military occupation in war's aftermath (with its ruins, corpses, and psychically traumatized survivors) summoned an uncanny relationship to the home, the homeland, and history.

Film spectatorship, at once strange and familiar, may have channeled that uncanny sense of history's return through a paranoiac fear that the Americans were not reeducating the Germans out of their enslavement to Nazi doctrine, but may in fact have unintentionally encouraged a return to this way of thinking. That the Hollywood films discussed thus far were part of the reeducation initiative designed to cure Germans of the paranoia born out of the pathology of National Socialism suggests that, as a cure, these films were, at best, a homeopathic remedy. As Freud himself conceded, "there is in fact some truth" in the paranoiac's sense that "everything he observes in other people is full of significance," especially when those other people are a foreign military whose designs on your country and, for that matter, on your mind, may not be transparent.[6] The question, however, is this: how might the occupation's uncanny resonances and paranoiac spectatorship address the particularities of occupation subjectivity as it intersected with the democratic imperative? Were there any Hollywood films that might direct this paranoia and the fear of history's return toward democratic ends?

If most of this book has detailed the unwitting failures of film to reeducate from the perspective of the occupier, this chapter considers its unwitting success from the perspective of the occupied through the rather unexpected genre of the gothic, in particular the female gothic or paranoid woman's film, several examples of which played in occupied Germany, including *The Spiral Staircase* (Siodmak, 1945), *Suspicion* (Hitchcock, 1941), *Shadow of a Doubt* (Hitchcock, 1943), *Jane Eyre* (Stevenson, 1944), and the nodal film for this chapter, *Gaslight* (Cukor, 1944). Dana Polan remarks that the female gothic film combines the strains of uncanny dread and paranoiac fear because the genre is chiefly concerned with the strangeness of domestic space, where "the geography of the home becomes a potentially paranoid space—each object turning into a possible threat, a betrayal."[7] This move from the "uncanny" to the "gothic" to the "female gothic" is deliberate. For insofar as war is the experience of men, occupation—especially in the wake of "total" war—is principally the experience of women. And the genre that best captures the fate of women caught in the wave of extreme, even brutalizing political change and democratic reform is the female gothic.

The Politics of Gothic Subjectivity

In the typical female gothic plot, an innocent, orphaned girl is hastily married to an older, foreign man with a dark and mysterious past. After a whirlwind honeymoon, the young wife suspects that her new husband not only does not love her, but may in fact be trying to kill her, perhaps to usurp her property and wealth. Though she is saved in the end, usually by another, less sinister man, the gothic heroine spends much of the film trying to confirm that her sense of persecution is justified and not merely a paranoid projection.[8] As Mary Ann Doane explains, this subgenre of the woman's film became codified during and after World War II when women, then Hollywood's primary audience, were left to manage the affairs of house and homefront while their husbands went to war.[9] The paranoid woman's film is of particular interest because it enacts the very impossibility of feminine subjectivity that we find in most Hollywood films, but it does so at a moment in U.S. history when women enjoyed provisional emancipation from the house by doing men's work and thus enjoying a measure of economic and social freedom. In addressing itself to a predominantly female audience, Hollywood developed women's films that, Doane argues, may read as "symptoms of ideological stress which accompany the concerted effort to engage female subjectivity within conventional narrative forms" (13).

The problematic of female subjectivity is emplotted through an oedipal scenario that dooms a girl to become her mother, "as if history were bound to repeat itself" (142). Indeed, in most of these films we come to learn that the heroine's mother, or mother figure, may have come to a violent end that the heroine is fated to suffer. This crisis of history is connected to the heroine's seeming inability to achieve a sovereign identity distinct from the mother and free from the controlling, reprimanding husband/father. In these films, the heroine's subjectivity always falters: her voice-over trails off and her subjective perceptions are not so clearly marked. Because paranoid women's films fail to sustain or clearly delineate the heroine's point of view, we cannot always differentiate between the objective world of the diegesis and the heroine's mental projections onto that world. The final descent into complete abnegation, however, comes with the almost insufferable failures of these heroines to possess the gaze or to become the gaze's desirous object. When she herself looks or is looked at, the paranoid woman is always punished. Though it would seem that these films dramatize the violence of the husband/father "as the figure of the law," in fact Doane concludes that they work through the woman's rejection of the "maternal space" (145, 147).

But Doane says very little about the originary politics of pre-cinematic female gothic or paranoia, nor does she speculate on why in the 1940s we see a resurgence in narratives about paranoid women in the *Victorian* Age. The history of the gothic can help us to unpack the ways that the crises of feminine subjectivity and historical experience may be connected to occupation and democracy.

Diane Long Hoeveler writes that the woman's gothic novel emerges in the eighteenth and nineteenth centuries in tandem with a radically new bourgeois order as signaled by industrialism, the rise of patriarchal capitalism, and the creation of separate, gender-coded public and private spheres. Such social forces brought about republican reform and wider political representation but also reified gender roles and spaces. Witness to the new democracy, women were politically disenfranchised and increasingly socially secluded. Thus, many female gothics revolve around questions of property and inheritance, isolation, and scenarios of rescue and capture, for without a man a woman had limited rights and was thus vulnerable to all manner of villainy (6–7). In contrast to the gothic male hero who conventionally finds the source of his torment within himself, the gothic heroine's ideological enemies, however internally she may experience them, are external to her and typically of some legal consequence (9). Hoeveler finds that these novels do not merely dramatize female victimization and disenfranchisement, as Doane finds of the films; they offer female readers the means of coping successfully in this new world order (but more on this in a moment). The literary female gothic, then, addresses the very real and concrete problems of female disinheritance, economic dependence, and disenfranchisement that would find a psychic resurgence in the United States in the 1940s, when women once again found themselves on the cusp of newfound freedom.

As a political genre, however, the gothic is not merely about the experiences of women. It first came into English parlance to capture a range of disparate anxieties around questions of Englishness and national identity in the eighteenth century. Fred Botting explains that, historically, the Goths were a Germanic tribe "whose fierce avowal of the values of freedom and democracy was claimed [by the English] as an ancient heritage." "Opposed to all forms of tyranny and slavery" the Goths are credited with having dismantled the Roman Empire, which they believed had been corrupted by the Catholic Church.[10] Ian Duncan notes that, on one hand, "Gothic" culture was identified by the more radical strains of the English polity as the "ancient constitutional source of British liberties usurped by the Norman Conquest and the subsequent aristocratic rule." "At the same time," he writes, "the establishment conception of 'Gothic' was that of barbarian forces that had overthrown a civilization, and the long cultural darkness haunted by despotism and anarchy, superstition and enthusiasm out of which the present British dispensation, modelling itself on classical principles, has only lately emerged." In this regard, the gothic potentially summoned at once a radical democratic impulse and a fear of foreign invasion. Or, as Duncan writes, "The Gothic novel describes the malign equation between an origin we have lost and an alien force that invades our borders, haunts our mansions, possesses our souls."[11] In English political culture, it was the menacing, barbarous elements of the gothic that dominated public thinking, and the traditional (masculine) gothic narrative was consistently suspicious of revolutionary movements. The female gothic, however, focusing on the women who democracy had left behind, did not suggest that the liberal movements of the past had in contemporary times gone too far, but that they did not go far enough. My point here is that if the gothic is a genre that tethers democracy to the trinity of foreign invasion, loss of sovereignty, and violent regime change, with all of the destruction and regeneration this cluster summons, and if the gothic may also give expression to the ways these possibilities are differently experienced by men and women, then the gothic may well be the genre of occupation, especially in Germany. In 1945 the Allies declared Germany "liberated" in the same breath that they declared sovereign rights over the country to impose a new democratic order. Moreover, as I elaborate later, this subjugated population was comprised predominantly of women. The gothic, perhaps more than any other genre, captures this interpretative and epistemological ambiguity and the terror that accompanies the occupied subject's loss of sovereign identity, as well as her liberation from tyranny.

We should also note that the paranoia associated with this genre—what gothic novels attribute variously to sublime justice and persecution—is not only psychically but politically anchored in Wilhelmine Germany, as evidenced in the famous case of Judge Daniel Paul Schreber, whose memoir of mental illness became the basis for Freud's theorization of paranoia. In his study of what he called Schreber's "own private Germany," Eric Santner argues that the symptoms Freud attributes to homosexual panic—Schreber's fear that God was turning him into an impregnable voluptuous woman, and Schreber's fantasy that his psychiatrist was controlling his thoughts in absentia—were politically symptomatic as well. The onset of these paranoid delusions was concurrent with Schreber's appointment of *Senatspräsident,* judge to the Saxon Supreme Court of Appeals. In this official capacity, he had to negotiate the turbulence of postunification judicial reform and the codification of German law. Santner explains that Schreber's experience of his own bodily etiolation and decay "found its source of rot much closer to his professional home."[12] The legal system over which he would preside idealized (positivist) Roman law but was under constant pressure from new constituencies born of industrialization and urbanization (15). Legal debates ensuing from these pressures brought into the open a certain arbitrariness of the

law and its potential failure to produce absolute justice and meaning. More damaging still, these debates exposed the delegitimiz-
ing violence of the law that conditions of political stability typically repress. This violence, Santner remarks in reference to Walter
Benjamin, is most evident in the death penalty:

> What manifests itself as the law's inner decay is the fact that the
> rule of law is, in the final analysis, without ultimate justification or
> legitimation, that the very space of juridical reason within which
> the rule of law obtains is established and sustained by a dimen-
> sion of force and violence that, as it were, helps the place of those
> missing foundations. At its foundation, the rule of law is sustained
> not by reason alone but also by the force/violence of a tautologous
> enunciation—"the law is the law!" which is for Benjamin the source
> of a chronic institutional disequilibrium and degeneration. (10)

Indeed, Benjamin's critique of the law is, as Santner points out,
indebted to Friedrich Nietzsche, whose formulation of the state of
emergency or exception fundamentally revised the notion of history as progress. Or, as Santner writes:

> For Nietzsche, the state of emergency is where the performative
> magic that animated all rites of institution is as its highest potency:
> at the moment of emergence of a new order of institutional condi-
> tions or interpretations. Nietzsche's name for this performativity
> was, of course, *will to power,* and his radical conclusion from the
> omnipresence of its effects was a view of history as nonteleological
> series of ruptures and usurpations. (14)

Schreber's most pronounced bout of paranoia, coincident with
his legal appointment at a moment of heightened social insecurity,
was as much a response to repressed sexual desire as to a broader
crises of post-Enlightenment reason, wherein the violent mechanisms of control in the law were exposed as such. In Santner's
reading, Schreber's memoir "tells the unnerving story of a massive return of this repressed knowledge" (12). If Germany was
later diagnosed as suffering from national paranoia, this mental
illness may be traced back to this period of epistemological tumult.
Schreber, however, stands in contrast to his compatriots who would
go on to embrace that collective insanity called National Socialism.
Rather than repudiate his sense of his feminized (indeed Jewish)
unmanning by "reclaiming the phallic emblem and the symbolic

authority attached to it," Schreber, Santner explains, "reiterates its 'miraculous' ruination" (144). That is, Schreber finally embraced his feminization, where the majority of German men fell headlong into the abyss of paranoid masculine culture.[13]

In keeping with Nietzsche's view of history, Germany continued to experience a series of ruptures and usurpations. In the teens and twenties Germans witnessed the failed communist revolutions. In the thirties and forties the Nazis countered with their anti-revolutionary fascist regime. And in 1945 the occupation forces imposed a democratic revolution from without by dismantling German institutions, de-Nazifying its population, and, under the legality of the Allied court, sentencing to death those who had committed crimes against humanity. Under occupation, under foreign martial law, Germany was in the most literal legal sense in a state of emergency until such time as these conditions would give way to the emergence of the West German state. Those who lived through the pre- and postwar political sea changes and the unprecedented violence of the Third Reich could well imagine what Donna Heiland calls "the gothic possibilities of everyday life" (3).

A Woman's Occupation

The mise-en-scène and plot elements of the female gothic (the haunted house or gothic ruins, the mysterious foreign husband, supernatural possession of homes and property, scenarios of rescue and capture) give outlandish expression to the abstract status of nineteenth-century feminine legal and psychic subjectivity. For those living in the postwar rubble, these conditions could not have been more concrete. Above all, however, occupied Germany, even more than in the postwar United States, witnessed the most pronounced "surplus of women" on whom fell the burden of clearing the debris, providing for the family, and living day to day in the most *unheimlich* ruins they once called home.[14] Elizabeth Heineman argues that the period of 1942 to 1948 was temporally condensed in the mind of survivors as "the hour of the woman."[15] It was predominantly women who greeted the Allied "liberators" or foreign men, who in many instances proved to be not only disappointing, but in some cases outright terrifying. While any number of genuine romances and friendships developed between Germans and Allied soldiers, during the first year of occupation, in the Soviet Zone especially, rape, pillage, and murder by the liberating forces was the order of the day. Atina Grossmann writes that the virtually systematic rape of German women by Soviet troops was the one postwar phenomenon rightly anticipated in Goebbels's propaganda. "So much so," she writes,

> that many women reported feeling that they were reenacting a scene in a film they had already seen when the drama they were expecting actually unfolded: soldiers with heavy boots, unfamiliar faces (invariably coded as Mongol), and shining flashlights entered a darkened cellar, searched for weapons and watches, and then revolver in hand, commanded the proverbial "Frau, Komm."[16]

For many Allied troops such action was justified given Nazi atrocities in German-occupied territories and the wide civilian support for Hitler's genocidal regime.[17]

For men and women the first years of so-called liberation felt more like the unconditional surrender marking the end of Germany as they knew it. The conditions across Germany did not improve in 1945 but steadily worsened, especially during the severe winters of 1946 and 1947.[18] The U.S. military government surveys note a steady decline of German confidence in American occupation authority, particularly when food was scarce and war reparations stripped Germany of the infrastructure necessary to rebuild.[19] In the spirit of the female gothic plot, not a few Germans, believing themselves historically innocent, felt that the end of the war "represented the exchange of one form of oppression for another. Germans, first victimized by demonic Nazis, were now victimized by the Western Allies, who were shortsighted, inefficient and incompetent at best and deliberately vengeful at worst."[20] The paranoid fear that your Allied protector—this emissary of democracy—is in fact out to harm you, steal your property, commandeer (literally occupy) your body and house, and drive you mad encapsulated the gothic's political ambivalence. That women were the primary targets of this violence brings us more squarely into the field of the female gothic.

As Heineman explains, for German women the occupation was the moment of their "forced emancipation" (115). Now, with few men to protect them, women learned to become entirely self-sufficient. This freedom came at the price of physical and psychic violation and a lasting embitterment as women felt not just abandoned but betrayed by their husbands and brothers who waged war but who proved inept at navigating ordinary life in war's aftermath (76, 115–17). Women with husbands felt the triple duty of being wife, provider, and protector, while women whose husbands never returned, Heineman writes, "dream[ed] of rescue in the form of a man" (111). Whatever the mixed feeling, such liberation was rather short-lived. In West Germany, women were no sooner brought into the workforce than they were requisitioned back to the house to make way for wage-earning returning soldiers. Heineman's summary of women's experience of occupation describes so well the gothic heroine's predicament: "The disruption of conjugal life might suggest victimhood; it might provide the opportunity for emancipation; or it might set the stage for moral degradation" (77). Dennis Gress and David Bark write that for German men and women alike, the experience of war, defeat, and occupation produced what they call the "basic emotion," an affective response to "skepticism regarding masculine and military values, loss of faith and interest in ideology, and distrust of the older generation." This emotion, they argue, coalesced into an overwhelming collective wish: "Never Again!" (45). In postwar Germany, vigilance against history's repetition and faith in its mutability were not merely a matter of gothic subjecthood but a world-historical imperative. That the population was unanimously mistrustful of masculine and military values suggests that the occupation was, in the best sense, perhaps, a feminizing experience.

A Tale of Two Surveys

With this context in mind I turn to two surveys of motion picture audiences that the U.S. military government commissioned in the American zone. The first, conducted in the fall of 1945 and the first months of 1946, revealed that 94 percent of the respondents longed to see old German films because they "made more sense, were more beautiful, or were more personal." Asked to select from the American films then playing, respondents singled out *Madame Curie* (LeRoy, 1943) as a favorite, and, though they believed it an accurate account of Nazi war crimes, German audiences least enjoyed *Death Mills*.[21] In 1948, at a time when *Madame Curie* was still in circulation and a number of older and new German films (including *Der Apfel ist ab*) were in theaters, the U.S. military government commissioned a second survey, this time of Munich movie audiences. The report concludes that "though the number of German titles mentioned as favorites exceeded that of any other country," the film overall (including German *and* American titles) receiving the most positive votes was *Gaslight*, George Cukor's 1944 canonical female gothic (256–57).[22]

There are some striking and, given the postwar German audience, expected points of similarity between the two favored films. Both *Madame Curie* and *Gaslight* feature female protagonists who live in western Europe during the turn of the century. Both heroines survive their husbands and both must, at some point, prove the validity of their thinking by challenging patriarchal forces. We might say that both women triumph in the end, but the narrative trajectory that vindicates them, and the lessons offered, are quite different. In *Madame Curie,* our heroine, Marie (Greer Garson), is the first woman Nobel laureate in science. In several scenes, Marie's husband and companion-scientist Pierre (Walter Pidgeon), gently interrogates Marie to help her refine her intuitions and sharpen her methods. Their marriage is a model of equality and mutual understanding that leads both to tenderness and to great, paradigm-changing discoveries. *Madame Curie* is not simply a biopic celebrating their marriage and the arduous work to discover radium; rather, it is a paean to scientific inquiry and rational thinking. We watch the couple carry out experiments; we listen as they interpret results; and we marvel at how Marie, encountering data that does not fit, forges new explanatory models. In the final scene of this film, Marie Curie, feted by the faculty of science of the University of Paris, offers an inspirational address in which she declares that science's "great spiritual strength will in time cleanse this world of its evils, its ignorance, its poverty, diseases, wars, and heartaches." And though this film also tells of Pierre's tragic early death, this story of her life bears out the promises of the speech. For it was only a few scenes earlier that the all-male scientific body who now celebrates her work refused to give her a well-equipped lab because she was "young, inexperienced, and a woman." But in this linear narrative, there is no need to look back or dwell too long on yesterday's losses. Science is about the future, and through sound empirical methods humanity may overcome all manner of past suffering. In her parting words, Marie bids her audience to go and build "the Paris of tomorrow."

We may argue that Marie's belief in the curative and futural powers of science was shockingly undercut by *Death Mills,* which, this survey confirms, played in Germany at the same time. As I have discussed earlier, this documentary describes the concentration camps in terms of methodical process and capitalist efficiency. Medical experiments carried out on inmates are unspeakably cruel and inhumane, and the film gives witness to the unprecedented violence and backwardness of German racial science. The coincident screening of these two films in Germany performs Adorno and Horkheimer's famous critique: by the mid-twentieth century, Curie's world of rational scientific thought had not delivered humanity into "a truly human state" but had self-destructed, plunging humanity into "a new kind of barbarism."[23] "The curse of irresistible progress," this film pairing intimates, "is irresistible regression."[24] Though audiences did not necessarily experience these films in dialectic relation, there is no doubt that as the reality of the Holocaust hit Germans through the distribution of this documentary and extensive coverage of the Nuremberg trials, it was increasingly untenable to have faith that science, especially as practiced in Nazi Germany, could eradicate war, heartache, and misery.[25] It was also likely that as the conditions of life under occupation further deteriorated it was difficult to embrace the optimism of *Madame Curie* or the film's conspicuous melding of scientific triumph and marital happiness.

It is perhaps fitting that the favorite film of 1948 was in the tradition of the gothic—the genre, according to Fred Botting, that undercuts modernity's progress "with counter-narratives" that display "the underside of enlightenment and humanist values."[26] If *Madame Curie* is about enlightenment, progress, and the future, *Gaslight* is about regression and the past. In this film Ingrid Bergman's Paula is duped into marriage after a two-week courtship with the mysterious composer/pianist Gregory Anton (Charles Boyer). She no sooner believes herself in the throes of conjugal bliss than she becomes prisoner in the London home where her aunt was brutally murdered decades earlier. Haunted by that violence, fearful that she too may suffer a similar fate, Paula is slowly driven mad by her husband, who secretly schemes to usurp her inheritance. From the energetic and inexperienced youth that she is at the beginning of the romance, Paula ages but also devolves into an uncertain, weary, and wary hysteric. Because she is isolated and fragile, Paula cannot trust what she sees or hears, as when the gaslight dims every evening and someone, or something, prowls on

German handbill for *Gaslight* (George Cukor, MGM, 1944), which was distributed in Germany as *Das Haus der Lady Alquist (The House of Lady Alquist)*. Courtesy of Deutsches Filmmuseum/Deutsches Institut für Filmkunde, Frankfurt.

the floor above her. In contrast to Marie, for whom aberrations occasion new scientific possibilities, Paula, unable to assimilate experience, grows fearful of her environment and suspects the violent past—her aunt's murder, her mother's madness—will revisit themselves on her body and mind. As Mary Ann Doane notes, because "the very process of seeing is now invested with fear, anxiety, horror," the paranoid woman's film creates a world in which "epistemology has gone awry."[27] The film teases us with the possibility that these may indeed be Paula's delusional projections and that she may in fact be losing her mind just as her mother did (or so Gregory tells her). In the end, however, Paula is saved by yet another unbidden foreign man—an America named Brian Cameron (Joseph Cotten), who verifies her perceptions and emancipates her from her husband's femicidal plot.

Film Criticism and Occupation Life

Prompted by this survey and the history of the gothic I have outlined thus far, I want to make the argument that *Gaslight* offered an emotional and political experience that was especially resonant in occupation life and that, as such, may help us to theorize occupation subjectivity. Because the surveys offer little explanation for the results, however, I want to buttress this proposition by turning to reviews for this and other films then in circulation. As we will see below, film reviewers in occupied Germany conspicuously engaged films not as self-contained aesthetic objects but as ideological and even ethnographic texts that were meaningful within the wider discursive environment of occupation. Reviews trained readers to understand film culture politically. They also, at times, reported on audience reactions to the films in the theater, providing a historical record of spectatorial effect. Using reviews to construct as far as is possible a horizon of reception, I consider not only the broad criteria used to assess films like *Gaslight*, but also how reviews activated vectors of spectatorship that rippled far beyond the local theater.

For many German audiences *Gaslight* was important for its star, Ingrid Bergman, who appeared to viewers in this film as well as in the OWI documentary *Swedes in America* (1943) (discussed in chapter 2) and in the feature film *The Bells of St. Mary's* (1945), which was released in Germany the same week as *Gaslight*. Where these two feature films were compared in the same review,

St. Mary's bells rang a hollow note, despite Bergman's luminous performance. *Bells of St. Mary's* takes place in a struggling parochial school whose building is slated to be condemned. To the rescue comes the crooning Father O'Malley (Bing Cosby). In the course of the film, O'Malley manages a number of improbable feats: he succeeds in softening the strict Sister Benedict (Bergman) and persuading a hard-boiled, selfish businessman to give over his new building to the parish school (for which the nuns have long been praying). He also reunites the estranged parents of a troubled student and all the while takes advantage of every opportunity to belt out a tune.

As the film reviewer at *Telegraf* remarked in reference to its singing priest, friendly nuns, and mawkish plotting, *St. Mary's* "is a film that exhibits a specifically American character. Only he who has patience and who will indulge the film's foreign peculiarity will enjoy watching it."[28] The *Berliner Zeitung* reported that without Bergman, "this emotionally overwrought clerical film would be hardly bearable." Cited in the same review, *Gaslight* "offers much more than an engaging criminal story. . . . The mental torment of the poor lady who is nearly driven mad by her rogue husband is outstandingly acted, and the spectator's nerves are spared nothing."[29] *Der Tagesspiegel* likewise noted that the "pious lessons" imparted by the *Bells of St. Mary's* "contradicts our [German] attitude and taste"; its "sentimental episodes work against European sophistication." However, this reviewer does not dismiss the film outright. Not only does Bergman transcend the film's material with her "fantastic sincerity" (indeed, the reviewer offers a rhapsodic tribute to Bergman's vitality, "equal only to Garbo's . . . that shines through the cold gaze of objectivity"), but *St. Mary's* opens a window onto American culture. As the critic explains, because the film was popular with U.S. audiences, profitable at the box office, and featured Hollywood's most celebrated actors, on the basis of its appeal to American audiences alone the film "offers insight into the religious mentality of the country from which it comes." Thus *St. Mary's* should be studied more than simply endured. But *Gaslight* appeals on its own merits as an aesthetic object without excuses or special dispensation. This same reviewer goes on to praise Cukor for masterfully creating the environment of turn-of-the-century London, and he lauds the story for its captivating suspense. Where *St. Mary's* presents us with the "straw-hat wearing," "tear-jerking" Crosby, in *Gaslight* Bergman plays opposite Charles Boyer, whose character "embod[ies] a demonic ambiguity" at once "scintillating and bewitching."[30]

We may also consider how *Gaslight* compared to other gothic-themed films. *Jane Eyre* premiered in July 1947 under the title *Die Waise von Lowood (The Orphan from Lowood)* three months before *Gaslight*'s release. The German reviews were roundly critical of *Jane Eyre*'s special effects and gothic tendencies that did not enhance but rather obscured the social polemic of Brontë's original. Attentive to the political history of the female gothic novel, *Die neue Zeitung* declared, "Charlotte Bronte's old novel, a clear and indicting report on the condition of orphan houses and an attack on marriage laws in England one hundred years ago, has by chance in our century become an almost unbearable gothic drama." The critic concludes the review warning that "[o]nly audiences who can take a dramatic punishing will find they can be satisfied with this horror."[31] The critic for the left-leaning *Socialdemokrat* also attacked the film for its gothic and melodramatic effects that not only dilute the novel's politics (the critic writes that "the gripping fate of the heroine is rendered insignificant") but produced unintended responses in audiences. Reversing typical methods of plotting, this film uses Jane's story as "merely a backdrop for Rochester's Scottish estate with all of the Hollywood trappings. The melodrama is laid on so thick that it elicits our laughter when really tears of compassion should be flowing."[32] Similarly *Nachtexpress* reported that audiences in Berlin's Kronen-Lichtspiele movie theater snickered at the film: "Only at the beginning, when the little orphan [Jane] like a feminine Oliver Twist is tortured in the religious poor house, did audiences not laugh." But once little Jane (Peggy Ann Garner) turned into adult Jane (Joan Fontaine)—"the virtuous young governess who walks like a blonde angel through the sinister manor belonging to noble Rochester"—"all reverence vanished." The film descended into "kitsch" and the audience dissolved into mocking laughter.[33]

Where *Jane Eyre* faltered for not being political enough, Robert Siodmak's *Spiral Staircase* was dismissed because its strange politics ventured a bit too close to home. The film's villain, Professor Warren (George Brent), is a Darwin-obsessed zoologist driven to serial murder to rid his town of its women less fit for survival. Our heroine, Helen (Dorothy McGuire), a hysterical mute, is Warren's next victim. She also works for Warren and thus turns to him for protection from the murderer at large. As Lutz Koepnick explains, critics were outspoken in their hostility to this film, especially in the context of post-Nazi spectatorship. *Der Tagesspiegel*, Koepnick writes, "censured the film as an absurd amalgamation of colportage and bogus psychotherapy, a typically American invitation to moral corruption."[34] And in the pages of the *Tägliche Rundschau Berlin*, film critic Hans Ulrich Eylau wrote, "Whoever as a victor of a war waged in the name of ethical principles, assumes the responsibility of reeducating and spiritually reshaping the Germans, should be able to recognize that murder films are not exactly an appropriate instrument to eradicate fascistic convictions."[35] On the other hand, Hitchcock's *Suspicion*, starring Cary Grant and Joan Fontaine, was widely hailed as a masterful manipulation of audience expectation. Writing for the *Der Tagesspiegel*, Friedrich Luft echoed the enthusiasm of his fellow critics when he summed up the plot and its effect: "The woman must imagine that [her husband] is a murderer. She must finally fear becoming his victim. Every gesture raises suspicion; with his every word her fear grows until the very end when the tension is released in innocence and happy union. [This film plays] a smart game with our easily deceived and far too hasty discernment. And so well made!"[36] If these reviews are in any way reflective of public sentiment, they demonstrate that *Gaslight*'s appeal was not merely for its star or its generic formulation. Nor was it received as merely a curious artifact of American cinematic taste or misguided reeducation propaganda. Like *Suspicion*, *Gaslight* attracted audiences with its tale of paranoiac ambiguity and phantasmic madness in a way, I argue below, that amplified occupation experience.

I conclude this section by way of a detour, specifically by way of a film review that in its itinerant musings manages to all but circumvent the film itself. Friedrich Luft's pithy and allusive 1947 review of Otto Preminger's film noir *Laura* (1944) maps the spatial and psychological terrain that connects the experience of film spectatorship explicitly to the experience of the occupation and recent history. Writing for *Die neue Zeitung* (published in Germany by the U.S. military government), Luft begins the review by offering this impressionistic description of the film's decadent mise-en-scène and dastardly characters:

The people in this film walk on the thick carpets of affluence. They sit on the golden stools of prosperity and are comfortably secure in their bank accounts. Still murder lies in wait, and envy, greed and ill-will circulate. Occasionally something is tormented. It is Busoni's heart, over whose grave, on a narrow pedestal, sits the mourning figure created by the genius of Kolbe, a figure flanked by two weeping willows.[37]

After a vague, three-sentence nod to this film about graven affluence, which seems to interest him not in the least, Luft abandons Friedenau's Kronen-Lichtspiele theater where *Laura* is showing and wanders over to Friedenau's famous cemetery.[38] Here lies buried the modernist composer Ferruccio Busoni, whose tomb is marked by a statue created by the great modern sculpture Georg Kolbe (who himself died in 1947). But Luft senses that something torments Busoni, something related to this film and this occupation. Perhaps Busoni agonizes in response to Laura's favorite tune that serves as her ever-present leitmotif. Even Laura's unrefined lover Shelby (Vincent Price) describes the melody as "not exactly classical, but sweet," just before he and Detective McPherson (Dana Andrews), typical Hollywood American men, bond over the fact that they both sleep through classical concerts. For Luft, it is clear that it is not just the film's saccharine score or uncultured characters that stir Busoni's heart (in fact, Luft says nothing more about the film after this opening paragraph). It is rather the recent cultural history of this Berlin neighborhood now under American occupation that strikes a pessimistic note, a history that Luft proceeds to sketch for his readers.

Host to the first bicycle race before World War I, known for its quirky apartment buildings and small gardens in the 1920s, Friedenau was a provincial district. Its bookstores, "not a bad gauge for a settlement's intellectuality," writes Luft, "were seldom centers of intellectual vitality, stocked as they were with nationalistic and reactionary Feuilletons." We may surmise from Luft's account that Friedenau is not where high culture thrived; it is rather to Friedenau's cemetery that it came to die. But the occupation is the last nail in Friedenau's coffin. As he makes his virtual way to the neighborhood's shopping district, Luft observes that "the Schloss street today looks like an American main street. . . . The

Tatania-Palast [Steglitz's premier Weimar-era film palace] in its outmoded modernism is the entertainment center for the occupation troops." With dry cynicism Luft observes that "this city district was razed by bombs. It probably had it coming." But what remains is hardly an improvement over what came before: "Today it is perhaps a symptom that the Schlosspark theater, which in its history managed to deliver neither art nor profit, is now flourishing and has achieved a place for itself among Berlin theaters."

Watching *Laura,* a decadent American film noir, Luft is compelled to leave the theater, cut short his review, and take stock of his surroundings. Where we might expect him to express an embittered nostalgia for a bygone era, he instead proffers a weary ambivalence channeled through the local cemetery where rests a composer associated with Berlin's once-flourishing city center. This center is now decimated, divided, decentered. If I am reading Luft correctly, he is struck that this formerly unimportant Berlin suburb is now itself a center, not of high culture but of lowbrow, mostly American culture. It is now a neighborhood populated by occupation troops who, in seeking entertainment, have helped to boost the profile of the uninspiring Schlosspark theater. In keeping with the gothic relationship to extreme historical change, the war and occupation are here regarded as both transformative (downtown looks like an American main street) and regenerative (thanks to the occupation and to the destruction of the war, the once ailing theater is now thriving); but to speak of progress would be misleading. In fact, if *Laura* teaches us anything, we should regard these first signs of crass affluence in Berlin with due suspicion. For where there is prosperity, jealousy and murder lie in wait.

In *Laura,* however, it is not the coarse Americans who are dangerous, but the urbane cultural critic/columnist/aficionado of true crime Waldo Lydecker (Clifton Webb), who would rather see his beloved Laura (Gene Tierney) dead and disfigured rather than leave her to "the vulgar pawing of a second-rate detective who thinks [she's] a dame." Luft does not fall prey to this kind of eviscerating logic for Berlin (the Allies have already seen to that), but neither does he rejoice in the presence of these soldiering Americans or their movies. Where just a year before he praised Hitchock's *Suspicion* that played in this very theater, Luft now associates American films with the *longue durée* of occupation and its long-term cultural effects. I cannot help but point out one, surely unintended parallel between *Laura* and the Luft review. In the film's final scene Lydecker is proven to be the heel we have taken him for as he threatens Laura with a rifle. But he is introduced as a murder suspect in the film's opening scene, when McPherson confronts him about a review he wrote. As McPherson explains to Lydecker, "Two years ago in your October seventeenth column, you started out to write a book review, but at the bottom of the column, you switched over to the Harrington murder case." Drawn to this essay's erratic form, McPherson finds that Lydecker's identification of the Harrington murder weapon was incorrect, but it accurately describes the shotgun Lydecker would later be found guilty of using. In this way, Lydecker's column serves as an admission of guilt before the fact. But we may compare the structure of this suspended book review (which catches McPherson's eye) to Luft's own film review cum meditation, which also "switches over." Though Luft says little about the film, he knowingly (or not) models his own column after Lydecker's and has thus in some way internalized the film's own symptomatology and perhaps even Lydecker's disdain for what now appears to be a more enduring presence of vulgar American detectives in the local movie theater.

Luft's review, which reads local culture and film culture symptomatically, is itself symptomatic of the associative logic informing occupation spectatorship that flits from the film to the theater, to the shifting topoi of local culture and history. Far from distracting Luft from the politics of defeat, filmgoing is one activity in which the experience of occupation and the stakes of its cultural influence, especially as the occupation wore on, are strongly felt. In Germany, film spectatorship and occupation subjectivity were always in intricate relation. With this in mind, I now consider what it was about *Gaslight*—a female gothic, not a standard criminal noir—that may have captured something about the experience of occupation life, something that attracted audiences to the theater to watch the film rather than luring them to the cemetery nearby where they could avoid it.

Gaslight, or Is This Madness?

Of course West Germany's cold war quandary is uncannily mirrored in *Gaslight* as Paula is herself positioned between her malicious, mystifying East European husband, Gregory (who we later learn is Sergis Bauer from Prague), and her kindly, demystifying

Paula (Ingrid Bergman) comes to her senses, thanks to the American Brian
Cameron (Joseph Cotten) in *Gaslight*. Production still courtesy of Photofest.

American rescuer, Brian Cameron, a fetching gentleman detective in league with London's Scotland Yard. The charismatic tyrant who would commandeer Paula's wealth and sanity and who
subjects her to all manner of sadistic manipulation, Gregory is the
gothic, totalitarian dictator onto whom we could variously map
the Hitlers and Stalins of Europe. Gregory marries Paula not out of
love for her or concern for her well-being, but only to have access
to the jewels she unknowingly inherited from her famous, opera-
singing aunt. To maintain his power over Paula, he manipulates all
aspects of her public and private life as well as her affective relationship to the past and present. In this way Gregory determines to
pervert Paula's psyche, have her committed, and thereby lay claim
to her estate. Cameron, on the other hand, acts in the interest of
justice and perhaps in the spirit of genuine friendship; he embodies the qualities we would hope to find in any democratic liberator.
Not only does Cameron restore to Paula her rightful inheritance,
he (like Leon in *Ninotchka*) brings Paula back to her senses.

At the same time, however, life with Gregory bears some comparison with the occupation. Where he produces a visual and sonic
environment designed to drive Paula mad, we may recall from

chapter 1 that the Americans regarded Germany under occupation as possessing "the same conditions of control as a scientific laboratory."[39] By manipulating cinematic projection, the Americans, who diagnosed Nazi Germans as suffering from group paranoia, hoped to drive them sane. In contrast to Marie Curie, the exemplary scientific subject, Paula, like a person under occupation, is the scientific object. Gregory sets out to discipline Paula so that she learns to recognize the signs of her own madness. He essentially tutors her in paranoiac behavior while unwittingly providing the optical sources of her terror when the gaslight dims. Reeducation was likewise predicated on the instrumentality of carefully calibrated external phenomena that would alter the deep structures of the German collective psyche. We could say that *Gaslight* offers its German spectators a national script of female victimization, authoritarian manipulation, and perhaps also liberation that could find wide historical application. However one reads the source of her torment, Paula is never anything but innocent prey to Gregory's malevolent mechanizations. But beyond this obvious and (given the year of *Gaslight*'s production) serendipitous nod to geopolitics, this film may also appeal for the way it contrasts with other female gothics: namely, in the representation of Paula's presumed paranoia.

For Mary Ann Doane, *Gaslight* is a prime example of the paranoid woman's film in that it provides the aural and visual registers of feminine desubjectification, according to which the heroine, like the paranoiac, experiences a "collapse between internal/external, subject/object" (144). Paula cannot discern if noises in the attic emanate from within her or from without, nor, putatively, can she distinguish fantasy from memory, as when Gregory declares that the letter she found earlier in the film signed by Sergis Bauer was merely a figment of her imagination. It is in this scene that Paula is forced to confront that which she most fears. Gregory announces that Paula is fated to end as her mother did: alone in an asylum, "with no brain at all." Though Gregory menaces Paula, it is her mother (or her mother's fate) and her aunt's violent death that Paula must escape. Because in the oedipal scenario girls are locked into a narcissistic relationship with the lost object, "the female subject does not institute a search to 'refind' the object; she becomes that object" (144). Thus, in this subgenre, when gothic heroines search the house for the source of their torment, what they find hidden are traces (or actually bodies) of another version of themselves—a mother, an aunt, a first wife, etc. Because these girls end up becoming the very women they initially feared, these films enact the inevitable cycle of history's repetition. Paula is bidden by those who wish her well and ill to "forget the past," to "never look back," to put behind her the aunt's gruesome murder. At the same time, these people mold Paula to her aunt's image as if to resurrect the past she is meant to forget. As a child, Paula is sent away from London to Italy, where she studies opera with her aunt's own teacher. Some years later, Gregory convinces Paula to take up residence in her aunt's London home. And when Cameron spies Paula at the London tower, she looks so much like her aunt that, as he later recalls, "I thought she was Alice Alquist come back to life." For Doane, these films are less about "the loss of [feminine] identity" than "a return to the locus of its unthinkability," for it would seem that Paula has no identity to lose (145). Here it is worth remembering the difference between masculine and feminine paranoia. As Freud explains, in the former, delusions of persecution ward off male homosexual desire and castration anxiety so that the proposition "I (a man) love him (a man)" becomes "I do not love him—I hate him because HE PERSECUTES ME."[40] In the latter, as Doane emphasizes, castration anxiety is not an option. One cannot fear losing what one does not possess. The female paranoid delusion then is a symptom of the woman's fear, not simply of loving another woman, the mother. It is the fear of becoming her, of complete narcissistic collapse with the maternal signifier. Such a reading not only elucidates *Gaslight,* it provides an interpretative framework for understanding how this subgenre problematizes the very concept of feminine subjectivity and female spectatorship and perhaps also, in the political sense, a nonsovereign subjectivity.[41]

And yet this emphasis on paranoia as a completely delusional state may cause us to overlook *Gaslight*'s unique narrative twist. Unlike Joan Fontaine's Lina in *Suspicion,* whose fear of her husband is produced by a paranoiac *misreading* of clues and against Doane's generalization about the paranoid heroine, Paula is not delusional. Rather, she is beholden to a violently irrational environment under the control of a jewel-obsessed sociopath. We come to understand before Paula does that Gregory orchestrates her phantasmic world of disappearing objects and inadvertently produces the dimming lights and ruckus above. We also understand why it is that she sensibly thinks herself mad. Bessie, the maid, has gone nearly deaf and thus cannot hear the noises above Paula's room, and Paula is always alone the moments the lights dim. She can find no plausible cause for the things she hears, sees, and is accused by Gregory of doing. But rather than suspect her husband of plotting against her or entertain the possibility of supernatural hauntings or divine possessions, Paula jumps to a more logical conclusion: because she believes that the world and other people are rational, she presumes that she is insane. Ironically, Paula's problem is not that she is paranoid; if anything, given Gregory's scheme, she is not paranoid *enough*. Likewise, this film is not about empiricism gone awry so much as a crisis that arises when the world exceeds rational explanation. When finally we learn the truth of Gregory's history and unpack his present motivation, it is little wonder to us that Paula cannot get her head around her dire circumstances. "Why? Why?" she asks, would Gregory lie to her? Why would he sneak up to the attic and search through Alice Alquist's trunks? Why would he want to drive her insane?

The fact is, Gregory is himself phantasmic. Cameron explains to Paula that more than ten years ago Gregory (then Sergis Bauer), a young pianist from Prague, followed Alice to London and broke into her house hoping to steal the crown jewels secretly given to her by a mysterious royal admirer. Startled by the sounds of someone (Paula, as it turns out) approaching in the house, Gregory strangled Alice but did not manage to find the gems. Undeterred, he plotted for ten years to find the grown-up Paula in Italy, who he then seduced, married, and nearly drove crazy in hopes of having her committed so that he could control her estate and search for the jewels at his leisure. As the police detective earlier made clear, these precious stones are too famous to sell, trade, or wear in the open. Whoever steals them does so only for the pleasure of possessing their luster. When Cameron apprehends Gregory he accusingly asks, "How does it feel to have planned and killed and tortured for something, and then to know it's been for nothing?" Though Cameron is referring to the fact that Gregory no sooner finds the jewels than his scheme is uncovered, there is something literal in the question Cameron asks. All of this suffering just for sparkles? If it were told from Gregory's perspective, this film would be the incredible saga of outlandish fetishism. Experienced from Paula's point of view, however, this becomes a cautionary tale of how an innocent but rational girl can be seduced by a murderer, how she is capable of falling in love with, marrying, and initially defending a man whose jewel lust renders him homicidal. It also shows us how far madmen can go before someone from the outside finally intervenes. For those living through the occupation who were themselves perhaps once swayed (and later felt themselves betrayed) by the chimera of Nazi pageantry—for those who now endured a world of a radically different order under the jurisdiction of unbidden foreigners—this film is attractive as a story in which madness is the rational response to a volatile world and a wicked man. But in the context of occupation, this madness may mean something more.

Paula's paranoia is not nearly so striking as her gullibility. As Andrew Sarris remarks of the plot, "Much of the time the situation verges on farce as the wife makes of herself an emotional doormat for her husband." As he notes, however, her "incredible lack of perspicacity," as untenable as it may seem, is necessary to "elaborate her husband's villainy" and set up the final, quite satisfying scene of retribution.[42] Diane Long Hoeveler offers a rather radical reading of the female gothic that applies especially well to *Gaslight* and addresses Paula's discomfiting naïveté. Noting that gothic heroines are typically propertied and rewarded for their innocence, Hoeveler argues that these are not tales simply of victimization. They instruct their readers in "gothic feminism," "an ideology of female power through pretended and staged weakness" (7). Rather than cave to the demands of "raving, lustful, greedy patriarchy," gothic heroines manage to subvert the system, feminize the husband, and make the home safe for themselves and their mothers by "carefully cultivating the appearance of their very powerlessness" (10, 7). In this pose, or masquerade, women feign conformity to patriarchal norms. That is, they pretend to be the disempowered, fragile innocents in need of protection that patriarchy takes them for. The effect is that when, in the end, they win back their property (often by inadvertently killing off or emasculating their husbands) we bear them no grudge. Unjustly persecuted, the gothic feminist gets what she deserves. Or, as Hoeveler nicely phrases it, by posing weakness, "the meek will inherit the gothic earth" (19). Paula, of course, ends the film in full possession of not just her wits but her aunt's prestigious London home. And she does so escaping the dreadful fate of both her aunt and her mother.

Paula receives the revenge she is owed by enacting her insanity, perhaps throughout the film (in Sarris's estimation) but especially at the end. In the penultimate scene, Cameron has exposed Gregory's treachery and murderous past, thus confirming Paula's sanity. After a scuffle between the two men, we find Gregory bound by rope to a chair in the attic, where Paula speaks to him for the last time. Hoping Paula is still too enfeebled to protest, Gregory entreats her to help him escape. Instead, Paula taunts him. He asks her to retrieve a knife and cut him free, but seeing the knife in the drawer she pretends not to find it. Then, moments later, having found the knife, Paula pretends to lose it. She puts the problem to him rationally:

> PAULA: How can a madwoman help you escape?
> GREGORY: But you're not mad!
> PAULA: Yes, I am mad, as my mother was!
> GREGORY: No, Paula. That wasn't true! Help me.
> PAULA: If I were not mad, I could have helped you. Whatever you had done, I could have pitied and protected you. But because I am mad, I hate you. Because I am mad, I have betrayed you, and because I am mad I am rejoicing in my heart without a shred of pity, without a shred of regret, watching you go with glory in my heart! Mr. Cameron, come. Come, Mr. Cameron. Take this man away!

After suffering through innumerable humiliations of her husband's concoction and nearly succumbing to his farfetched plot, Paula confronts Gregory not as the sane woman she now knows herself to be, but as the madwoman he had nearly convinced her she was.[43] In her parting words, Paula explains the logic of her newfound gothic feminism: a sane woman would forgive her husband his unpardonable crimes; she would stand by the vow of marriage over and above the law of the state (and her own best interest). But a mad and vengeful wife, a paranoid wife, rejoices in the force and even the violence of justice. Paranoia, or its pose, is not simply a rational response to an irrational world; it is a madness that gives way to anger that erupts in the face of criminal domination, and it is the pose that attracts the attention and support necessary to temper such dark forces.

Paula's savvy is further reinforced when at the end, released from Gregory's control, she is duly cautious of a new romance or marriage. In the final scene she guardedly accepts, instead, Cameron's proposal of friendship. In keeping with Hoeveler's analysis, this film, like the female gothic novel, does not promote a fantasy of revolution or complete and self-actualizing liberation (after all, Paula could not have regained her sanity without Cameron's help), but neither does it cage its heroine in an impossible or unsustainable subjectivity. As Hoeveler explains, it offers instead a practical lesson

> that patriarchy is a gigantic protection racket; there is no protection for women unless they too get a big stick behind them any way they can. If there is a system of "traffic in women," then sell yourself to the best (read: most controllable) bidder, the man with the most effective system of protection behind him. (36)

For the gothic heroine this is good advice. Cameron respects Paula's rights and carries the stick of Scotland Yard. Writing specifically of *Gaslight,* Diane Waldman puts the narrative transition squarely in the terms of modern politics, whereby Paula overthrows "the patriarchal tyrant" and replaces him "by a gentler, more democratic type."[44]

In this respect, the pose advocated by gothic feminism stands in intriguing contrast to the mimetic registers of reeducation. Where U.S. officials proposed that Germans rehabilitate themselves by imitating their occupiers, the female gothic proposes a different strategy. Rather than ape authority, the heroine adopts the pose of a person in need of rehabilitation and protection. As Hoelever explains, rather than internalize and replicate the laws and institutions that oppress her, "[the gothic heroine] must redeem those institutions and mark them as female controlled and female identified." In other words, the gothic feminist domesticates the masculine order and bends it to her needs and manages to engage it on a more equal footing (22). Though I am loath to press the analogy too far, this paradigm of the pose that yields protection aptly describes the realpolitik of the soon-to-be sovereign West Germany negotiating a place for itself in the gigantic protection racket of the cold war. And it captures the political spirit of Munich in 1948, when, after once being the capital of the Nazi Party, it became the center of a short-lived revival of the leftist Social Democratic Party (SPD). Kurt Schumacher, leader of the SPD, imagined a distinctly German model of democratic nationalism that rejected both the fierce jingoism of Nazism and the historically determinative Marxist orthodoxy of communism, especially as practiced in

Stalin's Soviet Union. But the SPD was also critical of American capitalism and Allied designs on Germany. Schumacher advocated strongly for German sovereignty and independence as the basis for any negotiations with the Allies and made clear that only "as a free man" could Germany accept responsibility for its history.[45] The connections then between madness and justice, between gothic feminism and cold war politics, anticipate another crucial question: beyond merely reflecting an occupational disposition, how might *Gaslight* foster a democratic subjectivity?

Gothic Citizenship and the Future of German Democracy

In *Democracy and the Foreigner*, Bonnie Honig offers an interpretation of democratic myths that can begin to help us answer this question. As she notes, democratic theory typically likens the people's relationship to the law as a romance or happy marriage; the problem is only "to find the right match between a people and its law, a state and its institutions."[46] Yet so many of the founding stories of democracies from Rousseau's *On the Social Contract*, Freud's *Moses and Monotheism*, and even the myth of immigrant America have recourse to foreigners who must reenchant the people once their marriage with the law falls apart. Foreigners engage these people through shared mistrust and anxiety. Honig asks:

> What genre best fits a work of political thought in which a people with a great deal in common decide to share the burdens and pleasures of a life together only to find that they have cast in their lots with a bunch of untrustworthy strangers? What genre dictates that, when their joint project founders, a mysterious foreigner will appear on the horizon to rescue these wayward people from their misfortune? What genre then trades on the reader's uncertainty as to whether that apparently rescuing foreigner is really a hero or villain? (109)

Read through "the female gothic lens," democratic theory elucidates this scenario and justifies the "mutual mistrust" between the people and the foreigner who founds or rescues them. For Honig the female gothics "[work] out certain ambivalences that are social and political rather than strictly familial" (111). Such a reading allows Honig not only to locate the political in these tales of domestic terror, it also brings focus to the foreign elements of democracy—the foreign founder, the "alienness of the law"—and offers an emplotment of how democratic citizens, like the gothic heroine, may be haunted by both the violence that founds (and continually refounds) their nation and the overpowering foreign agent that calls (and may recall) them into being. Indeed, stories detailing the gothic heroine's paranoid fear of husbands and father figures who offer her romance only to victimize her may well foster in readers just the kind of skepticism necessary to uphold a democratic society (115):

> What [female gothics] provide us with is not a sense of paralyzing paranoia in the face of monstrous forces beyond our control, nor a clear distinction between the forces of good and evil, but a healthy caution to be wary of authorities and powers that seek to govern us, claiming to know what is in our best interest. From female gothics, we get a valuable exhortation to take matters into our own hands. (118)

The heroine comes into a more responsible citizenship by investigating her husband and taking it upon herself to learn about his often homicidal, secret past. Though she may require the help of another man, who himself may have murderous designs, the heroine matures in these stories and eventually learns that scenarios of rescue and abandonment, liberation and captivity, are always in antinomic relation with power. Like Hoeveler, Honig finds that these narratives are not celebrations of unbridled liberation, nor do they comfort us with the knowledge that historical evil has been completely excavated and dispelled. The new man may have evil intentions and the past may still be opaque. Instead they teach us "the powers but also the limits of self-conscious agency" (118). Translated into a civic sensibility, the female gothic constructively channels the "sense of terror of belonging," and "the hope and betrayal that comes with inextricable intertwining of people in one another's lives across lines of difference and power" (121). As she concludes, gothic citizenship is far preferable to the happy marriage of people to their law or leader, especially, I want to emphasize, in the case of post-Nazi Germany:

> Exhorting citizens to return to the nation and relate to it or to its good guys in unambivalent terms is not the way to (re)inaugurate a vital and magnanimous democratic politics, though it may serve

the rather different cause of nationalism or patriotism. Instead, we
need a politics that acknowledges our passionate ambivalences and
engages them by pluralizing our attachments so that the nation-state
is just one of several sites of always ambivalent attachment rather
than the sole and central site of simply romantic love. (121–22)

To go back to two earlier examples, we might remark that where
Ninotchka allows herself to be seduced by capitalism, the gothic
heroine would be suspicious of the regime that lures her. She would
be wary that this new government may harbor a violent history
and may be just as untrustworthy as the regime it replaces. Read
through the female gothic lens, Käutner's *Der Apfel ist ab* becomes
a great tale of vindicated paranoia, wherein Adam is truly at the
mercy of celestial power and godly ineptitude. Like a good gothic
heroine, the feminized Adam (it is *he* who picks Eden's forbidden
apple) is equally dubious of "good" heaven and "evil" hell, and in
feigning, perhaps, his indecision and immaturity, he manages in
the end to get a woman he wants. Indeed, in exactly the ways that
Apfel fails as satire, it succeeds in the spirit of the female gothic
in capturing a distrust of power and limits of self-actualizing
sovereignty.

Gaslight too promotes a version of passionate ambivalence advocated by Honig. Paula learns the folly of falling too quickly and
too completely for the man who would rescue her from her dark
past, and she learns that the only way to avoid history's return is by
knowing that history to the best of her ability. But it is in relation
to the other Hollywood films in Germany that *Gaslight* offers an
important corrective to the very reeducation campaign of which
it was a part. Against the ethnographic wisdom that we find in
the psychoculturalist approach to the German problem, but also
in Hollywood's bald ethnographic imaginary as demonstrated especially in *Human Comedy*, *Gaslight* reminds us that we cannot
always tell a person (a tyrant or a savior, an American or an immigrant) just from looking. Ethnography's faith in observation is
undercut in the female gothic world in which things and people
are never quite as they appear to be. Gregory seems so charming
at first, so truly in love with Paula. But later in the film his vi-
ciousness is matched only by Cameron's kindness. And yet, had
Paula watched American movies in occupied Germany, she would
know to keep her distance from Cameron, her American rescuer

Young Charlie (Teresa Wright) shrinks from her serial-killing Uncle Charlie (Joseph Cotten) in *Shadow of a Doubt* (Alfred Hitchcock, Universal, 1943). Production still courtesy of Photofest.

played by Joseph Cotten. Not only might she have associated him with the violent beginnings of American democracy and the exclusionary politics of its history as dramatized in American westerns, musicals, and noirs, she might have recognized that the man who saves her in Victorian England is played by the same actor who in Hitchock's *Shadow of a Doubt* (in circulation in Germany in 1945) is the Merry Widow murderer—the jewel-obsessed psychopath who poses as a model citizen to cover his true identity as a strangler of rich women. In displaying America's brutal history through the Hollywood films it imported, the American military government may have provided Germans with the best kind of education: one that does not cure or completely evacuate paranoia but redirects it from masculine delusionality toward feminine, rational, even gothic skepticism. And this skepticism would make Germans wary not only of the return of their own national socialist past, but duly attentive to the violence of law and vigilant against succumbing to power (even a foreign military power) in the future.

Epilogue
Berlin Fifty Years Later

As a technology of political pedagogy, cinema in occupied Germany was also an instrument of historical reckoning. By watching Hollywood films, occupied spectators were supposed to come to an understanding of their own past misdeeds, to renounce their collective superiority, and to disassociate themselves from the structures of national feeling upon which territorial expansion, war, and genocide are founded. Though many of the Hollywood films screened in Germany fostered precisely these sentiments in their American viewers, German audiences were themselves conditioned by the experience of occupation to reread American history on and through film for its negative and positive examples. In the case of *Gaslight,* films might help to condition a skeptical relationship to history when its violence threatens to return. It is interesting, in this light, that the occupation of Germany has made a comeback in American political discourse in order to condition our relationship to history as it is currently unfolding. By way of commenting on this occupation revival, I conclude this book with a reflection on the efficacy of reeducation and German democracy under American military rule.

Berlin Fifty Years Later . . .

To commemorate the Berlin airlift and bolster support for Chancellor Helmut Kohl's unsuccessful bid for reelection, President Bill Clinton—or "dear Bill," as Kohl referred to him—undertook a short, whirlwind tour of Germany in May 1998. The *New York*

Times reported that the two world leaders "looked and dressed like brothers: grinning, burly, silver-haired, ruddy-faced brothers in dark suits, white shirts and yellow ties." Though the likeness to this reporter's eye was not perfect ("more accurately, the much broader Mr. Kohl looked like Mr. Clinton seen in a fun-house mirror"), this calculated staging of similitude was part of a larger politics of comparison that would ripple far beyond the presidential tenure of either man and morph into equivalencies far stranger than this fun house duo.[1] But at this moment in May, these fraternal leaders were the most *visible* and—thanks to the occupation— perhaps *predictable* signifiers of German-American goodwill and ideological mutuality. One could imagine them posed like *Hallo, Fräulein!*'s Tom and Walter in a hotel room at the end of the day, wearing similar clothes and sharing their last cigarette. As Clinton and Kohl toured the now unified Germany, they embodied the triumphant abundance of democratic capitalism (both men were known for their robust appetites) and the success of the occupation in transforming Germany into a model nation for the rest of post-Soviet Europe to imitate.

Though Clinton's speeches in Germany focused on "the next fifty years," his tour with Kohl was resolutely grounded in a sentimental nostalgia for the occupation past. At the joint news conference at Potsdam, Kohl observed that the last American president to visit this site came to sign the Allied four-power agreement that partitioned Germany and set forth the terms of its unconditional surrender. Kohl remarked that at that time "Germany and the chances of Germany belonging to the free nations of our continent looked very bad. . . . [T]he fact that we've been able to overcome that part of our history is something we owe . . . to our American friends."[2] At Tempelhof International Airport, to rousing applause from German civilians and American pilots, Clinton celebrated the Berlin airlift as the event that transformed the Allies into "protectors, instead of occupiers." With "democratic Russia" now a partner, Clinton could look back on the cold war as history and the airlift as the inauguration of the German-American "fight for freedom."[3] In the annals of official memory, the American occupation of Germany was not a gothic romance but a buddy movie.[4]

The airlift and occupation also served to positively dispose Germans, Americans, and the rest of the world to a new era of U.S. foreign policy and a battle against a new global threat. On the tarmac at Tempelhof, Clinton and Kohl spoke as they were framed between an old C-54 transport plane named *The Spirit of Freedom* that flew in the original mission and the new C-17 Globemaster III, which Kohl christened *The Spirit of Berlin*.[5] As Clinton urged on that day, "A new generation must relearn the lessons of the airlift and bring them to bear on the challenges of this new era." Already Germans had themselves embarked on humanitarian ventures when they delivered "the modern equivalent of CARE packages . . . to Bosnia, Afghanistan, and other places ravished by war."[6] But *The Spirit of Berlin*—in both senses of the phrase—would turn up in several other, increasingly incomparable ventures.

Consider these three examples:

1. Just a few months after his German visit, Clinton summoned the airlift again, this time to characterize the U.S. relief effort in Honduras following a hurricane. A national security adviser explained that this use of military power for humanitarian work sent a message to the people of Latin America that the United States is no longer a partner with oppressive regimes but a source of aid and hope in difficult times.[7] If in Germany the airlift made friends of former enemies who had fought on opposite sides of a world war, this relief effort was both an admission and apology that the United States had allied itself with violent dictators in Latin America against the wishes, freedom, and best interests of the people.

2. In October 2001 the United States carried out air raids in Afghanistan in retaliation for the 9/11 attacks on the World Trade Center. During this mission, the *Spirit of Berlin* cargo plane (operating out of the U.S. base in southeast Germany) dropped from dangerously high altitudes ready-to-eat meals over Afghanistan to demonstrate, as one reporter explained, "that the air strikes that began about the same time were not directed against ordinary Afghans" but against the hunted Al Qaeda terrorists. Wrapped in yellow plastic, each bag addressed its hungry recipient in English: "Food gift from the people of the United States of America."[8] In contrast to the original Berlin mission, these meals were not delivered in the war's wake to recondition Afghans' relationship to the U.S. military. Rather, food was dropped in between the "relentless" bombing raids. One U.S. commander observed that this alternating pattern between bombs and food was "unprecedented," despite that the name of the Globemaster suggested that this food drop was in the same "spirit of freedom" as was the airlift over Berlin.[9]

3. By 2003, the *New York Times* reported that Geraldo Rivera "gallantly" hailed the Berlin example to describe U.S. efforts to resupply *American* ground troops with food and *arms* in Iraq.[10] In this admittedly hyperbolic comparison, the airlift does not connect peoples of different countries who like to be free, nor does it make friends of former enemies. Instead, the heroics of the airlift are invoked to describe American military efforts to resupply its own troops for a war against a foreign country. From *The Spirit of Freedom* to *The Spirit of Berlin,* what began as raisins over Germany in 1948 is, by 2003, the supplying of bombs over Iraq.

Before pursuing the uses and abuses of the airlift and occupation any further, however, I want to return to 1998 and the movie theater. Five months after Clinton's visit, Steven Spielberg's *Saving Private Ryan* (1998) premiered in Germany while still enjoying its wide North American release. Acclaimed by the *Washington Post* as "the best war film of our era," this high-budget, sentimental feature, whose gruesome Normandy beach scene earned the film an R rating, was hugely successful in the United States, earning in 1998 alone more than $103 million.[11] For many German reviewers, Spielberg's film was a puzzling return to, and an almost encyclopedic index of, classical Hollywood's formulas. To these critics, *Ryan*'s commercial success was a sign that Americans longed for a narrative of a morally unambiguous, if brutal, war against an uncomplicated enemy.[12] Watching the film in Santa Monica, California, *Die Zeit* film critic Andreas Kilb offered his readers a glimpse into U.S. audiences. American women wept anytime "a bullet, a blade or a bit of shrapnel bore into an American body, or when a youth from either Iowa or Brooklyn exchanged his life for freedom." Men in the audience, however, managed to compose themselves until Tom Hanks's character (Captain Miller) died and the film returned to its present-day framing narrative. "Once again we saw the old man at the cemetery, once again the flag, once again the resounding trumpets. When the lights in the theater came up, everyone was crying."[13] Though no German critic commented on the fact that *Saving Private Ryan* was a loose remake of *The Sullivans* (Bacon, 1944), a war film first screened in Germany during the occupation to model immigrant American life for German imitation,[14] at least one reviewer noted Spielberg's clichéd formulation of the soldierly group ("a Jew, an Italian, and one from the

Midwest—each different and yet all united"). He admitted that even fifty years later, this part of the film was an important celebration of America's "multicultural society" and an always-welcome condemnation of "Nazi racism and ethnic cleansing." Yet he observes that in this film the German solider cannot signify as anything other than a Nazi: "The soldier, the soldierly person as such has, like the two hundred years that imprinted Germany's national spirit, landed on the wrong side of history."[15] This is by no means an embittered response to the war but a reminder that America's moral and military victory of 1945 continued to be differently experienced on both sides of the Atlantic (not surprisingly), despite that politically Germans and Americans were supposed to look and feel the same. Indeed, *Private Ryan*'s tear-jerking patriotism and its final emblematic shot of the U.S. flag reassured Americans poised at the dawn of a new era that however tattered and bleached from debacles of Vietnam, Nicaragua, and Somalia (to name just a few), these were still *their* lucky stars and stripes. It is perhaps not surprising, then, given the moral clarity and patriotic pride evoked by the memories of World War II and the American-led postwar reconstruction, that the ethos of this era and the occupation of Germany became convenient models for promoting the American occupation of Iraq.

Germany and Iraq Fifty-five Years Later

In August 2002, Vice President Dick Cheney defended America's proactive war in Iraq through the narrative of "other times." Evoking World War II, he explained:

> The United States defeated fierce enemies, then helped rebuild their countries, forming strong bonds between our peoples and our governments. Today in Afghanistan, the world is seeing that America acts not to conquer but to liberate, and remains in friendship to help the people build a future of stability, self-determination, and peace. We would act in that same spirit after a regime change in Iraq.[16]

In July 2003, a television journalist in Germany asked Condoleezza Rice if the United States' position in the world (and, in particular, its operations in Iraq) might be compared to the Roman Empire. Rice deflected the implicit critique of U.S. foreign policy with an alternative analogy:

I think rather of what happened after World War II, when the
United States . . . came back to Europe and helped to create a
whole set of institutions . . . and to contribute to the creation of
a new kind of Germany that became an anchor for a democratic
Europe. We're now trying to do that, in a sense, in the Middle East,
with Iraq and with the Palestinian state and with what we've done
in Afghanistan. And there, again, it is the spread of values that will
make the U.S. more secure. And so I think of this rather as a period
of the triumph of states that are committed to a set of values, not
the triumph of the United States alone.[17]

That we may interpret U.S. intervention in Iraq and Afghanistan as
versions of the occupation of Germany and not the imperialism of
the Roman Empire or the neocolonialism of Vietnam, or other less
flattering examples, the Bush administration has urged its critics to
imagine the Iraq war through the experiences of our happier national past: to see, in other words, Saddam Hussein as a latter-day
Hitler; the Baathists as Nazis; and U.S. military incursions in the
Middle East not as a war against the people but as their liberation
from a tyrannical leader.[18] Paul Bremer III, former administrator of
the Coalition Provisional Authority in Iraq, forthrightly compared
Hitler's Germany to Saddam's Iraq when he explained: "Saddam
explicitly modeled his efforts to control Iraqi forces on the Nazis.
Mein Kampf was required reading for members of his intelligence
services."[19] For Bremer, the traces of Nazism in Iraq justified the
U.S. decision to foster not just regime change, but the creation of
"a new Iraq" under American tutelage. The "de-Baathification" of
Iraq, a phrase and process adapted from the "de-Nazification" efforts, suggests both how Germany and the Nazis became shorthand for Saddam's regime, and how the American-led reeducation
effort in Germany became the model for Iraqi political rehabilitation.[20] At the same time, the administration has invoked Nazism
and fascism to describe politically radical Islamism.[21] Against both
Islamic extremism and Saddam's Baathist regime, American liberalism is promoted as the universal standard for global democracy.
Or, as Rice declares above, we should understand U.S. foreign
policy today not as the triumph of American power but as an actu-
alization of a shared "set of values."

Though Iraq is not Germany, nor radical Islam Nazism, and
though today's neoconservatives are not yesterday's cold war lib-

erals, we again find the vocabulary born of the American occupation of Germany circulating in the public domain. The Bush administration has contextualized its Iraq policy with reference to the American national character, "democratic culture," and the centrality of the immigrant experience to U.S. democracy.[22] Traces of psychoculturalism were evident when George W. Bush spoke of how U.S. aid and free trade encourage "the habits of liberty" in Africa and the Middle East. While one did not hear him speak of reeducating or reorienting the Iraqis, Bush has promoted the Iraqi mission as the spreading of "universal values" cherished by the rest of the "civilized world."[23] And anthropology has continued to inform how the U.S. military handles its wards. Seymour M. Hersh reported that the startling U.S. military abuses in Abu Ghraib were informed by Raphael Patai's 1973 book on the Arab national character, *The Arab Mind*, the "bible" to the U.S. administration on Arab behavior.[24] Patai, who like Mead taught cultural anthropology at Columbia University, unwittingly delineated for Washington modes of sexual conduct deemed demoralizing in Arab culture. The U.S. military, in turn, used techniques of sexual humiliation (among other things) as a technology of torture. Germans were not tortured as a matter of official policy. But the very use of an ethnographic study of national character to formulate occupation policy is grounded in the post–World War II era. Just as "enlightened" Germans had immigrated to the United States, proving that not all were paranoid, Patai found that as Arabs were embracing ideas of history and the value of education and sanitation, they too were moving, but only begrudgingly so, toward Western norms.[25]

The German analogue serves to simplify the enemy and manufacture nostalgia for America's last great war. But above all, this antecedent has functioned to whiten, Westernize, and politicize a military occupation that has been deeply inflected by race, religion, and cultural otherness. If the Americans wanted to teach Germans to see race as culture to impose in Germany a politics and capitalist economy compatible with U.S. cold war interests, today the U.S. administration bids Americans to see Iraqi culture only as politics to deflect attention from the brutalizing and homogenizing force of military occupation. America's experience in Iraq, comments Anthony Shadid, is a "microcosm of America's broader struggle with the Arab world, a generational battle . . . waged by two cultures so estranged that they cannot occupy the same place. . . .

Whatever its intentions, the United States was a non-Muslim in-
vader in a Muslim land."[26] Blind to this cultural estrangement,
Bush has declared of the terrorism that continues to plague occupation forces in Iraq: "None of this is the expression of a religion. It
is a totalitarian political ideology, pursued with consuming zeal,
and without conscience."[27] Even as Bush has maintained the insep-
arability of democracy from American culture, he has insisted on
the depoliticization of Islam and separation of Islam from the Iraqi
people, who share "a need for freedom as deep as our own." In this
formulation, the universality of American citizenship is fully consistent with Iraqi culture, because, free of Hussein on the one hand
and radical strains of Islam on the other, Iraqis are really just like
us. Echoing Mead, Brickner, and Patterson discussed in chapter 1,
Bush has found proof of this compatibility by pointing to the millions of Muslims who have immigrated and contributed to Western
"democratic societies," many of whom are now in the service of
the (cultural army of) occupation.[28]

   With this prompt we should return to the import of the immigrant example and the democratizing powers of American culture. In the 1950s Erik Erikson found that American liberalism
produced and exacerbated the very markers of racial and ethnic
difference that the political system tried to manage and erase.
For Erikson, postwar American national identity was wholly inadequate for democracy and genuine liberalism, not least because
"self-contradictions in American history" (he specifically cites the
"open roads of immigration and the jealous island of tradition")
"may expose her youth to an emotional and political short circuit
and thus endanger her dynamic potential."[29] Though he worked
with Mead and Brickner on the "Germany after the War" conference, Erikson was dubious of American normalcy and was far
more attentive to the experiences of American minorities. In his
canonical *Childhood and Society,* Erikson argued that the United
States attempts to create a "super-identity out of all the identities
imported by its constituent immigrants" that adheres to the norms
of white, Anglo-Saxon Protestantism. Within these norms, the
typical American family fosters a kind of democracy that is tolerant
of "different *interests,* but not of different *beings*" (317, emphasis
in original). American schools, likewise, promote "the standardi-
zation of individuality and the intolerance of 'difference'" (245).
Indeed, the average American youth—white, vaguely Protestant—

"more or less sonambulistically moves in a maze of undefined privileges, licenses, commitments and responsibilities"; his "restricted vision" makes him blind to his "less fortunate mates of darker shades, whom he excludes from his home, his clique, and himself, because to see and to face them as actual human beings might cause vague discomfort" (315). "Functioning without friction" is the motto of the individual American, of the family, and of the polity (311). It is the motto of majoritarianism, which responds not to a greater sense of universal justice or pluralism, but adopts a course of action that "is least unacceptable to anybody concerned" (317).[30]

For those who fall outside of the American identity, assimilation (in the case of blacks and Jews) and "reeducation" (in the case of Native Americans) do not bring out their better selves or truer nature but produce the condition of a double exile. Not fully welcome or comfortable in white American society, these physically and culturally marked individuals become estranged from the familial/ ethnic culture in which they were raised. As a result they may develop defensive pathologies that produce the ethnic stereotypes that further mark their difference from American "normality."[31] If, as Erikson maintained, "a sense of identity provides the ability to experience one's self as something that has continuity and sameness, and to act accordingly," the American experience systematically stripped minorities and immigrants of this necessary sense of self and, in its strikingly contradictory history, short-circuited the development of an authentic selfhood even among its majorities (42). In contrast to Mead and Brickner, Erikson, particularly later in his career, found that American modernity was not Nazism's opposite, nor was America's modern industrialization "civilizing" at home or abroad (186). Though not as ruthless as Nazi Germany, the United States, like its Axis enemies, was a military superpower "consolidating human gain" and replacing "universality" with "world domination."[32]

Speaking in 2004 to the global rise of jihadist violence, Olivier Roy argues that the most politically radical, neofundamentalist strains come not from Arab countries but from minority Muslim immigrant populations in Western Europe who, separated from Arab countries, have experienced the "deterritorialization" and "deculturalization" of Islam, which in turn, and in some communities, has encouraged an identification with a Muslim *ethnic* identity and neoreligious commitments.[33] In a similar vein, Susan

Buck-Morss writes that "American hegemony is constitutive of the fundamentalist Islamism that opposes it: U.S. and Israeli state terror is not only the effect but also the cause of the terror that resists it."[34] The pressure of assimilation in the United States and Europe and its "universalizing" foreign policy may well produce the insurgency Americans are attempting to suppress in Iraq.

We Are Not All Americans

While U.S. leaders summon the American occupation of Germany as the "enabling precedent" for regime change in the Middle East, Anne Sa'adah argues that Germans "tend to draw skeptical, even pessimistic lessons from their experience, and they often emphasize its unique and disquieting aspects." As both a "highly exceptional *and* importantly paradigmatic" example, postwar Germany, "'happy ending' notwithstanding . . . should be viewed as a cautionary tale" of regime change and externally imposed democratic formation.[35] Germans emerged from the occupation, she writes, with profound disillusionment over the political maneuvers that brought West Germany into being. Because postwar democracy required that the anti-Nazis find space in the polity for the Nazis, by the 1950s political appeasement prevailed over justice. The rules of law rarely give way to a new era, Sa'adah argues. Instead (and in the spirit of satire) they promote "the survival of yesterday's understanding of justice." Democracy in the wake of revolution, dictatorship, and violent upheaval is necessarily riven with compromise because it is incumbent upon the new regime to accommodate and give political representation to the very people who thwarted democracy (or worse, actively supported violent dictatorship, ethnic cleansing, and terrorism) in the first place.[36] Germany is both exceptional and paradigmatic because its democracy was achieved and sustained through anticommunism, a "reflex" that provided continuity between the new democratic government and the old authoritarian regime, especially under Chancellor Konrad Adenauer, who, Sa'adah writes, "had little difficulty formulating anticommunist appeals unadorned by affirmation of democratic values."[37] The communists were politically neutralized while Jews and other ethnic minorities "were physically eliminated as a significant demographic or political force," thus minimizing the retaliatory impulse for justice. Postwar Germany was ethnically, if not (thanks to anticommunism) politically, homogeneous (308).[38]

Under the American leadership, West German democracy suffered a crisis of legitimation that did not come into full public recognition until the East and West German reunification. In the 1990s, the "us and them" paradigm of the cold war was no longer a sustainable marker of democratic citizenship, and this new political landscape forced Germans to reconstitute and question their liberal commitments.[39]

German skepticism over the experiences of occupation and the limits of postwar democratic invention may also explain why in 2002 Helmut Kohl's successor, Chancellor Gerhard Schröder, ran his faltering reelection campaign not as George W. Bush's doppelgänger, but as an outspoken critic of U.S. foreign policy. The war and subsequent occupation of Iraq precipitated a split between Germany and the United States for the first time since World War II, a break that seemed shocking after more than fifty years of friendship. Constitutionally forbidden to go to war without a UN mandate, Germany, Schröder said, would not join the United States in its attack on Iraq (not even *with* a UN mandate). His minister of justice turned the fun house mirror back on the United States and purportedly accused Bush of mustering support for his war through techniques comparable to Hitler's. And even Schröder's challenger, Edmund Stoiber, critiqued Bush's unilateralism and goal of regime change in Iraq.[40] For many, the breakdown in U.S.–German relations was inconceivable and, in light of the airlift, most certainly ungrateful. *New York Times* Berlin correspondent Steven Erlanger pondered the meaning of these developments:

> Is this shift a reflection of a significantly changed Germany, no longer beholden to its conqueror and liberator from across the sea? Or of a chancellor in trouble using a delicate issue to try to squeak by? Or of a Bush administration that is failing to bring along its own allies? Or of a true friend to America, as Mr. Schröder insists he remains, who is simply speaking truth to power, as a real friend should?[41]

Where in 1949 the *New York Times* could not discern if Germans were really like Americans or just pretending, now the question was whether Germans had really become so *different* from Americans or if they were just acting like it. Stephan Szabo explains that this turn in U.S.–German relations had as much to do with the personalities of two world leaders who rubbed each other the wrong way as it was a consequence of bungled diplomacy on both sides of the Atlantic.[42] But the cultural history of the occupation I have set forth here may also help to explain why Germans might reject participation in a foreign war and nation building explicitly modeled on their own postwar experience. Sensitized to the culture of occupation, disappointed by their own national experience of democracy, and loath to remilitarize in the name of a preemptive war, Germans rejected the politics of American similitude at the moment Germans were asked to help the United States shape another people and government in the American image and to reproduce in Iraq the occupation of Germany. Contra the claims of the *Tomorrow—the World!* Germans had learned that, to rephrase Leona's sermon, "It *does* matter where you are from. We are not all alike, and we are not all American."

Acknowledgments

I have no autobiographical hook that connects me or my family to the American occupation of Germany, and yet because I have spent most of my adult life researching and writing this project, it could not be more personal. Over the years, I have indebted myself to several people and institutions who made this book possible.

This project began as a dissertation in film studies at the University of Wisconsin, where I was fortunate to work with David Bordwell and Vance Kepley Jr. Vance, as both adviser and friend, taught me not only the intricacies of film historiography but the fundamentals of college basketball fandom; both skill sets have served me well in my first job. Marc Silberman shared his video archive of occupation cinema and was equally generous with his time and feedback on my work both during and after graduate school. I feel lucky to have gone through the program with Christine Becker, Lisa Parks, and Michael Kackman. My Madison years were profoundly shaped by Daniel Kowalsky, who endured all of my Sturm und Drang.

The intellectual environment in the Department of English at Michigan State University has enabled me to turn that dissertation into this book. My department chair, Patrick O'Donnell, has supported my work and teaching through his administrative savvy and warm friendship. I thank my perspicacious colleagues Zarena Aslami, A. C. Goodson, Ellen McCallum, Sandra Logan, Judith Stoddart, Karl Schoonover, Stephen Rachman, Judith Roof, Ellen

Pollak, Jeff Wray, and Scott Michaelsen, all of whom contributed in some meaningful way to my academic and social well-being. I'm especially grateful to Justus Nieland, who read and offered incisive feedback on most of this book, even as he was writing his own; I could not ask for a more exemplary colleague or friend. Scott Juengel pored over, commented on, and copyedited every page . . . a few times.

I must acknowledge two especially important teachers during my undergraduate years at Indiana University. Barbara Klinger was my first professorial model, and I still look up to her example. William Rasch, who introduced me to the world of Büchner, Hoffman, and Brecht, has come back into my academic life as a formidable political theorist, mentor, and fellow traveler through Germany's postwar rubble. His encouragement and substantive feedback on the manuscript have made all the difference to this book's completion. Scott Curtis amicably read drafty drafts and helped me plug many holes. This project is also better for having been vetted by Thomas Elsaesser and Heide Fehrenbach, whose work on German cinema and film history have been foundational to my own research. I thank Andrea Kleinhuber and Jason Weidemann at the University of Minnesota Press, the former for her initial enthusiasm for this project and the latter for expertly shepherding this book through to its final stages.

Not all support for this project has been moral and intellectual. Grants from the German-American Fulbright Commission, the German Historical Institute, and the Dissertation Fellowship from the University of Wisconsin Graduate School enabled me to carry out research in the United States and Germany in several archives. The Inter-mural Research Grant from Michigan State University gave me the time to work on the manuscript. For their kindness and professionalism, I thank Dorinda Hartmann at the Wisconsin Center for Film and Theater Research, Anna Kucypera at Frankfurt's Deutsches Filminstitut, and Wolfgang Theis at Berlin's Stiftung Deutsche Kinemathek.

I conclude on a more personal note of gratitude. Abby Wells, my guardian angel of higher education, has supported me financially and morally and with unfathomable generosity throughout my entire life. If I had the talent and space to do it, I would write in her honor a long poem in heroic couplets. Were it not for Abby, I would not be Dr. Fay. And were it not for my parents, Gae Galza and Tom

Fay, I simply would not be. I thank them for giving me life, taking interest in my life, and for encouraging me in my circuitous path to adulthood. My aunt L. Collette Galza (Loie) kept me flush with my favorite English tea snacks when the writing was particularly rough, and she kept me company (and well fed) in Frankfurt during my last tour of research. Because of Loie, I will now associate archival work with the conviviality of fun and loving family. Brendan Fay, Kathleen Fossan, Joan Squires, and Paula Page have given me their support throughout the many years of this project.

Most of all, I thank with all my heart my colleague, friend, and partner Scott Juengel. Other professors may thank their partners for reminding them that there is a world outside of academia, but I thank Scott for showing me the intimate and infinite pleasures of a shared intellectual life.

Notes

Introduction

1. Eric L. Santner also unpacks the layered definitions of *Besetzung* in reference to Anselm Kiefer's photographic series titled "Occupations." Santner, however, routes his etymology through Freud. See Santner's "The Trouble with Hitler: Postwar German Aesthetics and the Legacy of Fascism," *New German Critique* 57 (Winter 1993): 23.

2. Drew Middleton, "Vignettes of a Rudderless Germany," *New York Times,* May 8, 1949, SM10.

3. Stephen Tifft, "Miming the Führer: *To Be or Not to Be* and the Mechanisms of Outrage," *Yale Journal of Criticism* 5, no. 1 (1991): 17.

4. Waite quoted in Tifft, "Miming the Führer," 17.

5. Max Horkheimer and Theodor W. Adorno, *Dialectic of Enlightenment: Philosophical Fragments,* ed. Gunzelin Schmid Noerr, trans. Edmund Jephcott (Stanford, Calif.: Stanford University Press, 2002), 152.

6. Tifft, "Miming the Führer," 2.

7. Fritz Erler, *Democracy in Germany* (Cambridge, Mass.: Harvard University Press, 1965), 39. Erler was the leader of the Social Democratic Party in West Germany.

8. Lucius D. Clay, *Decision in Germany* (Garden City, N.Y.: Doubleday, 1950), 281–82.

9. Margaret Mead, *And Keep Your Powder Dry: An Anthropologist Looks at America* (New York: Berghahn Books, 1942, reprint 2000); Margaret Mead, "The Study of National Character," in *The Policy Sciences,* ed. Daniel Lerner and Harold D. Lasswell (Stanford, Calif.: Stanford University Press, 1951); and Richard Brickner, *Is Germany Incurable?* (New York: J. B. Lippincott, 1943).

10. Russ Castronovo and Dana D. Nelson, "Introduction: Materializing Democracy and Other Political Fantasies," in *Materializing Democracy: Toward a Revitalized Cultural Politics,* ed. Castronovo and Nelson (Durham, N.C.: Duke University Press, 2002), 4.

11. This reflexive pedagogy was, of course, the foundation of Soviet filmmaker and theorist Sergei Eisenstein's early model of film propaganda. He speculated that cinema could produce a series of calculated shocks to recondition the spectator's physiological relationship to Marxist-Leninist principles. These shocks in turn would lead to an intellectual understanding of and positive disposition toward communism. David Bordwell, *The Cinema of Eisenstein* (Cambridge, Mass.: Harvard University Press, 1993), 111–38.

12. Ali Behdad, *A Forgetful Nation: On Immigration and Cultural Identity in the United States* (Durham, N.C.: Duke University Press, 2005), 13. I return to Behdad's reading of immigrant America in chapter 2.

13. Challenging accounts of the wholesale Americanization of West Germany—recent scholarship on the postwar German culture and film especially—have emphasized the myriad ways in which Germans resisted, twisted, and improvised on American mass culture, thwarting U.S. domination and forging a post-Hitler identity and distinctly *national* culture. Heide Fehrenbach, *Cinema in Democratizing Germany: Reconstructing National Identity after Hitler* (Chapel Hill: University of North Carolina Press, 1995). Uta G. Pioger analyzes the oftentimes politically progressive appropriation of American popular culture in both East and West Germany as this culture redefined gender norms and racial relations during the cold war. *Jazz, Rock, and Rebels: Cold War Politics and American Culture in a Divided Germany* (Berkeley: University of California Press, 2000). Covering a later period in German-American cultural relations is Gerd Gemünden's *Framed Visions: Popular Culture, Americanization, and the Contemporary German and Austrian Imagination* (Ann Arbor: University of Michigan Press, 1998), in which he reads German high-art film and visual culture with and against American popular forms.

14. Erler, *Democracy in Germany,* 39–40.

15. Chantal Mouffe, *The Democratic Paradox* (London: Verso, 2000), 10. See also Norberto Bobbio, *Liberalism and Democracy* (London: Verso, 1998); Claude Lefort, *Democracy and Political Theory* (Minneapolis: University of Minnesota Press, 1988), especially part 1, "On Modern Democracy." For a discussion of this paradox as being democratically generative, see Iris Marion Yong, *Inclusion and Democracy* (Oxford, UK: Oxford University Press, 2000).

16. *Public Opinion in Occupied Germany: The OMGUS Surveys, 1945–1949,* ed. Anna J. Jerritt and Richard L. Merritt (Urbana: University of Illinois Press, 1970), 207–8.

17. Victoria de Grazia, *Irresistible Empire: America's Advance through Twentieth-Century Europe* (Cambridge, Mass.: Harvard University Press, 2005), 8. For a cultural history of consumer citizenship in West Germany, especially as it intersects with the construction of postwar femininity, see Erica Carter, *How German Is She? Postwar West German Reconstruction and the Consuming Woman* (Ann Arbor: University of Michigan Press, 1997).

18. House of Representatives, *Postwar Economic Policy and Planning Hearings before the Special Committee on Postwar Economic Policy and Planning*, 79th Cong., part 9, December 20, 1946 (Washington, D.C.: U.S. Government Printing Office, 1947), 2522.

19. Ibid., 2523.

20. Statement of Nathan D. Golden, consultant for motion pictures, Department of Commerce. Ibid., 2547.

21. This logic overlooks the fact that, until 1952, motion pictures were not protected under First Amendment rights, because they were considered commodities first and foremost. Neville March Hunnings, *Film Censors and the Law* (London: George Allen and Unwin, 1967), 151–222; Ruth A. Inglis, *Freedom of the Movies: A Report of Self-Regulation from the Commission on Freedom of the Press* (New York: Da Capo Press, 1974).

22. For a discussion of the Paramount case, see Ernest Borneman, "United States Versus Hollywood: The Case Study of an Antitrust Suit," in *The American Film Industry,* ed. Tino Balio (Madison: University of Wisconsin Press, 1985), 449–62. *Film History* 4, no. 1 (1992) is a special issue on the Paramount case.

23. Gerd Gemünden points out that Shylock's appeal, whose first line in the play is, "I am a Jew. Hath not a Jew eyes?" is purged of its Semitic signifiers. This omission, Gemünden notes, is largely a consequence of the Hollywood censorship code. I address questions of Hollywood's Semitic evasion in chapter 1. Here, for my purposes, it is significant that Lubitsch transforms the plea of the individual actor into a protest by the occupied Poles. "Space Out of Joint: Ernst Lubitsch's *To Be or Not to Be,*" *New German Critique* 89 (Spring/Summer 2003): 72–73.

24. Ibid., 72.

25. Four exemplary studies in film reception are Barbara Klinger, *Melodrama and Meaning: History, Culture, and the Films of Douglas Sirk* (Bloomington: Indiana University Press, 1994); Janet Staiger, *Interpreting Films: Studies in the Historical Reception of American Cinema* (Princeton, N.J.: Princeton University Press, 1992); Janet Staiger, *Perverse Spectators: The Practices of Film Reception* (New York: New York University Press, 2000); and Judith Mayne, *Cinema and Spectatorship* (London: Routledge, 1993).

26. See, for example, Robert R. Shandley, *German Cinema in the*

Shadow of the Third Reich (Philadelphia, Pa.: Temple University Press, 2001); Frank Stern, "Film in the 1950s: Passing Images of Guilt and Responsibility," in *The Miracle Years: A Cultural History of West Germany, 1949–1968,* ed. Hanna Schissler (Princeton, N.J.: Princeton University Press, 2001), 266–80; Wolfgang Becker and Norbert Schöll, *In jenen Tagen . . . Wie der deutsche Nachkriegsfilm die Vergangenheit bewältigte* (Opladen: Leske + Buderich, 1995); Betina Greffrath, *Gesellschaftsbilder der Nachkriegszeit, 1945–1949* (Pfaffenweiler: Centaurus, 1995).

27. Shandley, *German Cinema,* 167–74; Fehrenbach, *Cinema in Democratizing Germany,* 84–89.

28. Mary Louise Pratt, *Imperial Eyes: Travel Writing and Transculturation* (New York: Routledge, 1992), 4.

29. I am not the first to invoke the contact zone to characterize encounters in Germany. In his study of travel guidebooks, *German Travel Cultures* (Oxford, UK: Berg, 2000), Rudy Koshar uses Pratt's model to theorize the intercultural exchanges between travelers and natives (or what he calls "travelees") in nineteenth- and twentieth-century Germany (7). He also notes that American occupation soldiers thought of Germany as both a military territory and a tourist destination (180). Though without explicit reference to Pratt's work, Heide Fehrenbach in *Race after Hitler: Black Occupation Children in Postwar Germany and America* (Princeton, N.J.: Princeton University Press, 2005), also uses the "contact zone" to explain the often intimate interactions between German women and African American occupation soldiers and the way these relationships put pressure on American and German racial constructs (11, 17–18). Rather than use "contact zone" to describe intercultural exchange (as differentiated from unicultural domination) as Koshar and Fehrenbach do, I mean also to invoke the *colonial* context out of which Pratt's formulation emerges.

30. Eyal Benvenisti, *The International Law of Occupation* (Princeton, N.J.: Princeton University Press, rev. ed., 2004), 3.

31. Benvenisti explains that the international law of occupation as dictated by the Hague Regulation stipulates that the people in the occupied territory retain their sovereignty. In the case of Germany, however, the Allies claimed that the territory was under the proviso of "Deballatio" or "subjugation," such that "the defeated state is considered not to exist any longer." Though Japan was equally subject to radical reconstruction under U.S. occupation, it retained its sovereignty insofar as the Japanese government was not completely dissolved with the country's surrender. Benevisti, *The International Law of Occupation,* 91–96. Quote of German legal contestation from 92.

32. The Bush administration has compared Saddam Hussein to Hitler, the Baathists to Nazis, and the American occupation in Iraq to the

American occupation of Germany. See, for example, Paul Bremer, "The Right Call," *Wall Street Journal,* January 12, 2005, A10; Richard Bernstein, "New Agenda: Go It Alone. Remake the World," *New York Times,* March 23, 2003, A1. I return to these examples in the epilogue.

33. Kohl quoted in Eric Malnic, "Berlin Airlift of '48: Mission of Mercy," *Los Angeles Times,* June 28, 1998, A24.

1. Germany Is a Boy in Trouble

1. *Tomorrow—the World!* press book, *Cinema Press Books from the Original Studio Collection,* Wisconsin Center for Film and Theater Research (microfilm, Research Publications), section B, reel 36. All references to advertising, tie-ins, and promotional materials come from the press book unless otherwise noted.

2. Wallace radio address quoted in Uta Gerhardt's "Introduction," in *Talcott Parsons on National Socialism,* ed. Uta Gerhardt (New York: Aldine De Gruyter), 41.

3. Werner Richter, *Re-educating Germany* (Chicago: University of Chicago Press, 1945), 190–93; Richard M. Brickner, M.D., *Is Germany Incurable?* with introductions by Margaret Mead and Edward Strecker (Philadelphia, Pa.: J. B. Lippincott Company, 1943), 265, 299.

4. James F. Tent, *Mission on the Rhine: Reeducation and Denazification in American-Occupied Germany* (Chicago: University of Chicago Press, 1982), 13.

5. Richard Brickner, Talcott Parsons, Margaret Mead, et al., "Germany after the War," *American Journal of Orthopsychiatry* 15, no. 3 (1945): 386. This article was jointly written as the proceedings from a conference called by the Joint Committee on Postwar Planning. See also Uta Gerhardt's discussion of the conference in her introduction to *Talcott Parsons on National Socialism,* 48–52.

6. Erik H. Erikson, "The Legend of Hitler's Childhood," in *Childhood and Society* (New York: W. W. Norton & Co., 1950, 1963, reissued 1985), 326–58. Portions of this essay were first published in 1942 as part of a study Erikson conducted on Nazi character on behalf of the U.S. government. For a discussion of the essay's evolution see Lawrence J. Friedman, *Identity's Architect: A Biography of Erik H. Erikson* (New York: Scribner, 1999), 168–76.

7. In 1945, with little elaboration, Erikson proposed suggestions for the democratic revival of Germany that would posit "the very antithesis" to Hitler's imagery. A democratic Germany would emphasize not youth and masculine values, but rather "the family, the township, and the region as the basis of universal cultural life." Quoted in Friedman, *Identity's Architect,* 172.

8. "*Tomorrow—the World!* Prize Essay Contest Winner," *Senior*

Scholastic, Teacher's Edition 46, no. 15 (May 14, 1945): 32. The essay was first announced in *Senior Scholastic* 45, no. 15 (January 14, 1945): 29. The prizes for the winning essays, predictably enough, included war bonds and Harmon watches.

9. "What Would You Do with Emil Bruckner?" *Comic Cavalcade* 10 (Spring 1945), last page (unpaginated).

10. "*Tomorrow—the World!* Prize Essay Contest Winner," 32. Interestingly, Shirley struggles with American racism in her essay when she notes that Wilhelm would certainly encounter undemocratic facets of American life: "To show Wilhelm Krueger that a high ranking member of the Winfield basketball team is a Negro might have little effect after he had read of the race riots in Detroit. In spite of these handicaps, we know that the good examples could outweigh the bad." Thus, she opts not to teach Wilhelm about race relations but to expose him to American science, industry, and art.

11. For an intriguing examination of Hollywood's Semitic politics, see K. R. M. Short, "Hollywood Fights Anti-Semitism, 1940–1945," in *Film and Radio Propaganda in World War II*, ed. K. M. R. Short (Knoxville: University of Tennessee Press, 1983), 146–72. Short finds that during the war, the Office of War Information attempted to block films addressing Nazi and American anti-Semitism for fear that such themes would awaken American anti-Jewish sentiment or would function to confirm Nazi propaganda that, despite American claims to the contrary, anti-Semitism was an integral part of American democracy. By the time *Tomorrow* was released, the OWI no longer exercised such influence on Hollywood output. Still, the impulse to attenuate Leona's Jewishness in the film but scandalize it in the advertising reflects Hollywood's complicated wartime strategies for representing "the Jewish question." See also Steven Alan Carr, *Hollywood and Anti-Semitism: A Cultural History up to World War II* (Cambridge, UK: Cambridge University Press, 2001); and Gregory D. Black, *Hollywood Censored* (Cambridge, UK: Cambridge University Press, 1994), 70–71, 170–72. Black discusses the overt anti-Semitism of the Production Code Administration under Joseph Breen. Hollywood veered away from Jewish themes, Black argues, likely because of the widely held belief that Jews "owned" Hollywood and were responsible for the degradation of American youth and Christian values.

12. For an elaboration of how wartime Hollywood addressed a female consumerist gaze, see Mary Ann Doane, *Desire to Desire: The Woman's Film of the 1940s* (Bloomington: Indiana University Press, 1987), especially chapter 1.

13. Jean-Paul Sartre, *Anti-Semite and Jew: An Exploration of the Etiology of Hate*, trans. George J. Becker (New York: Schocken Books, 1948; reprint 1995), 57.

14. Two examples come to mind. The first is Rita Hayworth. Born Rita Cansino and the daughter of Spanish vaudeville entertainers, Hayworth began her career as a B-movie actress playing the "dark, full-blooded Latin American heroine." She achieved her A-list status after undergoing plastic surgery, elocution lessons, and a midwesternizing name change. Significantly she could then play, among other roles, Fred Astaire's Argentine love interest in *You Were Never Lovelier* (Seiter, 1942). For a short discussion of Hayworth's transformation see Lary May, *The Big Tomorrow: Hollywood and the Politics of the American Way* (Chicago: University of Chicago Press, 2000), 164–68. Hayworth stands in contrast to Carmen Miranda, whose overembodied ethnicity never allowed her to move beyond stereotypes of Brazilian excess, except insofar as Miranda mobilized her image as a self-parody or masquerade of ethnic performance. See Shari Roberts, "'The Lady in the Tutti-Frutti Hat': Carmen Miranda, A Spectacle of Ethnicity," in *Hollywood Musicals: The Film Reader,* ed. Steven Cohan (New York and London: Routledge, 2002), 143–53. Significantly, Hayworth's *You Were Never Lovelier* was among the first films selected for screening in occupied Germany.

15. Richard Dyer, *The Matter of Images: Essays on Representations* (New York and London: Routledge, 1993), 142.

16. The white actress, Dyer notes, is lighted so that she glows, her body luminous and ethereal. In contrast, darker and/or perspiring working-class subjects are lighted to reflect light so that their bodies' visible surfaces shine or glisten. Richard Dyer, *White* (New York and London: Routledge, 1997), 14, 122.

17. For a discussion of Brickner and other social science influences in U.S. policy, see Uta Gerhardt, "A Hidden Agenda of Recovery: The Psychiatric Conceptualization of Reeducation for Germany in the United States during World War II," *German History* 14, no. 3 (1996): 297–323.

18. Richard M. Brickner, "The German Cultural Paranoid Trend," *American Journal of Orthopsychiatry* 12, no. 4 (October 1942): 623.

19. Brickner, *Is Germany Incurable?* 139.

20. Brickner, "The German Cultural Paranoid Trend," 624.

21. Ibid., 625.

22. Brickner, *Is Germany Incurable?* 305–6.

23. Brickner, "The German Cultural Paranoid Trend," 627.

24. First published as Margaret Mead, *And Keep Your Powder Dry: An Anthropologist Looks at America* (New York: W. Morrow and Co., 1942). All references taken from the 2000 reissue by Berghahn Books, beginning here with page 165.

25. In addition to writing a preface to Brickner's *Incurable* and contributing to the "Germany after the War" conference, Mead served in England during WWII on behalf of the Office of War Information on

morale building. Her husband, Gregory Bateson, worked for the Office of Strategic Services on psychological warfare. Jane Howard, *Margaret Mead: A Life* (New York: Simon and Schuster, 1984), 228–42.

26. Margaret Mead, *And Keep Your Powder Dry*, 7.

27. Margaret Mead, "The Study of National Character," in *The Policy Sciences*, ed. Daniel Lerner and Harold D. Lasswell (Stanford, Calif.: Stanford University Press, 1951), 75.

28. In a footnote, Mead clarifies that this study of national character applies to the northern, midwestern, and western United States but not to the South, where the "bi-racial classification of humanity means that caste is sometimes a directly formative element in developing standards of behavior." *And Keep Your Powder Dry*, 14, fn.

29. I take this idea of the immigrant from Bonnie Honig, *Democracy and the Foreigner* (Princeton, N.J.: Princeton University Press, 2001), 47.

30. Mead, *And Keep Your Powder Dry*, 19.

31. The idea that Europe represents a place of the past is akin to Fatimah Toby Rony's discussion of ethnography's fascination with the "primitive" as prehistoric. When he or she visits a primitive culture, the anthropologist also travels back in time. Thus Rony finds connections between the ethnographic film and science fiction fantasy of time travel. See *The Third Eye: Race, Cinema, and the Ethnographic Spectacle* (Durham, N.C.: Duke University Press, 1996), 129–32.

32. Arjun Appadurai, "Putting Hierarchy in Its Place," *Cultural Anthropology* 3, no. 1 (February 1988): 37.

33. Mead, "The Study of National Character," 70–71.

34. For a discussion of Mead's national character study and its implication for U.S. wartime policy, see Federico Neiberg and Marcio Goldman, "From Nation to Empire: War and National Character Studies in the United States," in *Empires, Nations, and Natives: Anthropology and State-Making*, ed. Benoît de L'Estoile, Federico Neiberg, and Lygia Siguad (Durham, N.C.: Duke University Press, 2005), 108–134.

35. Mead, *And Keep Your Powder Dry*, 152.

36. Ibid., 138.

37. For a brief discussion of Mead's conservative turn, see Micaela di Leonardo, *Exotics at Home: Anthropologies, Others, American Modernity* (Chicago: University of Chicago Press, 1998), 197–98.

38. Mead, *And Keep Your Powder Dry*, 19.

39. Hervé Varenne, "Introduction" to *And Keep Your Powder Dry*, xii.

40. "Germany after the War," 385.

41. Mead, *And Keep Your Powder Dry*, 21–22.

42. For a critique of Hollywood's immigrant mythology, see Judith Mayne, "Immigrants and Spectators," *Wide Angle* 5, no. 2 (1982): 32–40;

and Miriam Hansen, *Babel and Babylon: Spectatorship in American Silent Film* (Cambridge, Mass.: Harvard University Press, 1991), especially chapter 2.

43. Emile De Brigard, "The History of Ethnographic Film," in *Principles of Visual Anthropology*, 2nd ed., ed. Paul Hockings (Berlin, New York: Mouton de Gruyter, 1995), 32. Brigard notes that this study inspired Columbia University's postwar Research in Contemporary Cultures Project under Ruth Benedict's leadership, which gathered researchers from various disciplines who analyzed films, literature, and art to study cultures "at a distance."

44. Gregory Bateson, "An Analysis of the Nazi Film *Hitlerjunge Quex*," *Transactions* 2, no. 4 (1943): 72–78; reprinted in *The Study of Culture at a Distance*, ed. Margaret Mead and Rhoda Métraux (Chicago: University of Chicago Press, 1953), 303 (hereafter *"Hitlerjunge Quex"*). A different version of this essay appears as "Cultural and Thematic Analysis of Fictional Films," in *Personal Character and Cultural Milieu*, ed. Douglas G. Haring (Syracuse, N.Y.: Syracuse University Press, 1949), 117–23 (hereafter "Cultural and Thematic Analysis"). In this discussion I will be referring to both versions of Bateson's essay.

45. Bateson, *"Hitlerjunge Quex,"* 306.

46. For a discussion of Norkus's story and the production history of the film, see Eric Rentschler, *The Ministry of Illusion: Nazi Cinema and Its Afterlife* (Cambridge, Mass.: Harvard University Press, 1996), 53–57.

47. Bateson, "Cultural and Thematic Analysis," 117–18.

48. Bateson, *"Hitlerjunge Quex,"* 311.

49. Bateson, "Cultural and Thematic Analysis," 122.

50. Like Bateson, Kracauer conducted his research at the Museum of Modern Art, which boasted an impressive archive of German cinema; Kracauer even cites Bateson's analysis of *Hitlerjunge Quex* in Siegfried Kracauer, *From Caligari to Hitler: A Psychological History of the German Film* (Princeton, N.J.: Princeton University Press, 1947, reprinted paperback, 1974), 262, n20.

51. Kracauer, "Propaganda and the Nazi War Film," in *From Caligari to Hitler*, 278.

52. Ibid., 303.

53. For a bibliography of Caligari reviews, see Thomas Y. Levin, "The English-Language Reception of Kracauer's Work: A Bibliography," *New German Critique* 54 (Fall 1991): 183–89.

54. Thomas Y. Levin, "Introduction" to Siegfried Kracauer's *The Mass Ornament: Weimar Essays*, ed. and trans. Thomas Y. Levin (Cambridge, Mass.: Harvard University Press, 1995), 15, 350, n30.

55. *From Calagari to Hitler*, 225–26. This argument is most explicit in Kracauer's discussion of *Emil und die Detektive* (*Emil and the Detectives,*

Lamprecht, 1931). Noting that the film approached the liberal spirit of its French and American inspirations, *Emil and the Detectives,* he argues, fails to express the "democratic spirit." Democracy "remains a mood, just strong enough to neutralize the patriarchal tendencies which try to assert themselves in sundry scenes of the film. . . . [T]he conclusion that the democratic attitudes behind the film lack vitality seems unavoidable." It is also striking that upon seeing examples of American postwar film noir, Kracauer became concerned for the health of American liberalism. See his "Hollywood's Terror Films: Do They Reflect an American State of Mind?" *Commentary* 2 (1946): 132–36.

56. Theodor Adorno, "The Curious Realist: On Siegfried Kracauer," *New German Critique,* trans. Shierry Weber Nicholsen, 54 (Fall 1991): 176.

57. Writing in 1944, Adorno and Horkheimer argue that the enlightenment project itself is not the opposite of fascism, as Kracauer maintains in *Caligari,* but, in its most realized form and tied to the demands of a far more insidious (American) capitalism, totalitarian. Moreover, in the famous "Culture Industry" chapter, they attack Hollywood for its complicity with the tyranny and mass deception of so-called liberal mass culture, which purports to serve art to diverse patrons, but in fact incessantly reproduces and masks the empty homogenizing logic of late capitalism. Hollywood films evacuate independent thinking with narratives about individual experience and triumph; these films harden pleasure into boredom and turn citizens into consumers. Max Horkheimer and Theodor W. Adorno, *Dialectic of Enlightenment,* ed. Gunzelin Schmid Noerr, trans. Edmund Jephcott (Stanford, Calif.: Stanford University Press, 2002), 94–136.

58. Confidential report from Office of War Information, London, "Film Policy toward Germany: Guidance for Selection of British and American Motion Pictures for Showing under Occupation," July 21, 1944, papers of the Office of Military Government, United States (hereafter OMGUS), folder 32–33, box 260-3, shipment 10, RG Z45F (microfiche), Bundesarchiv, Koblenz, Germany (hereafter BA).

59. U.S. Committee on Educational Reconstruction, "Re-education of Germany," June 15, 1945, OMGUS, folder 12, box 259-11, shipment 5, record group Z45F, BA.

60. W. D. Patterson to the Office of War Information, March 27, 1944, confidential interoffice memo, "Films for Germany," OMGUS, folder 13, box 17-3, shipment 10, RG, Z45F, BA.

61. Ibid.

62. William Harlan Hale to Dr. William D. Patterson, April 8, 1944, confidential interoffice memo, "Films for Germany," OMGUS, folder 13, box 17-3, shipment 10, record group Z45F, BA.

63. Bernard Barnes to All Division Chiefs and Section Heads (USIS), February 23, 1945, "Draft Operational Plan for Germany," OMGUS, folder 13, box 17-3, shipment 10, RG Z45F, BA.

64. Barrett (no first name given) to Robert McClure, Information Control Division, USIS, August 8, 1945, "Confidential Operational Priority," OMGUS, folder 9, box 17-3, shipment 10, record group Z45F, BA.

65. Elizabeth Stewart Roberts to W. D. Patterson, February 14, 1945, interoffice memo, OMGUS, folder 13, box 17-3, shipment 10, record group Z45F, BA.

66. William Harlan Hale to Dr. William D. Patterson, April 8, 1944, "Films for Germany," confidential interoffice memo.

67. I use the phrase "ethnographic artifact" in the spirit of Barbara Kirshenblatt-Gimblett's observation that objects of ethnography are not originally created as such but constructed by ethnographers through the process of removing objects from their place of origin and exhibiting them as anthropological fragments of a larger cultural whole. Barbara Kirshenblatt-Gimblett, *Destination Culture: Tourism, Museums, and Heritage* (Berkeley: University of California Press, 1998), 20.

68. Robert Joseph, Film Officer, Information Control Division, to Chief of Information Control Division, December 8, 1945, memo, OMGUS, folder 13, box 16-3, shipment 10, record group Z45F, BA.

2. Hollywood's Democratic Unconscious

1. Dennis Bark and David Gress, *A History of West Germany,* vol. 1, *From Shadow to Substance, 1945–1963,* 2nd ed. (Cambridge, UK: Blackwell Press, 1993), 32–33.

2. Norman Davies, *Europe: A History* (Oxford, UK: Oxford University Press, 1996), 1328.

3. W. G. Sebald, *On the Natural History of Destruction,* trans. Athena Bell (New York: Modern Library, 2004), 36.

4. Film, Theater, and Music Division, Information Control Division, "Report on the German Motion Picture Industry in the U.S. Zone," May 22, 1947, memorandum, Office of Military Government, United States, papers (hereafter OMGUS), folder 12, box 17-2, shipment 10, record group Z45F (microfiche), Bundesarchiv, Koblenz, German (hereafter BA).

5. Ibid.

6. Michael Hoenisch, "Film as an Instrument of the U.S. Reeducation Program in Germany after 1945 and the Example of 'Todesmühlen,'" *English Amerikanische Studien* 1–2 (July 1982): 201.

7. Harold Zink, *The United States in Germany, 1944–1955* (Princeton, N.J.: D. Van Nostrand Company, 1957), 244. David Gress and Dennis Bark note that the food crises in Germany at its nadir dropped

to a per capita intake of seven hundred to eight hundred calories a day in 1947, approximating those of the concentration camps (130–31).

8. Dana Adams Schmidt, "Our Movies Leave Germans Hostile: Political and Psychological Regeneration Fails—U.S. Prestige Suffers," *New York Times*, July 23, 1946, 33.

9. Eric Pommer, Film Production Control, Information Control Division, to the Chief, Film, Theater and Music Branch, "Reconstruction and New Organization of the German Film Industry," October 15, 1946, OMGUS, folder 10, box 267-3, shipment 5, record group Z45F, BA. Mark Woodward notes that through 1946, theaters in the American zone played exclusively American films. See his "Formulation and Implementation of U.S. Feature Film Policy in Occupied Germany, 1945–1948," Ph.D. diss., University of Texas at Dallas, 1987, 135.

10. For a discussion of German misinterpretations of Allied policy, especially in the first years of the occupation, see Josef Foschepoth, "German Reaction to Defeat and Occupation," in *West Germany under Construction: Politics, Society, and Culture in the Adenauer Era,* ed. Robert E. Moeller (Ann Arbor: University of Michigan Press, 1997), 73–89. Foschepoth notes that although the U.S. military government discarded collective guilt in 1945, this doctrine caught on with the German population as a means of explaining postwar privations.

11. For a discussion of the film's production and reception history see Hoenisch, "Film as an Instrument," 196–210.

12. While the German and English language print is the same, there are some differences in the translation. I had access to the English language print at the National Archives, Suitland, Maryland. This text is taken from the German language voice-over, translated in ibid., 210.

13. Information Control Branch condemned this compulsory viewing of the film as a misinterpretation of U.S. policy. J. H. Hills, Col. GSC, to the Chief of ICD, "Compulsory Showing of Atrocity Films," February 18, 1946, OMGUS papers, folder 10, box 17-3, shipment 10, record group Z45F, BA. Heide Fehrenbach also discusses the film's reception in Germany in *Cinema in Democratizing Germany: Reconstructing National Identity after Hitler* (Chapel Hill: University of North Carolina Press, 1995), 58.

14. Motion Picture Branch Report, "Film Situation in All the Zones of Germany, Dec. 1945–April 1946," May 5, 1946, OMGUS, folder 1, box 11-3, shipment 10, record group Z45F, BA.

15. *The Human Comedy* review, *Variety*, March 3, 1943.

16. Friedrich Michel to Filmkontrolle, Frankfurt, November 20, 1945, OMGUS, folder 13, box 16-3, shipment 10, record group Z45F, BA.

17. It is very likely that the military government would have paired *Human Comedy* and *The Town* on a film program.

18. Motion Picture Branch, "Operation Report," March 21, 1949, OMGUS, folder 4, box 265-1, shipment 5, record group Z45F, BA.

19. Carrie Tirado Bramen, *The Uses of Variety: Modern Americanism and the Quest for National Distinctiveness* (Cambridge, Mass.: Harvard University Press, 2000), 17.

20. "Film in Germany during the Period of Military Occupation," February 24, 1944, OMGUS, folder 13, box 17-3, shipment 10, record group Z45F, BA.

21. Office of War Information, Washington, D.C., "On Films for Germany," March 27, 1945, confidential memo, OMGUS, folder 13, box 17-3, shipment 10, record group Z45F, BA.

22. Office of War Information, London Office, "Film Policy towards Germany: Guidance for Selection of British and American Motion Pictures for Showing under Occupation," July 21, 1944, OMGUS, folder 32-33, box 260-3, shipment 5, record group Z45F, BA.

23. William H. Kennedy to William Patterson, "Memorandum: German Propaganda," February 6, 1945. OMGUS, folder 13, box 17-3, shipment 10, record group Z45F, BA.

24. Office of War Information, London Office, "Film Policy towards Germany."

25. "Films in Germany during the Period of Military Occupation" (summary of the German Subcommittee of the Psychological Warfare Division Meeting), February 2, 1944, OMGUS, folder 13, box 17-3, shipment 10, record group Z45F, BA.

26. Office of War Information, Washington, D.C., "Draft for Operational Plan for Germany," February 23, 1945, OMGUS folder 13, box 17-3, shipment 10, record group Z45F, BA.

27. Office of War Information, London Office, "Film Policy towards Germany."

28. "Films in Germany during the Period of Military Occupation."

29. Barrett (no first name given) to Robert McClure, Information Control Division, USIS, "Confidential, Operational Priority," August 8, 1945, OMGUS, folder 9, box 17-3, shipment 10, record group Z45F, BA.

30. For a summary of OWI pretests on German POWs, see Woodward, "Formulation and Implementation of U.S. Feature Film Policy," 763–69.

31. Ibid., 64–65.

32. OWI Survey Section Report No. 137, quoted in Woodward, 66.

33. Dana Adams Schmidt, "Our Movies Leave Germans Hostile," *New York Times,* July 23, 1946, 33. Among the thirty-five films to play in Germany during the first few months were *Across the Pacific* (Huston, 1942), *Action in the North Atlantic* (Bacon, 1943), *Air Force* (Hawks, 1943), *Covette K-225* (Rosson, 1943), *The Maltese Falcon* (Huston, 1942),

I Married a Witch (Clair, 1942), *Shadow of a Doubt* (Hitchcock, 1943), *The Sullivans* (Bacon, 1944), *Thirty Seconds over Tokyo* (LeRoy, 1944), *You Were Never Lovelier* (Seiter, 1942), *Sun Valley Serenade* (Humberstone, 1942), *Madame Curie*, (LeRoy, 1943), *Christmas in July* (Sturges, 1940), *The Gold Rush* (Chaplin, 1942 rerelease with sound), *The Human Comedy* (Brown, 1943), *The Navy Comes Through* (Sutherland, 1942), *Pride and Prejudice* (Leonard, 1940), and *My Sister Eileen* (Hall, 1942). List compiled from Robert Joseph, "Our Film Program in Germany: "How Far Was It a Success?" *Hollywood Quarterly* 2, no. 2 (January 1947): 124–25. Joseph worked in the Motion Picture Branch of the U.S. military government for Germany. See also Bernard Barnes, "Draft Operational Plan for Germany," January 20, 1945, OMGUS, folder 10, box 17-3, shipment 13, record group Z45F, BA.

34. For a list of all the Hollywood films that played in Germany during the occupation, see "OWI and MPEA Releases in Germany, 1945–1949," Academy of Motion Picture Arts and Sciences, Special Collections, Motion Picture Industry Council Collection, box 2, folder 15.

35. The MPEA companies were Columbia Pictures International Corp., Loew's International Corp., Paramount International Film, RKO-Radio Pictures, 20th Century Fox International Corp., Warner Bros. Pictures International Corp., and United Artists.

36. MPEA representative Francis Harmon describes this process in House of Representatives, 79th Congress, part 9, December 20, 1946, *Postwar Economic Policy and Planning Hearings before the Special Committee on Postwar Economic Policy and Planning* (Washington, D.C.: U.S. Government Printing Office, 1947), 2567–573.

37. Film Control Office of Film, Theater, Music Branch, memo, May 28, 1946, OMGUS, folder 1, box 11-3, shipment 10, record group Z45F, BA. In subsequent memos, Civil Affairs Division rejects this policy on the grounds that it is too inefficient and grants German critics too much authority over U.S. policy. See Nils Nelson, Chief of Film Control, to Chief of the Film, Theater, Music Branch, letter, June 3, 1946, OMGUS, folder 1, box 11-3, shipment 10, record group Z45F, BA.

38. W. D. Patterson, Office of War Information, to C. D. Jackson, interoffice memo, March 27, 1944, OMGUS, folder 13, box 17-3, shipment 10, record group Z45F, BA.

39. "Selection of Motion Pictures Shown to German Youth," Motion Picture Branch, September 20, 1946, OMGUS, folder 2, box 11-3, shipment 10, record group Z45F, BA.

40. Gunter Groll, "Im Atlantic nicht Neues . . . ," Munich, October 2, 1946 (I believe this is from the *Süddeutsche Zeitung* where Groll worked, but it is marked only by the date and city of origin). Press clippings for

Corvette K-225, Deutsches Institute für Filmkunde/Deutsches Film-museum, Frankfurt a. M (hereafter DIF).

41. Report quoted in Woodward, "Formulation and Implementation of U.S. Feature Film Policy," 234.

42. Herr Prof. Dr. Van de Well, Religiöse Gesellschaft der Freunde, to the Motion Picture Branch, Berlin, confidential letter, November 12, 1946, Eric Pommer collection, folder 8, box 8-2, shipment 4, Stiftung Deutsche Kinemathek, Berlin (hereafter SDK).

43. Information Control Division report #64, "German Reaction to American Films," 1946 (no month or day given), OMGUS, folder 10, box 267-3, shipment 5, record group Z45F, BA.

44. Information Control Division, "Reactions of German Civilians to a Program of Short Films," July 20, 1945, OMGUS, folder 32, box 260-3, shipment 5, record group Z45F, BA.

45. Information Control Division, "The Film Situation in All Zones," May 5, 1946, OMGUS, folder 1, box 11-3, shipment 10, record group Z45F, BA.

46. Gladwin Hill, "Our Film Program in Germany: How Far Was It a Failure?" *Hollywood Quarterly* 2, no. 2 (January 1947): 135. Hill was the correspondent for the Associated Press and *New York Times.*

47. ICD complains that the MPEA, concerned about its short-term profits, will not release its most prestigious films or provide a larger selection of films from which to choose. Information Control Division, "Motion Picture Program for Germany," confidential memorandum, August 25, 1945, OMGUS, folder 1, box 267-3, shipment 5, record group Z45F, BA. There is a similar discussion in 1946 when the Film Branch complained that the films on the MPEA list did not have clear reeducation messages and that the Film Division needed a greater selection of titles. Film Control to Chief of Film, Theater, and Music Branch, memo, June 3, 1945, OMGUS, folder 1, box 11-3, shipment 10, record group Z45F, BA.

48. Dana Adams Schmidt, "Our Movies Leave Germans Hostile," *New York Times,* July 23, 1946, 33.

49. Eric T. Clarke to Col. Kinard of Film, Theater, Motion Picture Branch, May 28, 1946, OMGUS, folder 2, box 11-3, shipment 10, record group Z45F, BA.

50. Ruth Vasey, *The World according to Hollywood, 1918–1939* (Madison: University of Wisconsin Press, 1997), 159.

51. Clayton R. Koppes and Gregory D. Black, *Hollywood Goes to War: How Politics, Profits, and Propaganda Shaped World War II Movies* (Berkeley: University of California Press, 1987), 71. For a discussion of the OWI Common Law in particular, see 63–81.

52. Sigmund Freud, *The Psychopathology of Everyday Life: The*

Standard Edition, ed. and trans. James Strachey (New York: Norton, 1965), especially "Combined Parapraxes" and "Determinism, Belief in Chance, and Superstition—Some Points of View," 295–355. For an excellent discussion of how Freud's formulation of parapraxis can model cultural studies analysis, see John Mowitt, "Stumbling on Analysis: Psychoanalysis and Everyday Life," *Cultural Critique* 52 (Fall 2002): 61–85.

53. Michael Walzer, *What It Means to be an American* (New York: Marsilio, 1996), 31, 35.

54. Bonnie Honig, *Democracy and the Foreigner* (Princeton, N.J.: Princeton University Press, 2001), 75.

55. Ali Behdad, *A Forgetful Nation: On Immigration and Cultural Identity in the United States* (Durham, N.C.: Duke University Press, 2005), 3.

56. Freud writes about perception as a reality testing mechanism that enables an individual to substantiate internal imaginings (images) against the external world (perception). As Freud explains, this reality testing is "not to *find* an object in real perception which corresponds to the one presented, but to *re-find* such an object, to convince oneself that it is still there" (668, italics original). What he calls the "reproduction of a perception as a presentation" is rarely faithful; it is always subject to distortions. Negation is one means by which an individual negotiates the gap between subjective images and objective perception and makes judgments about incorporation. Film images (which Freud does not, of course, discuss) would constitute an external perception even if the images themselves bear no relation to any kind of political reality. Sigmund Freud, "Negation," in *The Freud Reader,* ed. Peter Gay (New York: Norton, 1989), 666–69.

57. Diane Negra, *Off-White Hollywood: American Culture and Ethnic Female Stardom* (London and New York: Routledge, 2001), 87.

58. Anton Kaes, *M* (London: BFI, 1999), 57.

59. Promotional material quoted in Eric Rentschler, *The Ministry of Illusion: Nazi Cinema and Its Afterlife* (Cambridge, Mass.: Harvard University Press, 1998), 155. Also central to my argument, Rentschler explains that Nazi anti-Semitism hinges on the Jew's deceptive features that mask his racial origins to all but the most perspicacious observer. The Jew's facility for disguises is specifically dramatized in Veit Harlan's *Jud Süß* (1940). Rentschler, 149–69.

60. Kaes, *M,* 71.

61. Moto almost gets killed in the process but is saved at the last moment by Connie (Virginia Field), who turns on her traitorous boyfriend because in one of Port Said's local theaters she watches a Movietone newsreel about the fragile state of international peace and decides to help her country rather than her boyfriend.

62. Katrin Sieg, *Ethnic Drag: Performing Race, Nation, and Sexuality in West Germany* (Ann Arbor: University of Michigan Press, 2002), 85.

63. "How to Tell Your Friends from the Japs," *Time*, December 22, 1941, 33.

64. Stimson quoted in Michi Nishiura Weglyn, *Years of Infamy: The Untold Story of America's Concentration Camps* (Seattle: University of Washington Press, 1976, reprint 1996), 43.

65. Roger Daniels, *Prisoners without Trial: Japanese Americans in World War II*, rev. ed. (New York: Hill and Wang, 2004), 46.

66. John W. Dower, *War without Mercy: Race and Power in the Pacific War* (New York: Pantheon Books, 1986), 530–57.

67. Capra's *Why We Fight* series along with *Know Your Enemy, Japan* were inspired by the rousing visual effects and persuasive graphics of Riefenstahl's *Triumph of the Will*. Claudia Springer, "Military Propaganda: Defense Department Films from World War II and Vietnam," *Cultural Critique* 3 (Spring 1986): 151.

68. I borrow the phrase "Hollywood Indian English" from Charles Ramírez Berg, "The Margin as Center: The Multicultural Dynamics of John Ford's Western," in *John Ford Made Westerns: Filming the Legend in the Sound Era*, ed. Gaylyn Studar and Matthew Bernstein (Bloomington: Indiana University Press, 2001), 88.

69. Ibid., 76.

70. See Lang's unfinished autobiography in Lotte H. Eisner, *Fritz Lang* (New York: De Capo Press, 1976), 14–15.

71. Sieg explains that this fantasy of the Wild West was derived principally from Karl May novels, such as the *Winnetou* trilogy first published in 1893. These narratives were revived as stage plays and films in the postwar period as responses to the Hollywood westerns Germans encountered during the occupation. In May's novels, the German "westmen" befriend the Indians and try to repair the "colonial atrocities" they suffer at the hand of white American frontiersman (78). In addition, the Winnetou series was the backdrop for the annual festival that began in Bad Segeberg in 1952, which includes in its many installations the Indian Village. Sieg argues that May's Wild West fantasy, reinvigorated through the generic vocabulary of the American western, gave Germans a generative, dehistoricized myth through which they could cope with the historically specific crises of postoccupation, post-Holocaust German identity. In particular, these dramas "substituted guilt with pride and facilitated an imagined trading of places between the victors and the victimized" (81). The myth of the American West functioned for Germans like the myth of immigrant America for citizens of the United States; that is, as Behdad theorizes, a forgetful narrative, or what Sieg calls a "technology of forgetting." *Ethnic Drag*, 73–84.

72. Lutz Koepnick, *The Dark Mirror: German Cinema between Hitler and Hollywood* (Berkeley: University of California Press, 2002), 102.

3. Garbo Laughs and Germans Eat

1. Despite this shift in policy, most of the feature films discussed in chapter 2 remained in circulation until 1949.

2. Otis Ferguson, "Mr. Capra Goes Someplace," *New Republic* 100 (November 1, 1939): 370.

3. Philip T. Hartung, "Garbo Laughs!" *Commonweal* 31 (November 3, 1939): 47; "Ninotchka," *Time* 34 (November 6, 1939): 76. On audience laughter, see Frank S. Nugent, "Entirely a Laughing Matter: Garbo's Ninotchka," *New York Times*, November 19, 1939, X5; "Movie Humor—No Laughing Matter," *New York Times*, March 3, 1940, 105.

4. *Daily Mirror* quoted in the *Sunday Worker* (New York), November 19, 1939. *Ninotchka* press clippings, Press Archive, Academy of Motion Picture Arts and Sciences, Margaret Herrick Library, Los Angeles.

5. C. L. Sulzerberger, "Foreign Affairs: American Seen through a Glass Darkly," *New York Times*, April 13, 1955, 28. For the Soviet protest of *Ninotchka*'s Italian release see "Russians Protest Film," *New York Times*, March 31, 1948, 31; and "Italians Refuse to Ban Film," *New York Times*, April 2, 1948, 27.

6. For a discussion of the Soviet reeducation program, see Norman M. Naimark, *The Russians in Germany: A History of the Soviet Zone of Occupation, 1945–1949* (Cambridge, Mass.: Harvard University Press, 1995), 398–464.

7. "Russian Film Principles," *Der Tagesspiegel,* translated in "Motion Picture Branch Report," December 13, 1947, Office of Military Government, U.S. papers (hereafter OMGUS), folder 6, box 11-1, shipment 10, record Group Z45F (microfiche), Bundesarchiv Koblenz, Germany (hereafter BA).

8. Files of the Motion Picture Branch, OMGUS, 1946–1952, Eric Pommer Collection, box B, folder 10, Cinema and Television Library, University of Southern California.

9. "Reports, 28 May 1948–2 June 1948," Film Section, Information Control Branch, May 20, 1948, Carl Winston Papers, Stiftung Deutsche Kinemathek, Berlin (hereafter SDK).

10. A brief description of these plays is found in Naimark, *The Russians in Germany,* 426–27.

11. Chief, New York Field Office, to Chief, Civil Affairs Division, Washington, D.C., "Proposed Information Policy," July 20, 1948, OMGUS, folder 22, box 261-3, shipment 5, record group Z45F, BA.

12. Victoria de Grazia, *Irresistible Empire: America's Advance through*

Twentieth-Century Europe (Cambridge, Mass.: Harvard University Press, 2005), 8.

13. These surveys, conducted on average every third week, were circulated among the highest levels of occupation authority and were instrumental in the formulation of American information policy. See Anna J. Merritt and Richard L. Merritt, "Introduction," in *Public Opinion in Occupied Germany: The OMGUS Surveys, 1945–1949*, ed. Anna J. Merritt and Richard L. Merritt (Champaign: University of Illinois Press, 1970), 3–16.

14. "Attitudes of AMZON Germans Towards Government and Politics," Report No. 74, October 27, 1947, in *Public Opinion in Occupied Germany*, 178–79.

15. My discussion of choiceworthiness (and the very term itself) is indebted to Bonnie Honig, *Democracy and the Foreigner* (Princeton, N.J.: Princeton University Press, 2001).

16. "Proposed Information Policy," July 20, 1948.

17. Woman quoted in Naimark, *The Russians in Germany*, 427.

18. Film Section Report 119, "Opening of *Ninotchka*," December 27, 1948, OMGUS, folder 6, box 2-3, shipment 4, record group 260, Eric Pommer Papers, SDK.

19. John Borneman, *Belonging in the Two Berlins: Kin, State, and Nation* (Cambridge, UK, and New York: Cambridge University Press, 1992), 78–79 (all quotes hereafter refer to these two pages).

20. Ibid., 79. For other discussions of the West German satiric state, see Friedemann Weidauer, Alan Lareau, and Helen Morris-Keitel, "The Politics of Laughter: Problems of Humor and Satire in the FRG Today," in *Laughter Unlimited: Essays on Humor, Satire, and the Comic*, ed. Reinhold Grimm and Jost Hermand (Madison: University of Wisconsin Press, 1991), 56–78.

21. Jeffrey Herf, *Divided Memory: The Nazi Past in the Two Germanys* (Cambridge, Mass., and London: Harvard University Press, 1997), 201.

22. Robert R. Shandley, *Rubble Films: German Cinema in the Shadow of the Third Reich* (Philadelphia, Pa.: Temple University Press, 2001), 151–80.

23. Borneman, *Belonging in Two Berlins*, 16.

24. Hannah Arendt, "The Aftermath of Nazi Rule: Report from Germany," *Commentary* 10 (October 1950): 343.

25. Heide Fehrenbach, *Cinema in Democratizing Germany: Reconstructing National Identity after Hitler* (Chapel Hill: University of North Carolina Press, 1995), 84–89.

26. "Warum ist der Apfel ab? Die geistigen Hintergründe einer 'Filmkomödie,'" *Westfälische Nachrichten*, February 10, 1949, press clippings

for *Der Apfel ist ab,* Helmut Käutner Archiv, folder 44, Stiftung Archiv der Akademie der Künste, Berlin (hereafter AdK).

27. "Der fröhliche Sündenfall: Uraufführung des Käutner-Films," *Hamburger Echo,* November 26, 1948, press clippings for *Der Apfel,* Helmut Käutner Archiv, folder 2143, AdK.

28. Shandley, *Rubble Films,* 1.

29. "'Wohin rollt der Apfel?': Ein Gespräch mit Helmut Käutner," *Die neue Filmwoche* 45 (December 5, 1948): 517.

30. For a discussion of the church's censorship rationale, see Heide Fehrenbach, "Persistent Myths of Americanization: German Reconstruction and the Renationalization of Postwar German Cinema, 1945–1965," in *Transactions, Transgressions, Transformations: American Culture in Western Europe and Japan,* ed. Heidi Fehrenbach and Uta G. Poiger (New York: Berghahn, 2000), 88.

31. "Das Publikom ist dran Schuld!" *Evangelischer Film-Beobachter* 3 (February 1, 1949): 27.

32. Alan Keenan, *Democracy in Question: Democratic Openness in a Time of Political Closure* (Stanford, Calif.: Stanford University Press, 2003), 11–12.

33. Ibid., 12.

34. One example of a foreign founder is Moses, an Egyptian (especially in Freud's reading *Moses and Monotheism*), who gives the Israelites the law as dictated by God. But once the people reach the promised land, Moses dies or disappears. Honig, *Democracy and the Foreigner,* 15–40.

35. "Trends in German Public Opinion: Report no. 175," June 1949, in *Public Opinion in Occupied Germany,* 294–95.

36. Ibid., 179.

37. Fehrenbach, *Cinema in Democratizing Germany,* 86.

38. Russell Merritt, *Democracy Imposed: U.S. Occupation Policy and the German Public, 1945–1949* (New Haven, Conn.: Yale University Press, 1995), 318–19.

39. Theodor W. Adorno, *Minima Moralia: Reflections on a Damaged Life,* trans. E. F. N. Jephcott (London: Verso, 1978), 209–12.

40. *Der Apfel*'s credit sequence pays ironic homage to *Welt im Film.* The newsreel title is superimposed over an image of the revolving Earth; Käutner's credits unfold over an image of a revolving cartographic apple that bears traces of the Earth's continents. This Earth/apple, however, is home to a hungry worm that has taken a bite out of Germany.

41. Roger Smither, "*Welt im Film*: Anglo-American Newsreel Policy," in *The Political Re-education of Germany and Her Allies after World War II,* ed. Nicholas Pronay and Keith Wilson (London: Croom Helm, 1985), 161.

42. *World in Film* episodes discussed in this essay are in German. All

translations are mine. Prints are located at the Motion Picture, Sound, and Video Branch, National Archives at College Park, Maryland.

43. Carolyn Woods Eisenberg argues that the currency reform was in clear violation of the Postdam Agreement and was thus initially unpopular with the international community. The Soviet blockade was an attempt to forestall the division of Germany, but as Eisenberg notes, this initiative backfired, producing instead a narrative of American humanitarianism in the face of Soviet brutality. *Drawing the Line: The American Decision to Divide Germany, 1944–1949* (Cambridge, UK: Cambridge University Press, 1996), 8–10.

44. "The American Note of July 6," *The Berlin Crisis: A Report on the Moscow Discussions,* 1948 (Washington, D.C.: U.S. Government Printing Office, 1948), 1–6.

45. "The Soviet Note of July 14," *The Berlin Crisis,* 10–14.

46. "Memorandum: The Soviet Election Propaganda Stressing U.S. Bombing of Berlin" to Cordon E. Textor, Colonel, Information Control Division (no author listed), December 3, 1948, OMGUS, folder 22, box 261-3, shipment 2, RG Z45F, BA.

47. Sergei Eisenstein, "The Montage of Film Attractions," in *The Eisenstein Reader,* ed. Richard Taylor (London: BFI, 1998), 40.

48. For a discussion of the airlift and the embodied stakes of American aid, see Petra Goedde, *GIs and Germans: Culture, Gender, and Foreign Relations, 1945–1949* (New Haven, Conn.: Yale University Press, 2003), 180–89.

49. This analysis is based on the English-language print at the Motion Picture, Sound, and Video Branch, National Archives, at College Park, Maryland. I assume that German audiences would have seen the German-language version almost identical to this one.

50. Benedict Anderson, *Imagined Communities: Reflections on the Origin and Spread of Nationalism,* rev. ed. (New York: Verso Press, 1991), 87.

51. David Campbell, *Writing Security: United States Foreign Policy and the Politics of Identity* (Manchester, UK: Manchester University Press, 1992), 56.

52. For the record, it was U.S. Air Force pilot Gail Halvorsen who first dropped the candy from the planes. Eric Malnic, "Berlin Airlift of '48: Mission of Mercy," *Los Angeles Times,* June 28, 1998, A24.

53. Harold Zink, *The United States in Germany, 1944–1955* (New York: D. Van Nostrand Company, 1957), 243.

54. Exhibitor quoted in Smither, "*Welt im Film,*" 161.

55. "Wochenshau im Spiegel der Offenlichkeit," *Film Echo,* June 10, 1949, 1.

56. Only in Berlin could audiences see newsreels produced by the French and Soviet government.

57. F. L., "Humorloses Weltgefühl: Neuauffürung von Lubitschs Ninotchka," *Die Welt,* July 13, 1955. Press clippings for *Ninotchka,* Deutsches Institute für Filmkunde, Frankfurt am Main.

4. That's Jazz Made in Germany

1. For a discussion of the American musical's celebration of American folk culture, see Jane Feuer, *The Hollywood Musical* (London: BFI, 1982), 1–22. A brief discussion of the German revue musical is in Sabine Hake, *German National Cinema* (New York: Routledge, 2002), 74.

2. Michael H. Kater writes that Hielscher, while employed at the Terra Filmkunst studio, was courted by Joseph Goebbels, whose typical seduction involved a private screening of *Gone with the Wind.* Leaving aside for the moment Goebbels's appropriation of Hollywood cinema as pornography, Kater notes that Goebbels was taken with Hielscher's resemblance to Vivien Leigh. Hielscher, however, was not particularly taken with Goebbels. When her singing career began to take off and as she modeled herself after American popular singers whose style the Nazis denounced, Goebbels took revenge on Hielscher, saying, as Kater recounts, "that her mouth was much too large, that it was an American mouth, 'not a good German mouth.'" *Different Drummers: Jazz in the Culture of Nazi Germany* (Oxford, UK: Oxford University Press, 1992), 183–84.

3. Margaret Mead, *And Keep Your Powder Dry: An Anthropologist Looks at America* (New York: Berghahn Books, 2000), 12.

4. Walter's line first came to my attention in Uta G. Poiger's brief discussion of this film in *Jazz Rock and Rebels: Cold War Politics and American Culture in a Divided Germany* (Berkeley: University of California Press, 2000), 70.

5. In her research on 1950s West Germany, Maria Höhn similiarly argues that German racism directed against black American GIs was not taken to be a vestige of Nazism. Rather, social conservatives "cited the model of racial segregation of their American mentor as informing their own convictions." *GIs and Fräuleins: The German-American Encounter in 1950s West Germany* (Chapel Hill: University of North Carolina Press, 2002), 14. See also 91–103.

6. Sally Marks, "Black Watch on the Rhine: A Study in the Propaganda of Prejudice and Prurience," *European Studies Review* 13 (1983): 297–334.

7. Adolf Hitler, quoted in Michael Burleigh and Wolfgang Wippermann, *The Racial State: Germany, 1933–1945* (Cambridge, UK: Cambridge University Press, 1991), 128.

8. Ibid., 37.

9. "Report of the Negro Newspaper Publishers Association to the

Honorable Secretary of War, Judge Robert P. Patterson, on Troops and Conditions in Europe," July 18, 1946, in *Blacks in the Military, Essential Documents*, ed. Bernard C. Nalty and Morris J. MacGregor (Wilmington, Del.: Scholarly Resources, 1981), 209–11.

10. Heide Fehrenbach notes that while most Germans initially greeted African American GIs with a mixture of "trepidation and disgust" (32), by 1948 many of the occupied came to regard black GIs as more open, friendly, and generous than their white American counterparts and that black soldiers finally found Germans to be far more accepting of racial difference than Americans back home. Fehrenbach emphasizes above all the intimate contact between Germans and black soldiers that created new networks of racial signification for both groups. *Race after Hitler: Black Occupation Children in Postwar Germany and America* (Princeton, N.J.: Princeton University Press, 2005), especially 17–45.

11. "Report of the Negro Newspaper Publishers Association," 211.

12. As Höhn notes, however, in the 1950s Germans came into increasingly intimate contact with black GIs. For many of these African American soldiers, the German tour "offered unprecedented levels of prosperity, social mobility, and freedom." Höhn cautions, however, that these experiences tell us more about American racisms and the intolerance these GIs experienced in the United States than it does about German acceptance of racial difference (103).

13. Secretary of War Robert P. Patterson to the deputy chief of staff, memorandum, January 7, 1947, in *Blacks in the Military, Essential Documents*, 216.

14. Elizabeth Heineman, "The Hour of the Woman: Memories of Germany's 'Crisis Years' and West German National Identity," *American Historical Review* 101, no. 2 (April 1996): 384.

15. Ibid., 387. In a similar treatment of a different occupation, Mary Layoun explores how the Turkish military invasion and occupation of Cypress are figured as rape in Cypriot fiction. Layoun, "The Female Body and 'Transnational' Reproduction, or Rape by Any Other Name?" in *Scattered Hegemonies: Postmodernity and Transnational Feminist Practices*, ed. Inderpal Grewal and Caren Kaplan (Minneapolis: University of Minnesota Press, 1994), 63–75.

16. For a broader discussion of Jews in postwar German film, see Frank Stern, "Film in the 1950s: Passing Images of Guilt and Responsibility," in *The Miracle Years: A Cultural History of West Germany, 1949–1968*, ed. Hanna Schissler (Princeton, N.J.: Princeton University Press, 2001), 266–80.

17. Information Control Division, Research Branch, to Chief, Information Control Division, "Comments on Lang ist der Weg," July 15, 1947, Office of Military Government, United States, papers (hereafter

OMGUS), folder 14, box 16-3, shipment 10, record group Z45F (microfiche), Bundesarachiv, Koblenz, German (hereafter BA) .

18. *Charly* was made by the Cinephon Film Company under the supervision of the British military government months before Jugert's film opened. I have been unsuccessful in finding a print of this film to watch. The plot descriptions here are based on the *12 Herzen für Charly* press books, Textarchiv, Das Deutsche Filminstitut Frankfurt, Germany (hereafter DIF).

19. *Die Neue Zeitung* quoted in the "Pressestimmen" page of the press book, ibid.

20. Arthur Mayer, U.S. Government, Motion Picture Branch, to Fortuna Filmverleih, GmBh, June 1, 1949, letter, OMGUS, folder 6, box 268-2, shipment 5, record group Z45F, BA. Fortuna distributed *Charly* in Germany.

21. Stuart Schulberg, "A Communication: A Letter about Billy Wilder," *Quarterly of Film, Radio and TV* 7 (1953): 435.

22. "Confidential Operational Priority," August 6, 1945, to McClure chief, Information Control Division, OMGUS, RG Z45F, shipment 10, box 17-3, folder 9, microfiche, BA. See also U.S. Military Regulations 21-606 and 21-606.1, quoted in Peter Pleyer, *Deutscher Nachkriegsfilm, 1946–1948* (Münster: C. J. Fahle Verlag, 1966), 26.

23. "Voluntary Self Control of the German Film Industry," May 1949, OMGUS, folder 2, box 245-2, shipment 5, record group Z45F, BA.

24. Carl Winston, Acting Chief, Motion Picture Branch, to Director, Information Services Division, "Self-regulation of the German Film Industry," May 5, 1949, OMGUS, folder 2, box 245-2, shipment 5, record group Z45F, BA.

25. "Zur Lage der Filmzensur," *Die neue Filmwoche,* March 20, 1948, 1.

26. Henry P. Pilgert with Helga Dobbert, *Press, Radio, and Film in West Germany, 1945–1953* (Bad Godesberg-Mehlem: Office of the U.S. High Commissioner for Germany, Historical Division, 1953), 97.

27. "*Hallo, Fräulein!* drehbuch fehlt," *Der Spiegel,* March 20, 1948, 24. The article makes special mention of Jugert's controversial subject of fraternization.

28. "Daily report," Motion Picture Branch, February 9, 1949, Eric Pommer Collection, box B, files of the Motion Picture Branch, Cinema and Television Library, University of Southern California, Los Angeles.

29. Michael H. Kater, "Forbidden Fruit? Jazz in the Third Reich," *American Historical Review* 94 (1989): 13–15.

30. Kater, *Different Drummers,* 32.

31. Paul Gilroy, *Against Race: Imagining Political Culture beyond the Color Line* (Cambridge, Mass.: Harvard University Press, 2000), 299.

32. See, for example, Uta G. Poiger, "Rock 'n' Roll, Female Sexuality, and the Cold War Battle over German Identities," in *West Germany under Construction: Politics, Society, and Culture in the Adenauer Era,* ed. Robert G. Moeller (Ann Arbor: University of Michigan Press, 1997), 373–410.

33. According to the Oxford English Dictionary, as early as 1924 "jazz" was a slang reference to sexual intercourse.

34. Kater, *Different Drummers,* 52.

35. Uta G. Poiger, *Jazz, Rock, and Rebels: Cold War Politics and American Culture in a Divided Germany* (Berkeley: University of California Press, 2000), 69.

36. Jeffrey Herf, *Divided Memory: The Nazi Past in the Two Germanys* (Cambridge, Mass.: Harvard University Press, 1997), 3.

37. Ibid., 112.

38. For a discussion of the Soviet arguments against jazz, see S. Frederick Starr, *Red and Hot: The Fate of Jazz in the Soviet Union, 1917–1980* (New York: Oxford University Press, 1983), 209–11. On East German jazz policies, see Poiger, *Jazz, Rock, and Rebels,* 150–54. In East Germany, jazz advocate Reginald Rudorf distinguished between commercial American dance music (a central component of American imperialism) and authentic African American jazz (one of many folk traditions that could positively influence East German dance music).

39. Herf, *Divided Memory,* 8.

40. Konrad H. Jarausch and Michael Geyer, *Shattered Past: Reconstructing German Histories* (Princeton, N.J.: Princeton University Press, 2003), 236–37.

41. According to the press releases, Hielscher's band initially comprised seven Americans who were then joined by a Dutchman, a Frenchman, a Swede, a Hungarian, an Italian, and a German who, despite not speaking each other's language, forged "out of the many, a single voice and produced a harmony, an entire sound." *Hallo, Fräulien!* Press Book, DIF.

42. Michael Rogin, "Blackface, White Noise: The Jewish Jazz Singer Finds His Voice," *Critical Inquiry* 18, no. 3 (spring 1992): 429.

43. Ibid., 447.

44. Kater, *Different Drummers,* 129; see also 249–50 n86.

45. Ibid., 131.

46. *Hallo, Fräulein!* press book, DIF.

47. Theodor Adorno, "The Perennial Fashion—Jazz," *The Adorno Reader,* ed. Brian O'Connor (Oxford, UK: Blackwell, 2000), 275.

48. Lorenzo C. Simpson, *The Unfinished Project: Toward a Postmetaphysical Humanism* (London: Routledge, 2001), 50.

49. Jane Feuer, "The Self-Reflective Musical and the Myth of Entertainment," in *Hollywood Musicals: The Film Reader,* ed. Steven Cohan (London: Routledge, 2002), 36.

50. Carol Clover, "Dancin' in the Rain," *Critical Inquiry* 21, no. 4 (Summer 1995): 742.

51. Eric Lott analyzes blackface minstrelsy as a performative, cultural invention based on both a northern fantasy of plantation life as well as interracial encounters. In this context, blackface minstrelsy was, "on the one hand, a socially approved content of institutional control; and, on the other, it continually acknowledged and absorbed black culture even while defending white Americans against it" (40). But minstrel representations were always a matter of white interest in and ownership of black performance. Eric Lott, *Love and Theft: Blackface Minstrelsy and the American Working Class* (Oxford, UK: Oxford University Press, 1993), 38–43.

52. "Address of Secretary of Defense Louis Johnson to Theater Owners of America," 1949 (month and day not given), Motion Picture Industry Council Collection, Ambassadors Abroad, box 1, file 1, Academy of Motion Picture Arts and Sciences, Margaret Herrick Library, Beverly Hills, California (hereafter AMPAS).

53. Both of these features played in Germany from 1945 to 1949. "OWI and MPEA Releases in Germany from 1945–1949," Motion Picture Industry Council Collection, box 2, folder 15, Special Collections, AMPAS.

54. Krin Gabbard, *Jammin' at the Margins: Jazz and the American Cinema* (Chicago: University of Chicago Press, 1996), 67.

55. Ibid., 87.

56. The Duke Ellington short was not approved for German audiences after a test screening with German POWs. "Film Exhibition in the American Zone," August 1945, Report of the Motion Picture Branch, Information Services Division, OMGUS, folder 9, box 17-3, shipment 10, record group Z45F, BA.

57. All reviews appear in translation in "Editorial Survey," April 19, 1948, Press Branch, Information Control Division, OMGUS, folder 6, box 11-1, shipment 10, record group Z45F, BA.

5. A Gothic Occupation

1. Gunter Groll, "Im Atlantic nicht Neues . . .," Munich, October 2, 1946. As previously noted, I believe this is from *Die Neue Zeitung*. The review is marked only by the city of origin and date. Press clippings for *Corvette K-225*. Deutsches Institute für Filmkunde, Frankfurt a. M (hereafter DIF).

2. F. L., "Humorloses Weltgefühl: Neuauffürung von Lubitschs Ninotchka," *Die Welt* (Hamburg), July 13, 1955. Press clippings for *Ninotchka,* DIF.

3. Sigmund Freud, "The Uncanny," *Writings on Art and Literature,* ed. Neil Hertz (Stanford, Calif.: Stanford University Press, 1997), 199.

4. Anthony Vidler, *The Architectural Uncanny: Essay in the Modern Unhomely* (Cambridge, Mass.: MIT Press, 1992), 7.

5. Vidler, *The Architectural Uncanny*, 35.

6. Sigmund Freud, *The Psychopathology of Everyday Life,* standard edition, trans. and ed. James Strachey (New York: W. W. Norton & Co., 1965), 326.

7. Dana Polan, *Power and Paranoia: History, Narrative, and the American Cinema, 1940–1950* (New York: Columbia University Press, 1986), 275.

8. Filmic variations on this theme include *Suspicion* (1941), *Gaslight* (1944), *Rebecca* (1939), *Dragonwyck* (1946), *The Two Mrs. Carrolls* (1947), *The Spiral Staircase* (1945), *Caught* (1949), *Jane Eyre* (1944), and *Secret beyond the Door* (1948), taken from Mary Ann Doane's discussion of the paranoid woman's film in *The Desire to Desire: The Woman's Film of the 1940s* (Bloomington: Indiana University Press, 1987), 155–75.

9. Ibid., 27–30.

10. Fred Botting, *Gothic: The New Critical Idiom* (London: Routledge, 1996), 5.

11. Ian Duncan quoted in Donna Heiland, *Gothic and Gender: An Introduction* (Oxford, UK: Blackwell, 2004), 129–30.

12. Eric L. Santner, *My Own Private Germany: Daniel Paul Schreber's Secret History of Modernity* (Princeton, N.J.: Princeton University Press, 1996), 9.

13. For other elaborations of Nazi masculine psychology, see Klaus Theweleit's two-volume elaboration of fascism as a rejection of feminine experience: *Male Fantasies*, vol. 1, *Women, Floods, Bodies, History* (Minneapolis: University of Minnesota Press, 1987); *Male Fantasies*, vol. 2, *Male Bodies: Psychoanalyzing the White Terror* (Minneapolis: University of Minnesota Press, 1989). See also work by Laurence A. Rickels, who discusses not only the Nazi ban on homosexuality but the Nazi use of psychoanalysis as homosexuality's cure for Aryan men. *Nazi Psychoanalysis,* vol. 2, *Crypto-Fetishism* (Minneapolis: University of Minnesota Press, 2002), 198–206.

14. Dennis L. Bark and David R. Gress, *A History of Western Germany,* vol. 1, *From Shadow to Substance, 1945–1963* (Cambridge, UK: Basil Blackwell, 1989), 42.

15. Elizabeth D. Heineman, *What Difference Does a Husband Make? Women and Marital Status in Nazi and Occupied Germany* (Berkeley: University of California Press, 1999), 115–16.

16. Atina Grossmann, "A Question of Silence: The Rape of German Women by Occupation Soldiers," in *West Germany under Construction: Politics, Society, and Culture in the Adenauer Era,* ed. Robert G. Moeller (Ann Arbor: University of Michigan Press, 1997), 41.

17. Bark and Gress, *From Shadow to Substance,* 31–41.

18. Joseph Foschepoth, "German Reaction to Defeat and Occupation," in *West Germany under Construction,* 83.

19. Public opinion surveys carried out in the American zone reflect the following trend: in 1945, 70 percent of German residents in the U.S. zone felt that the U.S. military government "has furthered rather than hindered" German reconstruction. In 1946 this number dropped to 44 percent. In January 1948, this number bounced up a bit, to 55 percent. Thus in 1948 almost half of the Germans living under U.S. authority felt that occupation forces were actually doing more harm than good in Germany. Anna J. Merritt and Richard L. Merritt, "Introduction," in *Public Opinion in Occupied Germany: The OMGUS Surveys, 1945–1949,* ed. Anna J. Merritt and Richard L. Merritt (Champaign: University of Illinois Press, 1970), 11–12.

20. Robert G. Moeller, "Introduction: Writing the History of West Germany," in *West Germany under Construction,* 14.

21. Merritt and Merritt, *Public Opinion in Occupied Germany,* 100–101.

22. Though this second survey involved fewer respondents and was concerned only with Munich audiences, Munich was the largest city in the American zone and the center of Bavarian political culture. It was the only *Land,* or German state, whose borders remained intact after the war. See Bark and Gress, *From Shadow to Substance,* 97. Because Bavaria was completely under U.S. control, the political sensibilities of Munich residents were especially important to American policy makers, as is evident in the commissioning of this survey.

23. Max Horkheimer and Theodor Adorno, *The Dialectic of Enlightenment: Philosophical Fragments,* ed. Gunselin Schmid Noerr and trans. Edmund Jephcott (Stanford, Calif.: Stanford University Press, 2002), xiv.

24. Ibid., 28.

25. Again, surveys show that in November 1946, when the trials were coming to an end, half of the respondents in the American zone reported that, in effect, the trials made them more aware of the "inhumanity of the concentration camps." Merritt and Merritt, *Public Opinion in Occupied Germany,* 123–24.

26. Botting, *Gothic,* 2.

27. Doane, *The Desire to Desire,* 129–31.

28. D. F., "Ingrid Bergman-Film," *Telegraf* (Berlin), September 7, 1947. Press clippings for *Glocken von St. Marien (Bells of St. Mary's),* DIF.

29. W. Lg., "Glocken, Tränen, Spannung," *Berliner Zeitung,* September 9, 1947. Press clippings for *Glocken von St. Marien,* DIF.

30. K. W. K., "Amerikanische Film: "Die Glocken von St. Marien""—

"Das Hause der Lady Alquist," *Der Tagesspiegel* (Berlin), September 7, 1947. Press clippings for *Glocken von St. Marien,* DIF.

31. F. T., "Die Waise von Lowood," *Die neue Zeitung* (Frankfurt, Munich), July 26, 1947. Press clippings for *Die Waise von Lowood (Jane Eyre),* DIF.

32. H. W., "Die Waise von Lowood," *Socialdemokrat* (Berlin), July 29, 1947. Press clippings for *Die Waise von Lowood,* DIF.

33. H. H., "Junge Waise, arm und edel . . . ," *Nachtexpress* (Berlin), July 26, 1947. Press clippings for *Die Waise von Lowood,* DIF.

34. Lutz Koeptnick, *The Dark Mirror: German Cinema between Hitler and Hollywood* (Berkeley: University of California Press, 2002), 193.

35. Hans Ulrich Eylau, "Film Export und Kunstgeschäft: Gedanken anläßlich der 'Weneltreppe,'" *Tägliche Rundschau* (Berlin), January 15, 1948, quoted in Koepnick, *The Dark Mirror,* 194.

36. Friedrich Luft, "Verdact," *Der Tagesspiegel* (Berlin), December 7, 1946. Press clippings for *Verdacht (Suspicion),* DIF. All of the reviews for the film in this file are positive and full of praise for Hitchcock's cinematography and masterful control of film style. And where Fontaine is the butt of the *Jane Eyre* jokes, the reviews for *Suspicion* celebrate her acting technique and inherent charm. In fact, the film critic for the *Spandauer Volksblatt* (Berlin) compared Fontaine to Germany's own beloved silver screen actress Marianne Hoppe. L. M., "Spielzeüg tanzt in den Neüen Scala," December 7, 1946. Press clippings for *Verdacht,* DIF.

37. Friedrich Luft, "Mord im Salon," *Die neue Zeitung,* May 10, 1947. *Laura* press clippings, DIF. My thanks to A. C. Goodson, who helped me to parse Luft's many cultural and geographical references to Friedenau's history.

38. The Kronen-Lichtspiele, located in the Berlin suburb of Friedenau, is the same theater where, in July 1947, audiences laughed at *Jane Eyre* and where in 1946 Luft himself saw and admired Hitchcock's *Suspicion.*

39. W. D. Patterson to the Office of War Information, "Confidential Inter-office Memo: Films for Germany," March 27, 1944, OMGUS papers, folder 13, box 17-3, shipment 10, record group, Z45F (microfiche), Bundesarchiv, Koblenz, Germany.

40. Sigmund Freud, "Psychoanalytic Notes upon an Autobiographical Account of a Case of Paranoia," in *Three Case Histories,* ed. Philip Rieff (New York: Collier Books, 1963), 139.

41. For a discussion of the relationship between psychic subjectivity, as constructed by psychoanalysis, and sovereignty, see Eric Santner, *On the Psychotheology of Everyday Life: Reflections on Freud and Rosenzweig* (Chicago: University of Chicago Press, 2001), 25–45. Here Santner considers the extent to which we, as psychoanalytic subjects, are formed by the institutions that "endow us with social recognition and intelligibility,

that produce and regulate symbolic identities." That is, he is interested in how both psychoanalysis and institutions preside over "the 'stuff' of sovereignty" (26–27). This model of institutionally produced sovereignty is in contrast to another possible model of the Freudian subject that is predicated more on the "singularity we assume thanks to what the biblical traditions understand as the blessings of divine love" (27–28). I gesture to this question of sovereignty merely to note that female paranoia, which threatens the complete annihilation of the subject, brings us closer to the crises of nonsovereign subjectivity than does the masculine paradigm of this perversion.

42. Andrew Sarris, "Two or Three Things I Know about 'Gaslight,'" *Film Comment* 12, no. 3 (May–June 1976): 23.

43. Doane also points out moments of feminine masquerade in women's films and even in *Gaslight*. For Doane, these are unsustained instances that briefly expose femininity as a patriarchal discourse. These moments—when Paula plays mad or when Stella (Barbara Stanwyck in King Vidor's *Stella Dallas* [1937]) parodies herself to convince her daughter to return to her father—show women audiences the perils of imitating essentialized visions of themselves. But these examples stop far short of creating the misrecognition in women spectators that is necessary for a truly feminist cinema, 180–82.

44. Diane Waldman, "'At Last I Can Tell It to Someone!' Feminine Point of View and Subjectivity in the Gothic Romance Films of the 1940s," *Cinema Journal* 23, no. 2 (Winter 1984): 38.

45. V. Stanley Vardys, "Germany's Postwar Socialism: Nationalism and Kurt Schumacher (1945–1952)," *Review of Politics* 27, no. 2 (April 1965): 220–44; "Social Democrats Win Bavarian Poll," *New York Times* (June 1, 1948): 16.

46. Bonnie Honig, *Democracy and the Foreigner* (Princeton, N.J.: Princeton University Press, 2001), 109.

Epilogue

1. James Bennet, "Help along the Campaign Trail from Kohl's Friend, 'Dear Bill,'" *New York Times*, May 14, 1998, A8.

2. "Remarks following discussions with Chancellor Helmut Kohl in Germany and an exchange with reporters in Potsdam, Germany (speeches by Pres. Bill Clinton and Kohl). *Weekly Compilation of Presidential Documents,* May 18, 1998 (Washington, D.C.: U.S. Government Printing Office), at http://www.highbeam.com/doc/1G1-20811569.html.

3. William J. Clinton, "Remarks at the Berlin Airlift Remembrance Ceremony in Berlin." *Weekly Compilation of Presidential Documents,* May 18, 1998 (Washington, D.C.: U.S. Government Printing Office), at http://www.highbeam.com/doc/1G1-20811573.html. In response

to these remarks, London's *Financial Times* noted that the fanfare and "razzmatazz" of Clinton's commemorative visit all but erased "those helpful Brits" who suffered the most casualties during the airlift. British authorities managed at least to change the official text of the Berlin city government's pamphlet before it went to press. "Airlift airbrush," *Financial Times* (U.S. edition), May 13, 1998, 11.

4. In the United States that year, the celebration of friendship continued on television. The Arts and Entertainment network premiered the two-hour special *Berlin Airlift: First Battle of the Cold War* (Robert Kirk, 1998), and CNN aired its twenty-four episode series *From the Bolsheviks to the Berlin Wall* (1998).

5. Kohl quoted in Eric Malnic, "Berlin Airlift of '48: Mission of Mercy," *Los Angeles Times*, June 28, 1998, A24.

6. William J. Clinton, "Remarks at the Berlin Airlift Remembrance Ceremony in Berlin."

7. John M. Broder, "Clinton Visit in Honduras Dramatizes New Attitude," *New York Times*, March 10, 1999, A1.

8. James Dao, "A Nation Challenged: The Aid," *New York Times,* October 9, 2001, B2.

9. Mark Skertic, "News Special Edition," *Chicago Sunday Times,* October 8, 2001, 2.

10. Geraldo Rivera's "gallant assessment" as reported by Alessandra Stanley, "A Nation at War: The TV Watch," *New York Times*, March 30, 2003, B15.

11. Box office gross from Angie Dullinger, "Jeder geger jeden und alle für einen," *Abendzeitung* (Munich), August 14, 1998; *Washington Post* quoted in Andreas Kilb, "Der Tod am Omaha Beach," *Die Zeit* (Hamburg), August 6, 1998; *Der Soldat James Ryan* press clippings, Deutsches Institut für Filmkunde (hereafter DIF).

12. Kurt Scheel, "Wer mag schon Kriegsfilme?" *Die Tageszeitung* (Berlin), November 3, 1999; Vera Graff, "John Wayne lebt nicht mehr," *Süddeutsche Zeitung* (Munich), July 30, 1998; Fritz Göttler, "Peter Pan im Nimmerland Normandie," *Süddeutsche Zeitung* (Munich), October 8, 1998, DIF.

13. Kilb, "Der Tod am Omaha Beach."

14. Doug Donovon notes *Ryan*'s clear debt to *The Sullivans*. "Saving the Sullivans," *Forbes* 162, no. 6 (Sept. 23, 1998): 289. For a short discussion of the reeducation policy statement discussing *The Sullivans,* see chapter 1.

15. Scheel, "Wer mag schon Kriegsfilme?"

16. Cheney quoted in Stephen F. Szabo, *Parting Ways: The Crisis in German-American Relations* (Washington, D.C.: Brookings Institution Press, 2004), 24.

17. "National Security Advisor Condoleezza Rice Interview with ZDF German Television," July 31, 2003. Transcript, at http://www.whitehouse .gov/news/release/2003/07/20030731-7.html.

18. David E. Sanger, "Witness to Evil, Bush Draws a Lesson," *New York Times,* June 1, 2003, A14; David E. Sanger, "Bush Asks Lands in Mideast to Try Democratic Way," *New York Times,* November 7, 2003, A1; Richard Bernstein, "New Agenda: Go It Alone. Remake the World," *New York Times,* March 23, 2003, E1.

19. Paul Bremer III, "The Right Call," *Wall Street Journal,* January 12, 2005, A10.

20. For just one example of how these terms are used in the public sphere, see the commentary by Daniel Johnson, editorial writer for London's *Daily Telegraph,* in which he argues that the de-Baathification of Iraq will operate in ways parallel to the de-Nazifying of Germany. Daniel Johnson, "De-Baathification," *Wall Street Journal,* April 24, 2003, A16.

21. Alexander Stille, "The Latest Obscenity Has Seven Letters," *New York Times,* September 13, 2003, B9; David S. Cloud, "Rumsfeld Says War Critics Haven't Learned the Lessons of History," *New York Times,* August 30, 2006, A4.

22. George W. Bush, "National Character Counts Week," a Proclamation, October 18, 2002, http://www.whitehouse.gov/news/releases/ 2002/10/20021018-9.html; George W. Bush, "President Bush Discusses Iraq Policy at Whitehall Palace in London," remarks by the President at Whitehall Palace, London, England, November 19, 2003. http://www .whitehouse.gov/news/releases/2003/11/20031119-1.html (Hereafter "Whitehall").

23. "Habits of Liberty" from Bush, "Whitehall"; "universal values," see Bush and Blair quotes in Warren Hoge and Don Van Natta Jr., "Today, Trailing Controversy over Iraq," *New York Times,* July 17, 2003, A10; Bush's comments about the "civilized world" from "President Outlines Steps to Help Iraq Achieve Democracy and Freedom," remarks by George W. Bush to U.S. Army War College, Carlisle, Pennsylvania, May 24, 2004, http://www.whitehouse.gov/news/releases/2004/05/20040524-10.html.

24. Seymour M. Hersh, "The Gray Zone: How a Secret Pentagon Program Came to Abu Ghraib," *New Yorker,* May 24, 2004, 42.

25. Raphael Patai, *The Arab Mind* (New York: Charles Scribner's Sons, 1973), 307–13.

26. Anthony Shadid, *Night Draws Near: Iraq's People in the Shadow of America's War* (New York: Henry Holt, 2005), 9, 212.

27. Bush, "Iraq and the War on Terror."

28. Bush, "Whitehall."

29. Erik H. Erikson,"Reflections on the American Identity," in *Childhood and Society,* 287.

30. The policy of offending the fewest people possible, we might note in passing, was also the motto of the Hollywood Production Code.

31. This double exile is most pronounced in Erikson's description of the Sioux girls who attend the white government-run school. "They are almost never given the opportunity, nor are they indeed prepared or willing, to live the life of an American woman; but they are only rarely able to be happy again in the spatial restrictions, the unhygienic intimacies, and the poverty of their surroundings." This ambivalence may produce cultural pathologies in the form of "alcoholic delinquency" and "mild thievery," or "in the form of a general apathy and an intangible passive resistance against any further and more final impact of white standards on the Indian conscience." "Childhood in Two American Indian Tribes," in *Childhood and Society*, 131.

32. Erikson quoted in Lawrence Jacob Friedman, *Identity's Architect: A Biography of Erik H. Erikson* (New York: Scribner, 1999), 188. Friedman here discusses the parallels Erikson found between the United States and Nazi Germany, two modern, military superpowers who, in their ruthless treatment of ethnic and racial minorities, betrayed the civilizing narrative of industrial progress (184–91).

33. I do not have the space here to fully elaborate Roy's argument. I wish merely to note that he finds jihad movements to be largely a product of globalized Islam and a response to Western discourses about Muslims as ethnic (as opposed to merely religious) minorities. Western multiculturalism ethnicizes Muslimism, which in turn fuels neoreligious movements. Olivier Roy, *Globalized Islam: The Search for a New Ummah* (New York: Columbia University Press, 2004), 100–147. Quoted words from 108, 109.

34. Susan Buck-Morss, *Thinking Past Terror: Islamism and Critical Theory on the Left* (London: Verso, 2003), 106.

35. Anne Sa'adah, "Regime Change: Lessons from Germany on Justice, Institution Building, and Democracy," *Journal of Conflict Resolution* 50, no. 3 (June 2006): 303–4.

36. Sa'adah elaborates on this dynamic in *Germany's Second Chance: Trust, Justice, and Democratization* (Cambridge, Mass.: Harvard University Press, 1998), 10–58.

37. Sa'adah, "Regime Change," 312.

38. Eva Bellin also notes that, in contrast to the political and ethnic divisions in Iraq, German and Japanese democracies were successful because of the "ethnic homogeneity found in their societies." "Democratic theory," she writes, "suggests that ethnic homogeneity is an important factor in shaping democratic outcomes." "The Iraqi Intervention and Democracy in Comparative Historical Perspective," *Political Science Quarterly* 119, no. 4 (Winter 2004/2005): 598. Both Bellin and Sa'adah stress

that Iraq's multiethnic composition alone speaks to the incomparability of these two occupations.

39. See Sa'adah, *Germany's Second Chance,* chapter 2.

40. Steven Erlanger, "Bush-Hitler Remark Shows U.S. as Issue in German Elections, *New York Times,* September 20, 2002, A1.

41. Erlanger, "Bush-Hitler Remark, A1.

42. For a detailed discussion of the German response to America's war in Iraq, and the numerous diplomatic fumbles in both Bush and Schröder's administrations, see Szabo, *Parting Ways.*

Index

Jennifer Fay is associate professor and director of film studies in the Department of English at Michigan State University.